Never Judge a Book
by its Cover

Never Judge a Book by its Cover

THE AUTOBIOGRAPHY

LISA RILEY

This edition first published in Great Britain in 2013 by Orion
an imprint of the Orion Publishing Group Ltd
Orion House, 5 Upper St Martin's Lane, London WC2H 9EA
An Hachette UK Company

1 3 5 7 9 10 8 6 4 2

A CIP catalogue record for this book is available
from the British Library.

Hardback ISBN: 978 1 4091 4734 3

Typeset by Input Data Services Ltd, Bridgwater, Somerset

Printed and bound by CPI Group (UK) Ltd, Croydon, CR0 4YY

The Orion Publishing Group's policy is to use papers that
are natural, renewable and recyclable and made from wood
grown in sustainable forests. The logging and manufacturing
processes are expected to conform to the environmental
regulations of the country of origin.

Every effort has been made to fulfil requirements with
regard to reproducing copyright material. The author
and publisher will be glad to rectify any omissions at
the earliest opportunity.

Photo Credits:
Fat Friends Fotoshoot and *Scott and Bailey* images: ITV/Rex Features
Strictly Wembley crew and Lisa at the TRIC TV and Radio Awards:
David Fisher/Rex Features
Lisa in lights: BBC/Guy Levy
Lisa with Bruce and Tess: BBC Worldwide

www.orionbooks.co.uk

For my beloved mum Cath, forever in my heart.
You have and always will be my guiding light.

And for Robin Windsor, King of my dance floor!
'We did it babes.'

Contents

Acknowledgements

I would personally like to thank the following very special people ...

Rebecca Cripps: for not only being the best listener (in our little white room) but being the best writer I ever could have had the pleasure of working with. I'm forever grateful.

Amanda Harris (Orion Books): from the first moment I met you, I saw your drive and passion for the job you do, a trait I believe we both share. See ... girl power lives on!

Beloved family, three words: 'I AM BLESSED'.

Forever loyal friends: you know who you are! Sometimes thank you just doesn't seem enough xxxx

My Godchildren: I will always guide you in life, but one thing is for sure ... always be who YOU want to be and don't CONFORM!!!

Boo and 'The Barlows': to say you are my rock is an

understatement. Honestly and truly sent from heaven.

Molly and Polly: too bloody young to be reading this book.

Phil Dale, my manager, and his PA Lucy Saunders: with all of your constant support and care, I feel together we are the 'Dream Team'. You both mean the world to me.

Mervyn Watson (*Emmerdale* producer): Mandy and the Dingles will always be yours.

PB and Steve: every word … every stitch … every tear … every cuddle … but mostly yellow dragonflies!!!!

Daisy Moore: you fought for me and made all of this possible – one in a million!

Jo Threfall: Mum's shoulder from the day you met to the very end … you are unique.

Artem Chigvintsev: for your constant patience, never, ever being 'the Russian Robot' and just … being my friend. Five, six, seven, eight, hold one.

Dr J Watts: for being so so so much more than a doctor – for being a friend.

Dr A Stewart and the staff at 'The Christie': all of you are true angels. You give the medicine; but one thing you can't get on prescription is what you, as people, give – love and support – every single day to every person who comes through your door! The Riley clan are truly lucky to have had the privilege to call you our friends.

Prologue

88–1

Sitting in my dressing room at the BBC, *Strictly*fied to the nines, I suddenly start to panic. What the hell am I doing? I think. Am I really wearing a crystal-encrusted dress, with eyelashes like claws and iridescent stocking shimmy on my bare legs, just minutes away from doing the cha-cha in front of thirteen and a half million people?

I have never, ever felt so nervous. I'm all over the place. What on earth was I thinking when I agreed to do *Strictly*? Performing live is always a risk, but this feels really dangerous. It's so much more intense than any other first night I've experienced, because I know that people are expecting me to fail.

I'm painfully aware that I could easily be a national laughing stock by the end of the evening, with omelette all over my face. I've watched the show year after year and I'm aware of how it works. It's obvious that I was picked to be this year's John Sergeant or Ann Widdecombe. There's always one, the token chubby contestant, the potential comedy figure of the series, the joke.

It's not looking good for me. Since the line-up was announced, every paper I've picked up has said something negative about me. The bookies have rated my chances of winning at 88/1 – in other words, not in a billion years – and the bookies tend to get it right. Then there are the dismissive comments on the TV and entertainment website forums. 'Oh, her from *Emmerdale*, she'll be one of the first to go.' 'All the smart money is on Victoria Pendleton. She's an Olympic gold medallist and she's got a body to die for.'

Everyone is predicting that I'll be voted off the show after a couple of dances. Even one of the *Strictly* judges has implied that he's expecting me to be rubbish. The night I was paired with my dance partner, Robin Windsor, Craig Revel Horwood said scathingly, 'Robin Windsor, good luck!' Clearly, if one of the judges is against me even before he's seen me dance, then the public vote isn't likely to go my way either. People are bound to be influenced by negative comments and sneering predictions. No doubt the rest of the panel think I'm going to be terrible, too. No one is on my side. The press, the bookies, the panel and the public are all waiting for me to make a fool of myself.

I felt like the happiest girl on the planet to be partnered with Robin. Thank you, Mum! I thought. I knew Robin was hoping for Kimberley Walsh, because he'd told me so, but when it was announced that we were together, he ran over and hugged me, looking elated. He's since admitted that he was thinking, What the hell am I going to do with her? But that was before he found out I had rhythm and could dance, before we started getting to know each other and hit it off. Now he tells me all the time that he's glad he's with me. I'm desperately hoping that I don't let him down.

That night, when we were given our dancing partners, my Twitter account went from about two thousand followers to thirty-seven thousand followers. I'd say that ninety-one per cent of the comments were positive but, oh dear, that other nine per cent! I felt utter disbelief that people could type the things they did. Some of the comments were downright cruel. 'You ugly fat mess!' 'You don't have a right to be on British television.' 'You're an obese waste of space.'

But you know what? I refuse to buy into all the negativity. That's just not the way I'm made. Instead of making my skin crawl, each insult is like a delicious morsel of food to me, and when I read a bunch of them together, it's like being given the best meal I could ever want. It makes me think, I'll show you! It makes me even more resolved to do well.

I have my mum to thank for that sense of determination. Mum gave me the confidence to believe that you can be who you want to be and do what you want to do. She had total faith in my abilities and always supported me one billion per cent. She taught me to hold my head up high when the chips are down and to laugh at the bad stuff that life throws at you.

Some of the vitriol and nastiness aimed at me online has been absolutely hilarious. In my mind, there's nothing else I can do except laugh at it. One of the funniest comments was on Twitter: 'Poor, poor Robin Windsor, you've been paired with Jabba the Hutt.'

No way! I thought. I cut out a picture of my head, glued it

onto a picture of Jabba the Hutt and took it to Robin in the practice room the following day. 'There you go, darling,' I said. 'Let's enjoy ourselves, shall we?' Robin was amazed. We laughed about it all day. Mum would have loved it.

I wish I could ring Mum. I'm used to speaking to her ten times a day. It's been a month since she passed and the pain is still unbearably raw. I miss her so, so much.

'What am I doing, Mum?' I'd ask. 'Am I totally insane?'

I know exactly what she'd say: 'Darling, just be yourself. I know you'll do well.'

Those were her words, a few days before she passed, when she heard that I was on the shortlist for *Strictly*. It was the best advice she could have given me and I've done my best to follow it by just being me, every minute of every day. Everything I'm doing now, I'm doing for her, my wonderful, amazing mum. It may sound strange, but I can feel her close by. I know she's watching over me. She's my guiding light.

When I said yes to *Strictly*, I made a choice: I could either have a good time and enjoy it for what it is, or I could be defeatist from the start. And since I'm my mother's daughter and I don't have a pessimistic drop of blood in my body, I made a conscious decision to have fun, to be giddy and to make the most of it, even though it's probably not going to last long. Yes, it is likely that I will be voted off the show very soon, but so what? I've had a ball with Robin in rehearsals. It's been a difficult time in many ways, but I've also had the most fun ever, ever, ever.

A lot of viewers may have already made their minds up about me, but I'm hoping they'll be nicely surprised when they see me dance. People like to put each other in envelopes, so if you're bigger, they think that you'll be out of breath, struggling to keep up and sweating like someone demented. But that's not the case with me. I'm very fit and I've got rhythm, like a lot of big girls. So I'm determined to go out there and show the nation that chubbers can move. And if anyone is wondering whether Robin will be able to lift me up, I hope they will enjoy what we've got planned for the end of our routine. Fingers crossed we can pull it off.

My nerves are getting worse now. I send a silent prayer up into the ether. 'Please, Mum, help me remember all my steps!' I'm terrified that I'll trip up or fall over myself. I can't even let those thoughts into my head. I have to stay positive.

The lovely lady who has dressed me tonight passes me a cool glass of water. Over the past few weeks we've got to know each other well. 'Your mum's with you,' she says gently. 'Just go out there knowing that she's with you.' Gratefully, I squeeze her hand.

I take one last look at myself in the mirror. I feel fantastic in my sexy dress, with my glossy hair and long eyelashes. I've spent my life playing mingers, with my hair scraped back or in a tangled mess. Often I've been lucky to get any make-up at all – and if I have, it's been grey circles under my eyes, to make me look like a druggie, and dirt under my nails. So words can't express how exciting it is to see my glamorous, shimmery *Strictly*fied self. I'm bowled over by how pretty I look.

'Go get 'em,' I say under my breath. 'Just be you.'

My heart starts thumping wildly. Oh my God, I'm on *Strictly*! I think, as if it's only just occurred to me. I'm about to appear live in front of half the nation, dancing a cha-cha in a competition that includes two Olympic athletes, an ex-supermodel and Nicky Byrne from Westlife. It's crazy.

The final call comes and I make my way to the TV studio. Robin's face lights up when he sees me. 'Wow, you look incredible,' he says appreciatively. I can tell he means it and I feel myself flush with pleasure. Robin's opinion means the world to me. He's been the most amazing support over the last few weeks.

'Positions, everyone!' the floor manager shouts. We take our place on the staircase.

The famous *Strictly* theme tune starts up. I'm so pumped I can barely breathe. I've never, ever experienced nerves like this before. Will I even be able to put one foot in front of another and make my way down the stairs to the dance floor? I turn to Robin and he lightly touches my shoulder, just as we've rehearsed. I instantly feel reassured. I raise my eyes to the roof of the studio and picture Mum smiling. Suddenly a sense of peace comes over me and I know that everything is going to be all right.

'Cath's here,' I whisper calmly, looking down at my shoulder. 'Mum's with us. We're going to be fine.'

Now it's time to go out there and give it my all. I've got one and a half minutes in which to change people's minds and show them what I'm made of. Robin puts his arm round my waist and leads me towards the dance floor. This is it, Mum, I think. Here I go.

Yellow brick road

'Oh, you're Lisa's mother,' said my form teacher, Sister Mary John, as Mum sat down to talk to her one parents' night when I was ten. 'I see. Does Lisa like chips?'

Mum wondered if she'd heard right. 'Pardon?' she said.

'Does Lisa like chips?'

'Well, yes, she likes loads of stuff.'

'Because she's quite plump, isn't she?'

'Right, my daughter's plump,' Mum said sharply. 'Well done, Sister. How very, very observant of you. Now can we talk about my child's education, please?'

'No, I want to say this,' Sister Mary John insisted.

'Either talk about Lisa's education, or I'm getting up now,' Mum said. 'Actually, you know what? I'm leaving. I don't care what you think!' She stood up and walked out.

Mum thought, I've got your number, mate! Don't you dare try to crush my daughter.

It said everything that Sister Mary John didn't talk about my efforts in mathematics or science before gently bringing up my weight. She didn't really want to address the issue. She wanted to undermine me. I was headstrong, confident and full of life and Sister Mary John preferred a more placid, docile kind of pupil.

But Mum wasn't having it. 'I don't suffer fools gladly,' she used to say, narrowing her eyes.

I come from a family filled with huge personalities and they've all had a massive influence on who I am now, but my mum was first and foremost among them. Mum was my life, my rock and my best friend. She defended me to the last. She made me who I am.

You could hear Mum's deep, irresistible laughter from three aisles over in the supermarket. 'Eh up, here comes Cath,' people would say. She was completely exuberant and she held court wherever she went. Everyone knew her as a total powerhouse.

Mum was fun, bubbly, strong and bolshy. She had a huge, huge heart and more friends than anyone I've known, but she was never bothered what other people thought of her. Her attitude was, 'If you don't like me, sod off!' I grew up with that attitude and I feel the same way. I don't care if someone doesn't like me. I know when to behave, but I will always be myself and I won't tread on eggshells for anybody.

Me and Mum formed our special, unbreakable bond on the day I was born at Fairfield Hospital, Bury, Greater Manchester, on 13 July 1976. From the moment I arrived, I was the apple of her eye. She absolutely doted on me. I was the kind of heavenly baby who ate well and slept through the night, apparently.

Mum always wanted the best for me, but no one was going to dictate to her how to be a mum. She remembers being told, 'You don't give kids dodies!' But she took no notice. She was her own person and she never conformed. Like the Bette Midler character in her favourite film *Beaches*, she did whatever you told her not to.

'You must breastfeed for a certain number of months,' the midwife advised her.

'I'll breastfeed for as long as I want to,' she replied. I'll do what I want to do when I want to do it, she thought.

Mum always said, 'There can be rules in life and I will adhere to rules, but only if they make sense.'

This attitude dated back to her schooldays. She and her older brother John had attended a very strict convent school in Burnley where they were caned and hit with rulers. They experienced the sort of fanatical discipline you see in a film like *The Magdalene Sisters* and, even today, my Uncle John trembles at the sight of bamboo. Their stories about the way they were treated were so horrific that I'd say, 'You're not telling me the truth now, are you?' But they *were* telling the truth. It was that bad. Mum knew all about nuns trying to stamp out individuality in their pupils.

There was a particular incident that she looked back on as a turning point in her life. One day, after the lunch break, she was sitting at the back of the classroom when she realised she needed the bathroom.

She put her hand up and said to the nun in charge, 'Sister, may I go to the bathroom?'

'No,' the nun said sternly. 'You should have gone at break.'

'But I didn't need it then,' Mum said.

9

'I said no!' the nun snapped.

Mum thought, In that case, I've no choice but to go to the bathroom right here. And that's what she did.

She was sent to the Mother Superior, who gave her a vicious beating. But, from that day onwards, she and the other children were allowed to go to the bathroom at any time of day, not just during the breaks. One point to Mum! She always maintained that she'd done nothing wrong.

Mum inherited her massive personality from her dad, William 'Bill' Pepper, my Poppa, who was successful, charismatic, generous, loving and opinionated. Poppa was the patriarch of the Pepper family, the leader of the pack, a regular Don Corleone. We nicknamed him 'Poppa Shango, the head of the Mafia' and he was always impeccably dressed, just like a Mafia boss.

At the end of a big family dinner, Poppa would clink his glass, ting-ting-ting, and everyone would stop to listen. You always wanted to listen when Poppa spoke. Although quite small in stature, he had a grandeur, a presence. Like my mum, he could hold court for hours on end.

After thanking everyone for coming and saying a few words about the family occasion we were celebrating, he would glance invitingly around the table and say, 'Sinatra, anybody?' Then he'd start into a Frank Sinatra song and all the Pepper men would join in. It was beautiful to hear and enthralling to watch. I was always wide-eyed around Poppa.

I'm definitely more Pepper than I am Riley and I love all the stories the Peppers tell. We used to have 'Pepper barbecues' at home, where all the Pepper women ended up in the conservatory and all the men in the kitchen, nattering away. It was often so loud that you had to sit with your ear next to someone's mouth to hear what they were saying. Everything was on show with the Peppers. Everyone was telling a story. It was always a question of, Who's got the limelight? Who's got the talking stick? I could have sat there and listened to them forever.

I used to say, 'Poppa, tell me more *Angela's Ashes* stories!'

'Well, it was bad. It was terrible,' he'd say. He found it quite difficult to talk about the dark days of his childhood.

Poppa was born into a very poor, very big Irish Catholic family in the Lancashire mill town of Burnley, in 1922. His mother gave birth to twelve children, two of whom tragically died in child-birth, followed by another two who died in early infancy. Poppa was the youngest of the boys. He and his brothers slept four to a bed and my Great-uncle John recalls saying to Poppa, 'Wee on us, Bill, to make the bed warm!' It was pure, Northern, hard living.

Communities were tight back then. When a baby was born, the neighbours would bring round a huge cottage pie and a trifle, which would last the entire family for four nights. The boys were encouraged to go out to work very young. My poppa was lucky and got a trade as a plumber. He was very driven. He did everything he could to leave behind the dirt and squalor of his childhood and with pure hard work he made a huge success of himself. I think that's partly why he was always immaculately turned out in later life. He wore tailored cream silk jackets and red silk ties with matching handkerchiefs. His beloved wife, my Nanna, was his perfect counterpart in her bright silk dresses and glamorous fur stoles. Nanna and Poppa were known among the Peppers as 'Taylor and Burton'.

The Peppers tend to be highly strung, very up and down. We call it 'the Pepper gene'. There are millions of them and they're all artistic. Depression was rife on that side of the family and Poppa's favourite sister, Nelly, suffered especially badly with it. She was given electroconvulsive therapy in an attempt to cure her depression and she later tried to kill herself. Mum couldn't understand why Nelly constantly wore roll-neck jumpers, because no one had told her what Nelly had tried to do. It was one of those secrets that families keep hidden, and everyone was very protective of Nelly. It crucified my poppa. Nelly's depression almost took her to the point of no return.

Like many families from the Manchester area, our roots are Irish: the Peppers were of Cork descent; and Nanna, whose maiden name was Mary Higgins, came from Tipperary. Nanna's father was a postman who wasn't getting the rounds that he wanted over in Ireland and was advised to come over to England, where he could make a good living. So that's what he did and he never looked back.

Nanna and Poppa met in 1945 at a church fundraiser Pop Higgins had organised at a Burnley club called the Mechanics. Poppa had come back from the war and Nanna was working as a clipper girl on the buses, where she was called Clipper Tipperary Mary. They went on to have a very happy marriage. It was a traditional relationship, where the man went out to work and the woman kept house and put the food on the table. Poppa was the great provider at work and Nanna was the great provider at home. She lived on her nerves and he spoke for both of them. They remained in Burnley and had two children, first my dear Uncle John, in 1948, and then my mum, Cath, who was born in

1954. These two were like chalk and cheese: John was timid and didn't like crowds; Mum was full of beans, the life and soul of every party.

Poppa's business went from strength to strength and Mum became quite spoilt as a result. After the family moved to Bury in 1961, she asked Poppa if she could have her own basin in her bedroom. Well, what Cath wanted, Cath got. She was Poppa's little princess, the ultimate daddy's girl. She was never in any doubt that he would have fought lions and tigers for her.

Mum was so bright and clever. She passed her Eleven Plus and could have done really well at school, but she rebelled against the harsh convent rules and was expelled at fourteen for truancy and smoking at the bus stop with her girlfriends. It was 1968 and the world was changing fast. Mum was eager to grow up and get a taste of the world.

Luckily for her, she could do no wrong in Poppa's eyes. She was never a spoilt brat, but she tended to get what she wanted. Not only did Poppa buy her a full-length caramel fur coat, but she was the first among her friends to have an all-in-one denim catsuit, which she wore with a fur bomber jacket. She liked to make an impact, did Mum. It's easy to see why people said of her, 'Once met, never forgotten.'

Aged sixteen, she and Jackie Barrett, her best friend at the time, used to sneak off to the Twisted Wheel nightclub in Manchester, which later became the Hacienda. Mum would tell Nanna, 'I'm stopping at Jackie's' and Jackie would tell her mum, 'I'm stopping at Cath's.' Then they'd get the late bus to Manchester and stay up all night dancing.

They were found out, of course, when Jackie's mum phoned

Nanna and asked to speak to her daughter. 'Isn't she at your house with our Cath?' Nanna asked.

This landed Mum in a lot of bother, but she always said that it was the best thing that could have happened. Since she wasn't allowed out after that, she set her sights on passing her driving test. If Mum put her mind to something, she'd do it, so she crammed and crammed. She was the only one of her girlfriends to pass her driving test first time, and she passed it with the minimum required hours of lessons.

Poppa rewarded her with an amazing car and for a while she was a crazy girl, a complete speed demon, always up to no good. Then she settled down a bit and got a job as a receptionist at the Gas Board, where she met two of her best friends, Joyce and Dilly. Auntie Dilly has never forgotten how all her colleagues came to work on the bus, but Mum would tip up in her Lancia sports car, which was smarter than the car their boss had!

Mum met my dad, Terry Riley, on a Tuesday night in June 1973 at a roller rink in Bury. It went on to be a nightclub called Sol Viva, but at the time it was called the Palladium. My dad was in there with his brother, my Uncle Graham; Mum was in there with Jackie Barrett. I think Dad loved the fact that Mum was confident and a little bit bonkers, but good bonkers. And she had the most incredible smile. 'Cath Riley's smile can melt butter,' everybody said. In turn, Mum loved the fact that Dad was a gentle, tender, cuddly giant. He was always her teddy bear, her rock, the stable one in the relationship.

I can see Dad's face now, watching Mum proudly as she held court among her friends or at a family gathering. The look on his face said, 'That's my girl.' Not that Dad's a wallflower, not at all. He holds his own. But he's that laid back, he's falling over. He's just happy in Terryland. He's always been the great provider for the family, but Mum wore eighty pairs of trousers in the relationship.

I love the story of when Mum took Dad home to meet Nanna and Poppa for the first time. 'Oh, you can marry him, he's got beautiful hands,' Nanna said approvingly.

'Good luck, son, you're going to need it,' Poppa said, thumping him on the shoulder.

Cath and Terry wed on 17 August 1975, introducing another über-personality into the family: my dad's mother, Gran Pat Riley. Bury born and bred, Gran was larger than life in so many ways. The epitome of the raw, wholesome, Northern woman, she said, 'kooking' instead of 'cooking', she was devoted to her family, she gossiped over the fence and she always had a fag on.

If you're familiar with Les Dawson's infamous creation Ada Shufflebotham, one of the Northern housewives in the 'Cissie and Ada' sketches, you'll have an idea of who Gran was. Just like Ada, she pursed her lips and silently mouthed the unmentionable things in life, rather than saying them out loud. This was known as 'mee-mawing' and it originated among the mill workers of Lancashire, because they couldn't be heard above the deafening noise of the looms, even when they shouted. After a while, mee-mawing became a part of daily life, especially when it came to discussing embarrassing or saucy topics. Basically, you mee-mawed anything you didn't want people to overhear, even when there was no one around to listen in.

Gran was tall and thin and bursting with confidence. 'I'm a peach, me,' she used to say. 'I'm gorgeous.'

That used to wind Mum up. 'Who in their right mind goes round telling people, "I'm a peach?"' she would complain. Well, the answer was, my gran! She was that woman. And in later life, somehow – anyhow – she would always manage to slip the words, 'My granddaughter is Lisa Riley' into a conversation, even if she was only buying a pound of Bourbon biscuits at Bury market. As for Granddad Sam, he was even more laid back than my dad. Gran was definitely the queen bee in that household.

Mum and Gran never really saw eye to eye, although they were alike in quite a few ways. They both had huge personalities and neither of them bothered about what other people thought of them. Gran thought Mum was a bit of a princess, I think. Gran was very traditional: Granddad's tea would be on the table at the same time every night and the week would take the same course, week in, week out.

In my gran's world, you did your shopping for the week on a Tuesday, whereas that kind of routine was abhorrent to my mum. Her attitude was: I'll do what I want; I'll make what I want; and if it's not there at six o'clock, so what?

There's a line in the film *Shirley Valentine*, when Shirley talks about her husband Joe always having to have his tea on the table at six. It used to make Mum roar. 'There are actually people like that!' she'd say, knowing full well that my gran was one of them.

We used to tease Mum about being a snob. We had this family joke that anyone who was anyone in Bury lived above the Citroën Garage just off the Tottington Road. Since Mum was brought up in the area above the garage, whereas my dad was born and bred below it, in 'real' Bury, you might say she had married beneath her, if she was that sort of girl, which she wasn't. Still, it didn't stop us teasing her about it, especially as she had an aversion to the sound of a really strong Bury accent, which is right loud and gruff. Quite a lot of people in Bury have booming voices, like they've got no eardrums. That's another knock-on from working in the noisy mills, I've heard.

'He's got a voice that breathed o'er bloody Eden!' Mum'd say, in a mock-snobbish way, whenever she heard a thundering Bury accent. She didn't put her nose in the air, but I suppose she had a high opinion of herself. Everyone knew that about her.

Anyway, whether or not there was a bit of a Pepper–Riley clash, the whole family was thrilled when I came along, just under a year after Mum married Dad. It was the height of the hottest summer on record and the sweltering heat meant that I gave Mum torture during the last month of the pregnancy, but the birth was easy and I arrived happy and healthy, weighing 7lb 1oz. Mum was desperately hoping that her first-born would be a girl. It wasn't for the whole pink thing, because Mum wasn't that sort of person. She put me in green and yellow, if anything, and in her book it was all right for girls to wear jeans. No, she wanted a girl because she wanted a mini-me, which she absolutely got! I am, without doubt, my mother's daughter, and she was ecstatic when she had me.

But then, seventeen months after I was born, Mum's world fell apart when Nanna died unexpectedly of a perforated duodenal ulcer. Cancer wasn't mentioned at the time, but a doctor cousin on the Pepper side thinks it probably would have been a cancer. It was devastating for Mum to lose her devoted mother Mary. It was such a terrible shock that her hair went white and grey within months. She had salt and pepper hair forever after.

To make things worse, Poppa collapsed with grief. He completely crumbled and had a full-on nervous breakdown. He was down for a long time. It was a double blow for my mum, who had just lost her mother. As well as grieving for Nanna, she was faced with the rawness of what Poppa was going through. She did her best to support him, but it was painfully difficult for her. Poppa had always been her safety net and now the roles were reversed.

When the chips are down on the Riley side, the violins are playing – they always love a drama – whereas when the Peppers are down, they tend to put on a front and pretend everything is OK. Their attitude is, 'Troop on! Troop on!' But from what I'm told, the chips were desperately down at this time and Poppa simply couldn't troop on.

Mum was twenty-three, with a newish husband and a demanding toddler, but when she realised the full extent of Poppa's breakdown, she and my dad made the decision to move in with him. It was brave of my dad to agree to it. He had to take a back seat and leave my mum to comfort Poppa and look after me. He remembers it as a terrible time. My dad loves his food – he's a big man – but they lived on soup. 'Lisa, you wouldn't believe how much soup we ate,' he says. That sums it up, for me. When people can't cope in life, they resort to soup.

We stayed with Poppa for two years. He stopped working and Mum's brother John, who worked with Poppa, took over. The business could have completely crumbled had it not been for the brilliance of Uncle John. He kept the candle lit, working all the hours he could to keep everything ticking over.

Mum often talked about that time. 'You were my comfort

blanket,' she used to say to me. She cuddled me endlessly and had me in bed with her every night, even though she'd been told that it was wrong to sleep with your baby. In the years that followed, she always liked to have me near, so I didn't go to nursery or pre-school. There was a Wednesday morning crèche held at our local church in Tottington, St Hilda's, where you could drop your child off for a couple of hours. Mum would take me there and Auntie Joyce would take her son Simon, but they never left us. Instead they sat and had a brew together while we played. Me and Si are twelve days apart in age, so we were the perfect playmates.

Despite the sadness and upheaval caused by Nanna's passing, I grew up happy and confident. My parents adored me, my grandparents treasured me and everyone encouraged me to be my own person. Obviously, I took them at their word and one Christmas Eve, when I was four, I became upset at the thought that Santa didn't want to wake me up for a chat when he came down the chimney. I had a beautiful pair of flamenco shoes that we'd brought back from a holiday in Spain and I felt sure he would want to see me dancing and clicking my castanets. Why wouldn't he?

After me and Mum had put some mince pies, sherry and a carrot on the hearth, I lay in bed and said, 'I have been good, haven't I, Mum?'

'Yes, of course. Why?' she asked.

'Why can't Santa wake me up and tell me I've been good? Wouldn't he like to see me do a flamenco dance in my shoes?'

I felt Santa had let me down by not wanting to see me dance. Then I wondered if he would like to wear flamenco shoes and do a Spanish dance too. I remember being swept away by the idea of Santa doing flamenco in my bedroom. I have no idea if that's a normal thought for a four-year-old to have, but it's typical of me. It was one of the first signs that I had of what Mum called my 'fairy-tale mind', something I don't think I've ever lost.

Like most little girls, I had a thing about shoes, especially grown-ups' shoes. What fascinated me was the sound they made when they clacked against the floor, particularly high heels. So, one day while I was at Gran's house, I decided to pop down to her neighbour Jean's house and borrow her shoes. Gran only wore flats and sandals, but Jean had the best footwear in the world. I desperately wanted to make that click-clack sound that she made when she left Gran's bungalow and walked down the steep slope to where she lived at the bottom of the brew.

So, off I went down the brew and knocked on Jean's door. She opened the door and looked down at me, astonished. 'Hi, it's me!' I said. 'Can I borrow your shoes?'

'What?' she spluttered.

'Please may I borrow your shoes?' I asked.

By now, Gran had noticed I was gone. 'Lisa!' she shouted frantically from four doors away.

'I'm fine, I'm at Jean's,' I called back.

Gran came running out of her front door. 'What the friggin' hell are you doing at Jean's?' she squawked.

To my delight and joy, Jean then handed me a pair of black patent court shoes. Up and down the road I walked in those shoes, clacking away, loving every second of it.

*

Eventually Mum had to let me go to school and I started at Holly Mount Roman Catholic primary school in Greenmount, Bury. Holly Mount was, and still is, a beautiful school, situated at the end of a long, narrow, treacherous lane. It was next to a church, which has since been converted into luxurious apartments.

Mum took up jogging on my first day at school. Auntie Joyce was astounded. 'Cath, jogging?' she said. Mum's daily run used to take her all the way up the lane leading to Holly Mount and past the school playground at precisely the time of my play break. Unbeknown to me, she'd be anxiously peering through the railings as she passed, feverishly checking that I was all right. She needn't have worried. I loved Holly Mount and all the new friends I was making, including Samantha, who remains my bezzie to this day. And it wasn't long before Mum and Gail, Sam's mum, became really close. Mum had so many friends it was insane. She had to be the most popular person in Bury.

A few months ago, Sam and Gail were discussing what to get me for my birthday. Gail went through some old photos and found a snapshot of me dressed as a sunflower, aged five. In costume for my first starring role, a song and dance at Holly Mount, I was wearing a green head-to-toe leotard and a headdress of yellow petals, with just my face showing.

Gail and Sam couldn't help laughing. 'It's perfect,' they agreed.

Gail decided to have the photograph mounted on canvas for my most recent birthday, partly because the petals are yellow, Mum's favourite colour, but also because she can remember watching me up there on the school stage like it was yesterday.

There I was, singing and dancing my heart out in the assembly hall, when Gail turned to Mum and said, 'She's a natural, Cath. She could end up doing that forever.'

'Don't be so bloody daft!' my mum said, swiping at Gail and laughing her famously infectious laugh.

2

You can take the girl out of Bury

I think of myself as a Northern lass, through and through. My hometown of Bury is in my blood and in my bones and I'm incredibly proud of my roots. But things could have been very different, because in 1981 we emigrated to Canada, after Dad was offered an amazing job there. Suddenly a whole new future loomed. Aged five, nearly six, I was set to lose my Northern identity and start speaking with a Canadian twang.

Dad had followed in his father's footsteps and become a printer, before branching out into graphics. He knew his trade inside out and was doing well in Bury, but the Canadian job was a once-in-a-lifetime opportunity. I think he relished the idea of leaving England and starting afresh, mainly because he wanted to give Mum and me a better life. I also get the impression that he struggled with a sense of living under Poppa's shadow, and that this was his chance to match Poppa materially.

At last he could give Mum everything that Poppa had given

her, and more. If Cath wanted a car now, she got a car. If she wanted the best velour curtains known to man, he could provide that for her. Not that Mum was demanding and she certainly wasn't materialistic. She just had a certain taste that I think she inherited from her mother. God, she'd love a Chanel handbag, simply because it was beautiful, but she wouldn't be bothered if she didn't have one. The label meant nothing to her and Dad knew that. Still, it didn't stop him wanting to give her the life he felt that she deserved.

Mum and Dad had a big emotional leaving party at the Walshaw Cricket Club. It was heartbreaking saying goodbye to all their friends and family, and especially hard for Mum to leave Poppa. In the early summer of 1981 we left for our new home in the Mississauga district of Toronto, on the shores of Lake Ontario. Mum loved it at first. Everything was new and exciting and she was the sort of person who made the best of everything. But over time she began to feel homesick. She desperately missed everyone back in Bury. Sometimes I saw her cry and I never understood why. It all makes sense now, but at the time I had no idea and she didn't tell me, not that I'd have understood at that age. All I knew was that whenever she got on the phone she'd burst into tears.

A couple of months after we arrived, she went to the hairdresser's and had her hair tinted a purply red wine colour. It was a radical move, as by now her salt and pepper hair had become her trademark, a statement, and she'd grown to love it. I've seen photographs of Mum with wine-coloured hair and she looks weird, so I can only think she was trying to reinvent herself for her new life.

Well, it instantly backfired. 'I can't bear it. I can't look at you!' Dad said when he saw it, and he persuaded her to grow it out. I think that's the only time Dad has put his foot down and got what he wanted. She never tinted her hair again.

There's a lot of snow in our photos of Canada. Snow and husky dogs. It does look a bit boring, really. Dad began flying people out to visit us, so that Mum would feel less homesick. Poppa came for two months, which was brilliant. There was one slightly sticky moment, though, on the day he arrived. Mum was still Poppa's little princess, to the point that she had managed to conceal from him that she was a smoker, even though she wasn't far off thirty. 'Someone's smoking!' he boomed, wrinkling his nose. He found Mum having a fag on the terrace and she finally had to confess.

Mum was broken when Poppa went home. I'll never forget it, because she didn't take me to school. Instead I got on the school bus, which was unheard of, Mum being as protective as she was. I asked her about it in later life, but she just shook her head.

'It's a pain that I never want to describe or revisit,' she said.

We flew home a couple of times, which must have been nice for her, although there was always the agony of leaving again. All I remember about those trips is that I had a horrific nosebleed on one of the flights because of the pressure of landing. For years after that I'd have nosebleeds every time I flew.

Back in Canada, we had more visitors, including my gran. Gran didn't cope very well with being out there. She wasn't well travelled. She came to see me, more than anything. There's a picture of her on her first day in Canada: she's half-heartedly waving a little Canadian flag and I'm doing a Debbie McGee, peering round her with my widest grin. There are loads of photos of me in Canada, on my roller skates or my bike. 'Take a picture of me!' I'd call out as I whizzed round a corner. It was clear, even then, that there was no way I was ever going to be a wallflower.

My memories of Canada are mainly happy ones. I enjoyed my new school and I was way ahead in class, because the English curriculum was a bit further ahead at the time. It drove Mum mad because she worried I wasn't learning anything, but it was great for me. I remember being thrilled to have a dog, a whippet called Junior, and I had a lovely friend next door called Kimmy. Best of all, our house had a massive basement with a ping pong table, a pool table and, in the corner, a wooden bar with several tall wooden stools. This little corner area was my stage. Stepping from one stool to another, I'd do a little performance on each stool top: I'd sing a song, recite a nursery rhyme or act out a character.

By now Mum was used to me acting out stories and letting my imagination run away with me. I had several 'My Little Pony' toys and Sindy dolls that I played with for hours on end, developing characters for them, giving them voices, putting them into different scenarios and doing all the sound effects. But she would go mental when she came down and found me doing my performances in the basement. 'Get off those frigging stools!' she'd yell, terrified that I was going to fall.

I tried to explain that it wasn't half as much fun doing my shows on the huge pool table. I think the precariousness of balancing on each stool gave the whole thing an edge that I enjoyed, and each little stage could be a different 'moment'. She wasn't having it, though.

Mum got so bored that she used to come into my school two days a week to help out as a classroom assistant. I had a very nice teacher called Mrs Bent, who later recalled me being fanatical about some baby chicks we were rearing as part of a nature project. I was given the task of putting them in a little incubator to keep them warm and I wouldn't let anyone else go near them.

'Come on, let someone else have a go,' Mum cajoled, in her role as classroom assistant.

But I wouldn't share them. 'No, *I'm* caring for them,' I said protectively. 'I have to make sure they're looked after.'

Like Mum, I could be a bit controlling! These days, my friends call me 'LL', which stands for 'Lisa Leader'. They tell me that this is because I'm bossy, though I'm not sure that's true. But if I have a bee in my bonnet, I certainly like things to go my way. I obviously had a bee in my bonnet about those chicks.

Mrs Bent has another particular memory of me, bless her. Apparently, when she asked me if I wanted to sit on a chair to read my book, I said, 'No, I'm fine reading on the floor, because I've got a built-in cushion.' It was me being camp, aged six!

We had been in Canada around a year when Auntie Joyce and Uncle Jesse came over to visit. In true style, they arrived with a bottle of Remy Martin brandy, which was downed on their first night.

Obviously, when Cath and her best friend got together with a bottle of Remy Martin, everything was fantastic, but the following morning, Mum said, 'I don't feel well.'

'That will be the brandy, my love,' Joyce said with a laugh.

'No, Joyce, you don't understand. I've been feeling sick for two weeks now and my boobs are killing me. What if … ?'

Joyce's jaw hit the floor. 'For God's sake, Cath, smell the roses. Get yourself to a GP, quick.'

Off Mum went to the doctor's. 'It's a bit more serious than a brandy hangover,' she announced when she got back. 'I'm three months pregnant!'

Although she'd been starting to suspect something was up, it was still a huge shock for Mum. She'd been thinking it was jet lag or the change of climate – anything apart from the obvious. Counting back, she realised that the date of the baby's conception coincided with the only three days in the six years since my birth that she had missed taking her contraceptive pill, in the time between losing her British GP and finding a Canadian one. My brother Liam, who was born six months later in June 1983, was *so* meant to be.

He wasn't planned and I've always joked about him being an accident. We laugh about it to this day. Even his twenty-first birthday invitation said, 'Please join the accident to celebrate his birthday!'

And when Liam asked me to be best woman at his wedding, I said in my speech, 'Ladies and gentlemen, I love my brother so much, but as you know, he's the worst accident that has ever happened to me, because he stole my thunder!' Everybody roared. 'I am glad, Liam, that you've turned out how you have.' I went on. 'Even though Mum did everything they tell you not to during the first few months of her pregnancy, you're such a bright boy and I'm so proud of you. Now here's a bottle of Remy Martin to celebrate your wedding night!'

Mum hadn't planned Liam, but she was thrilled that another baby was on the way. However, his birth was not straightforward and, after a long labour, the doctors resorted to forceps to deliver him. Mum had to stay in hospital for a few days afterwards. All well and good, except that anyone under sixteen was banned from visiting the unit where she was, because of the risk of spreading infection. Since Mum and I had only ever spent the night apart when I stayed at Gran and Granddad's back in England, Mum missed me desperately. No-rules Cath told the nurses, 'I want to see my little girl. I have to see her!'

Meanwhile, I was going crazy, because I hated being apart from Mum. 'You'd better let my child in here now. She's upset,' Mum said, but the staff were adamant that I wasn't allowed in.

So Mum and Dad hatched a plan, whereby Dad smuggled me into the hospital and hid me in a maintenance cupboard just along the corridor from where Mum was. At an appointed time, Mum told the nurses that she needed to have a walk and get some air. She slipped away from the ward and met up with me and Dad, so that she could give me some precious reassurance and cuddles.

Unsurprisingly, I wasn't too keen on Liam at first. It was a shock for me to have to share Mum all of a sudden and I struggled with how close she was to the new baby. When Gran heard about this, she sent me some tap dancing shoes from England, so that I wouldn't feel left out. I think the idea was for me to dazzle anyone who came near Liam's crib with a tap dancing Shirley Temple impression. I love that. Thank you, Gran.

Liam's birth changed everything. Until he was born, we had our life mapped out in Canada. Big house, two cars; Dad was doing tremendously well at work; I was doing great at school. But Cath, being Cath, couldn't handle not having someone to share the baby with. She had loads of friends in Canada, but they weren't the friends and family she really needed. And so the decision was made: we've got to go home, because Cath gets what Cath wants. Three months after Liam was born, we came back to England.

Isn't it weird what my life could have been? It freaks me out, it really does. It reminds me of the movie *Sliding Doors*: I look at Canada as the tube train I didn't get on. Who knows what would have happened if we'd stayed. I was still the same confident kid over there, but would I have gone on to be an actor? I hope so, but I sometimes wonder. Would Canada have flattened me?

I think Dad must have regretted coming home. We'd had the big lavish leaving party and within nineteen months we were back. Dad probably felt defeated; it's a male pride thing. That is the ballpoint truth. Anyway, why on earth would he have wanted to come home, when his future was so bright over there? As far as he was concerned, the move to Canada could be only for the good. If he'd had his way, which he never did, we would have stayed.

On our final return to England, my nose bled so badly when we landed that the stewards filled a bag with ice and packed it on my face. It was really worrying for Mum. All the other passengers got off the airplane, but they kept me on until last because my jersey was covered in blood. I remember everyone looking at me as they filed past. I felt suffocated and panicked. I didn't want the fuss and I had a horrible feeling of being hemmed in. To this day, I have a fear of confined spaces and I'm sure it dates back to that flight.

Back in Bury, we went to live with Poppa for seven months, until we found our own house. While we were in Canada, Poppa had moved to a beautiful house in Harwood called Salamanca, which had a sweeping drive leading up to the front door and a games room, with a snooker table in it. Poppa had come so far since his childhood. It makes me well up to think of it. Even to this day I like to watch the Barbara Taylor Bradford 1984 miniseries *Hold The Dream* and *A Woman of Substance*, which follow the rise of a determined young girl from kitchen maid to respected businesswoman. It always makes me think of Poppa. There's eight hours of it and I can easily spend a whole Sunday watching it.

As soon as Mum and Dad's friends and family heard we were coming back, they went round to Poppa's and dropped off a mountain of gifts for the baby. These were stored in the games room until you couldn't see the snooker table for presents and hampers. When we arrived, I couldn't understand why none of it was for me, but I nabbed some of it anyway. Nelly's daughter, Auntie Anne, remembers me using Liam's Johnson's Baby Talc as a pretend microphone.

I had my own room with an adjoining bathroom at Poppa's. Mum said that she felt history was repeating itself because she could see that I was Poppa's little princess, just as she had been. I was the apple of his eye. Poppa was the most generous person I've ever come across in my whole life. He provided for everyone in his family. It was never frivolous stuff, though. It was always clothes or books, because he liked to give you what would benefit you.

Officially, there was no longer space for me back at Holly

Mount primary school, so Mum had to charm and wheedle the head, Sister James, into finding room for me. I struggled with my lessons at first, because I was way behind in our curriculum. Still, it was great to be back with my bezzie Samantha and the rest of the gang and I soon settled in again. I was a popular pupil, quite naughty, but never cheeky or backchatty. Everyone described me as giddy and the teachers were constantly telling Mum that I was full of life. And although my studies didn't go too well, at least I was always the Angel Gabriel in the nativity play. I loved being an angel, with wings, booming forth from on high. I never wanted to be Mary.

On rainy days, instead of going into the playground, we were all made to congregate in a narrow corridor that led from the dining room to the playground. My fear of confined spaces meant that I hated being hemmed in there. And anyway, I thought, why can't we go out and play? I loved the idea of mucking around in the rain and not caring about getting wet. It appealed to my romantic streak.

What I liked best about school was entertaining people. I mimicked the teachers, impersonated the other kids and turned every situation into a comic skit. At home, Mum and Dad never had to say, 'Lisa, do that funny voice you do for Auntie!' because whether or not we had visitors, I'd start performing anyway. It was never in an over-the-top, stage school, jazz hands way. It was just something I did, constantly.

Mum would say, 'What do you want for tea?'

Instead of saying, 'Fish fingers', I'd operatically sing, 'Fi-i-sh fing-er-ers!'

Mum would sigh. 'Just talk, Lisa. Please, just talk.'

I was a little bit different from the other kids at school, something that was brought home to Mum one parents' evening at Holly Mount, when I was about eight. They had put teas and coffees on in the assembly room and all the mums gathered there after seeing the teachers. Mum was tired after a run of sleepless nights with baby Liam, so instead of holding court like she usually did, for once she sat back and listened as the other parents chatted about their kids.

A group of mums started talking about a character called Penfold from the cartoon series *Danger Mouse*, which was a major obsession among school kids up and down the country in 1984.

'My Colette can't stop talking about *Danger Mouse*!' one mum said.

'My Katie's writing a story about Penfold,' another mum chipped in.

'Penfold!' someone else said. 'I wish our Michelle would shut up about Penfold for just one minute!'

Mum frowned. She had never heard me mention Penfold or *Danger Mouse*. Is there something wrong with my child? she worried.

An image of me popped into her head, a vision of her eight-year-old daughter sitting in the window of our house strumming a plastic toy guitar and singing 'Moon River' over the window box. I just wanted to be Holly Golightly, the Audrey Hepburn character in *Breakfast at Tiffany's*. Gran had all the Audrey Hepburn films and I was always impersonating her. Gran encouraged me to show off. She loved watching me role play.

I suppose I was a little bit eccentric. Often when I went to Gran's, the first thing I'd say was, 'Please can we watch *Seven Brides for Seven Brothers*? Please, please, please?' It was either that or *Finian's Rainbow*. Gran and Granddad could leave me in a room with a video of *Finian's Rainbow* for hours on end and when they came back I'd still be fast-forwarding and rewinding to find the best bits, parroting the voices and copying the dances. I knew it verbatim, still do.

I didn't have a pushy mum at all, but I had a pushy gran. While Mum would say, 'Come on, that's enough now,' Gran always said, 'Go for it!' Instead of getting a draught excluder for the front door, she put up some drapes so that I'd have my own pair of theatrical curtains to burst through.

Whenever any of her relatives came over, Gran would say, 'Lisa, do that song from *Mary Poppins*!'

I'd jump up and run off to find a stick and some talcum powder, in readiness for the Bert and Mary song, 'Jolly Holiday.' I'd put the talc on the carpet so that it puffed up when I pretended to jump on Bert's chalk drawing on the pavement, like it did in the movie.

Gran always sat in the same place on the same couch. It was Gran's perch. 'Go on, stand over there,' she'd say, directing me to a carpeted step built into the wall, known as 'the plinth', which has since been replaced by a fireplace. That was my stage when I was a kid. 'Right, sing!' Gran would say. 'Sing louder!'

Standing on the plinth, *my* plinth, I'd sing songs, do dialogue from films and mimic everyone and anyone, from pop stars to Gran's neighbours and members of the family. The moment I heard something new, I had to mimic it, whether it was an accent, a turn of phrase or a particular sound.

I often went to Gran and Granddad's at weekends and then I started going there every Wednesday after school, so that Mum could have a girls' night out with Auntie Joyce and all her other friends. Gran and I used to cosy up in front of the telly and watch *Open All Hours*, *The Two Ronnies*, *Morecambe and Wise* and absolutely anything that had Victoria Wood, Maureen Lipman or Thora Hird in it. It fascinated me that Thora Hird could make me laugh simply by grimacing.

Weekends at Gran's revolved around *The Colbys* and *Dynasty*. I was obsessed with the drama, the glamour and what I would now describe as the drag queen make-up. As soon as the theme tune came on at the end of *Dynasty*, I'd be up on the plinth, imitating Joan Collins. 'Daahling!' I'd say, raising one eyebrow and pouting. 'I never buy *anything* on sale!'

Over time, Gran got rid of all the ornaments around the plinth. 'Once she starts, accidents happen,' she told my auntie, by way of explanation.

She was right about that. One Sunday when I was nine, I was up to my usual tricks while Mum and Dad were in the kitchen having a fag. You were only allowed to smoke in the kitchen at my gran and granddad's. When everyone had finished their fags, Gran would say, 'Come on, let's go into the house,' meaning the front room.

'Gran, we're already in the house,' I'd say, but she took no notice. I could never understand it.

Anyway, this particular Sunday, Gran watched in horror as I

did a cartwheel off the plinth, crashed into a huge plant pot and split my jaw open. There was blood everywhere. Mum and Dad rushed into the front room to find me laid out on the floor. They took me straight to A&E, where I needed fourteen internal and fourteen external stitches.

The doctor who treated me was Scottish, which I found intriguing. Hey, I've not heard that way of speaking before! I thought. I must try it. So I chatted away in a Scottish accent for the entire time the doctor sewed up my mouth and chin. He couldn't believe it; neither could Mum or Dad.

It was around now that Mum realised I needed a bigger platform for my performances – literally! At the same time, she started noticing articles about the Oldham Theatre Workshop in the *Manchester Evening News* and other local papers. Oldham Theatre Workshop was known for supplying *Coronation Street* with young actors like Anne Kirkbride, who went into the series in her teens and still plays Deirdre to this day – and later Sally Whittaker and Sean Wilson. Community-based and council funded, it was a place where kids really learnt how to act, which is why groundbreaking Granada TV dramas like *Cracker* and *Prime Suspect* later went there to cast younger actors. There was nothing 'tits and teeth' about Oldham Theatre Workshop. If you had the slightest leaning towards that style of performing, David Johnson, its brilliant founder and director, struck it out of you.

Each year, Oldham Theatre Workshop put on two shows: a Christmas panto or play that was performed in their upstairs studio, and a summer musical showcase that was staged at the Oldham Coliseum. In early 1985, Mum took me along to an audition for the next summer show. There were hundreds and hundreds of kids there and we were divided into groups of four and five and given role plays to enact. I vividly remember being asked to pretend to be a supermarket customer, while someone else was the cashier. It was just the sort of thing I loved doing, because I was constantly observing and imitating people. I based my role play on conversations I'd overheard when Mum and I went shopping together. I really got into talking about prices, special offers and what time the cashier clocked off.

As the day went on, each of us was given a red, an amber or a green spot. In the mid-afternoon, David Johnson clapped his hands and said, 'Everyone with a red spot, thank you, we'll be in touch.' Unfamiliar with audition etiquette, I didn't realise that these words meant the people with the red spots hadn't got through. Shortly afterwards, the people with the amber spots were asked to leave. I had a green spot, which took me through to the second stage of the audition.

Next, I had to sing a song. It was that clichéd stage school anthem 'Tomorrow' from the musical *Annie*, which was an interesting choice, because Oldham Theatre Workshop wasn't that kind of place. It wasn't like the Sylvia Young Theatre School and they weren't looking for the next Bonnie Langford, so I can only imagine 'Tomorrow' hits certain keys that prove whether someone can sing or not. I didn't particularly like *Annie* at the time and I didn't know the song; I had probably heard it along the way, but I'd never actually sung it. Bryn Taylor, the musical director, started playing it on the piano and I had to pick it up instantly and start singing.

I must have done OK, because I was called back for an interview with David Johnson. 'We want Lisa in the summer showcase,' he told my mother afterwards. 'She's definitely got something special and I think her future as an actor could be very, very bright.' My heart soared. I couldn't wait to come to my first Workshop session. I was going to be an actress!

'But I need to warn you now that I'm certain Lisa won't make it as a child actor, so she needs to keep concentrating on her education in the meantime,' he went on. 'It's important she keeps up her studies, so that she has something to fall back on.'

Whoops, I'm not sure I heard that last part. Or if I did, I chose to ignore it.

3

Educating Lisa

I wasn't a fat kid. I started out cuddly and then became a little bit podgy, but it wasn't until puberty at around twelve that the weight really went on. Before that, my size was nothing out of the ordinary, so it seemed weird to Mum that my form teacher Sister Mary John kept on at her about it.

If you're wondering why my mum sent me to a convent school after having such a terrible time under the nuns at her school in Burnley, the main reason was because Holly Mount was by far and away the best primary school in Greater Manchester. The other reason was Poppa. While Mum and Dad would probably have described themselves as lapsed Catholics, as would Gran Riley, who was snubbed by her church when she got pregnant with my dad out of wedlock at the age of seventeen, Poppa was still one of the faithful. He would have been furious if I hadn't gone to a Catholic school.

After walking out on Sister Mary John, Mum was tempted

to take me away from Holly Mount. But she recognised that I was very happy there and wouldn't have wanted to be split up from my lovely friends. My other bezzie, Kate, had joined the school by then and me, Kate and Samantha were inseparable. Our mums were mates too and at one point Mum, Sam's mother Gail and Kate's mother Pam had the bright idea of going to tap dancing classes together – all of us, mums and daughters.

The class was held in a room with a grotty wooden floor above a pub in Ramsbottom, which wasn't far away. It was a hideous experience for me, Sam and Kate. We were painfully embarrassed to be there with our mums, especially when Gail turned up with one black tap shoe and one white tap shoe. It soon became clear that it was just an excuse for the mums to get together in the pub afterwards, while we sat there, waiting to go home. We put up with it for about a term, and then refused to go back. By then I'd learnt the basics, so it wasn't a complete waste of time.

At eleven, I left Holly Mount and moved to St Gabriel's RC High School, and that's when I started gaining weight, during my first year. It didn't bother me at that age, like it doesn't bother me now. I enjoyed being different and the fact that I was a bit bigger just made me stand out more. My gran and mum called it 'puppy fat'; my dad was a bigger man; and my girlfriends at school said, 'Well, you're from a big family.' It wasn't an issue. People didn't call me fat, at least not to my face, and it didn't affect my friend-ships or how I felt about myself, which was lucky. I was a classic bully target, but no one bullied me or was nasty to me about my weight, perhaps because I was a bit crazy and I came across as strong.

Since I've become well known, I've had letters from girls who say they are so body conscious that they get their mothers to write them excuse letters to get them out of going in the showers, or to gym class. Reading their letters made me realise that I genuinely wasn't bothered about wearing a leotard at school, or shorts and a T-shirt, and I didn't think twice about going in the showers with everybody, because it was just the norm.

I think there must be more pressure on girls nowadays. They constantly read magazines that tell them how wonderful it is that a certain pop star has gone from a size 12 to a size 8, and they want to be like that pop star. I don't remember it being that way when I was growing up. One of my role models was Alexis Colby in *Dynasty* and *The Colbys*. I thought she was fabulous. It didn't matter if she was thin or fat. I just wanted her shoulder pads and the power they symbolised.

Later on, in my teenage years, Dawn French, Alison Moyet and Jo Brand were all really successful. I remember thinking, They're big; they're different; they're similar to me. None of the magazines I looked at said that there was anything wrong with them, or that the girls from Bananarama were how you should be. There might have been a magazine that said that, but I didn't read it, and I was reading everything from *Look-In* to *Vogue*.

The one problem I had was finding clothes that fitted me. I'll never forget the day I went shopping with my mum at C&A, where all my friends bought their clothes from the Clockhouse range. I was desperate to be trendy, but when we got there they didn't have anything in my size. 'None of it fits me, Mum!' I wailed in the dressing room, throwing a pair of mad-coloured leggings on the floor. It was really upsetting.

We ended up going to Marks and Spencer, which did bigger sizes, but wasn't nearly as trendy. I wanted to look funky like my friends but you couldn't find mad-coloured leggings at M&S. It was a turning point for me. Since I couldn't wear what everyone else was wearing, I realised that I would have to develop my own style and create my own trends. It wasn't long before I started to think, Why do I have to wear puffball skirts just because everyone else is? They didn't suit me. They looked completely wrong on me! After that, I went my own fashion route, mixing and matching clothes to create my own distinct look.

The whole ethos of Oldham Theatre Workshop was about being individual and being yourself. That was great, because I could have ended up feeling frumpy if I hadn't been creative with my style. As it was, I always had a terrible time getting ready for the school disco. 'What are all the other girls going to wear?' I'd think anxiously. It's every teenager's worry, but my size was an added factor. I didn't want to look like the other girls – I couldn't look like them, anyway – but I wanted to be trendy. My bedroom always looked like a volcano had gone off by the time I'd decided what to wear.

Luckily for me, school wasn't the only world I inhabited. Workshop gave my life another dimension and broadened my horizons, so school was never the be-all and end-all that it was for many of my friends. Going to Workshop was great for my confidence. Sally Ann Matthews was at Workshop when she got the part of Jenny Bradley in *Coronation Street* and press articles about her sometimes included the words: 'and Bury's own Lisa Riley also attends the Oldham Theatre Workshop,' much to my delight!

I loved every minute I was there. At first, I went on Saturdays from nine to three. Then I started going on Sundays from ten to six too, so sometimes my whole weekend was consumed by it. We'd always be working towards a show. The way it worked was that you paid your own expenses for auditions and show costumes, plus clerical costs for printing up scripts and other paperwork. Everything else was funded by Oldham Council. Luckily for me, my gran made me the most fantastic show cos-tumes. Gran was a great knitter and sewer, unlike Mum, who couldn't even thread a needle, bless her! That may have been another bone of contention between them.

Sometimes I was in a class of ninety or a hundred kids, plus all the mums and chaperones. We regularly did improvs and you really had to focus, because David Johnson might ask you to switch roles at any moment. First he would divide you into groups and give each little group what he called 'a situation'. So, you might be pretending to be a patient sitting in a doctor's wait-ing room, while someone else role-played the doctor. You had to think hard about how someone acts when they're waiting to see the doctor. People don't do a lot when they're waiting, but the small things they do can be quite revealing.

Then suddenly you'd be told to switch roles from patient to doctor. David would watch closely to see if you could create a distinct character. If you had acting in your soul, you'd make your doctor completely different from anyone else's. If you didn't, you'd be more likely to copy. I tried to be as versatile as possible and constantly put on different accents. At presentation time, we watched each other's dialogues and the situations the different groups had created.

I was like a sponge at Workshop. I listened intently to every word spoken by David and the musical director Bryn and I put a hundred per cent effort into my singing and acting. I did everything within my power to get things right, to listen and take in as much information as I possibly could, because I desperately wanted to stand out from all the other kids. But it wasn't until I was fourteen that I started getting major roles in the shows.

When it came to learning, I was like Dr Jekyll and Mr Hyde. At Workshop I was keen and obedient, but at school I felt totally unmotivated. Concentration was always an issue for me at St Gabriel's. I wish I had tried more, because these days I love information and if something's in the news, I want to talk about it. But I just switched off back then. I felt suffocated in class. 'I'm bored, bored, bored!' I kept thinking. It felt like I was wearing a big, heavy hat all day.

I loved drama and English literature, but the thought of talking about volcanoes in geography sent me to sleep. Presented with algebra homework I'd say, 'What's this? When will I use x over 5 in later life?' The hours spent wrestling with equations felt like wasted hours. Even now, I'd like to know how algebra has helped me get to where I am now. If someone can answer that question, I will absolutely listen.

The other day, I found some old school reports which showed a real division of opinion among my teachers. Most of them seemed to like me, but inevitably there were complaints about me mucking around in lessons. I'd do anything to get a laugh out of my mates and of course that was disruptive. My fairy-tale brain constantly whisked me off into some whimsical scenario and before I knew it, I'd be acting it out in front of the class. In business studies, I'd nick a pair of glasses from one of the lads, put them on, sit behind my typewriter like one of the girls from *Grandstand* and say in a soft, sexy voice, 'You boys had better do as I say.' I was always role playing.

The only subjects I worked hard at were drama and English literature. My drama teacher, Mr Keating, was very encouraging and he adored all my play acting and silly voices. A huge man, with the towering presence of Robbie Coltrane's character Hagrid in the *Harry Potter* films, he was a real disciplinarian. But he believed in my acting and could see that I was never going to be a physicist.

I also worked hard for Miss Maxfield, my English teacher, who was a lovely woman. Acknowledging that some of the other teachers complained about me in the staff room, she'd say, 'You're not the girl they all say you are!' That meant a lot to me. I would love it if my teachers looked at me now and said, 'Bless her!' but perhaps that's a hope too far.

St Gabriel's was a devout school. There was a girls' playground and a boys' playground and it was totally forbidden to stray into the wrong one. But, like my mum, I did whatever they told me not to. So I often went round to the boys' playground to see my mates there. I was constantly getting told off for it.

When I hit my teens, boys took on another dimension. In the third year, when I was thirteen, our class went on a field trip to Jodrell Bank Centre for Astrophysics, where we stayed the night in separate dormitories: the girls were on the ground floor, the

LISA RILEY

boys were one floor up and we had the teachers to the left and right of us. I was bored out of my head looking through telescopes at Saturn and Mars during the day, but I loved the feeling of freedom that came from being away from home, especially at night. After lights out, I had a captive audience in the dorm. One night, I got out of bed and started doing Mel and Kim impressions to make the girls laugh, until a couple of teachers came in and said, 'Lisa, please be quiet and get into bed.'

Next I decided I wanted to go and see the lads and maybe snog one of them. 'Go on, Lise!' whispered the others. They all wanted to see the boys, but I was the only one who dared to do it. So I snuck up the staircase towards their dorm. But, as usual, I was caught. My punishment was to sleep on the concrete floor next to a huge industrial vacuum cleaner for two hours, after which I was allowed back into the dormitory.

My first boyfriend was Gareth Davies. For a while he was the love of my life. I was smitten. It was a massive crush. I used to study my school timetable and work out that if I walked down a particular corridor at a certain time, when I was on my way to English and he had geography, we might pass each other in the corridor. Then I could say, 'Hi!' and scurry past. Back then, it was all about catching his eye in the dinner queue. But then we took things to another level when we snogged on the staircase at Altrincham Ice Rink one day after school, after which nothing ever happened between us again.

I was still pretty innocent. I knew I wanted to be with boys, but I wasn't sure what I wanted to do with them. I'll always remember one of the girls telling us about sex at Girl Guides. It sounded to me like she'd made it up, like she was romancing,

46

but I couldn't be absolutely sure. Although I'd heard rumours at school, nothing was clear in my head. 'Do you know about sex?' she said. 'Yeah, well, your mum and dad, right, they kiss each other all over and then he whacks her with his willy.'

Right, OK, whatever, I thought. That sounds fun. Shut up!

In time, you learn. There's always that one girl in your year who claims to have done it, eight times over, and our year was no exception. Desperate to find out the core details from her, we quizzed her constantly. But she was very vague about it. 'It's really great,' she said with a dreamy look in her eyes. Looking back, I don't think she had actually done it at all.

Of course, there were real boys and there were fantasy boys. New Kids On The Block were my teen idols. I had a huge poster of them on my bedroom wall. Obsessed! So I was absolutely elated when all the mums sorted us out front row seats for the band's concert at the Manchester Apollo. There were nine of us going, including Sam and Kate.

On the morning of the concert, I said to the girls, 'We're going to see New Kids On The Block! We need to go and get make-up and nail varnish!'

Sam was a Grade A student and bunking school was something she had never even dreamt of doing. Another friend, Suzanne Martin, was the same. But, believing my assurances that we wouldn't get caught, everyone followed me to Boots in Bury. Lo and behold, as we were browsing though different shades of metallic blue eye shadow, who should walk past but Mrs Pryce, Head of Maths. Busted! We were marched to Mr Hopkins, the school Head, and all our parents were told. I instantly owned up to the fact that it had been my idea. I didn't want them to be punished for following me to Boots.

It created a real dilemma for Mum. Normally she would have said, 'Whatever. It's fine. You've done wrong. Don't do it again.' But there were other parents involved, so she had to set a precedent. 'I have to be the disciplinarian here,' she told me. 'You're not going to the concert.'

Well, my life was broken. 'New Kids On The Block have come to Manchester, Mum! I can't miss them. They're my world.'

'Sorry, but you're not going,' she said.

She rang all the other parents up and told them what she had decided. Then, unbeknownst to me, she rang them all back and said, 'I can't do it to her! Believe me, I've tried, but I cannot deprive her of what she wants.'

Meanwhile, I went through school like a broken mess, dramarama. My life had ended. Everyone felt sorry for me. Still, I had to accept that it was no one's fault but my own. My head was hanging when Mum picked me up from school. 'Well, that's it,' she said. 'You've learnt your lesson.'

'I'll never do it again, Mum, ever in my life,' I said dejectedly.

'It's a good job, because you're going to the concert, and I'm taking you,' she said. I've never screamed so loudly in my life.

By now, I was really getting into clothes and fashion. Dressing was a way of expressing myself and I didn't hold back. I definitely had my own style and it wasn't only because I couldn't fit into trendy shop clothes. It was also because a lot of my mates were obsessed with Dash tracksuits for the first few years we were at St Gabriel's and I genuinely thought they were hideous.

Why would you want to wear a tracksuit? I thought. Boys wear tracksuits.

There was also a mass Goth thing going on during my teenage years that I couldn't understand. Why would you want to look like you're going to a funeral? I thought. It didn't appeal to me so, being me, I went completely the other way and dressed like a raving rainbow. I was obsessed with colour. Thinking I was kooky and funky, I would mismatch patterns, mix up colours and, later on, dye my hair different shades, from black to orange. I loved logo T-shirts, the madder, the better. I'd wear a Mr Bump T-shirt and knot it at the back to make it tighter and sexier. During my charity-shop phase, I thought it was off the hook to mix even more stuff up, so then I'd go and get a trainspotter's kagoul and knot it at the back to make it look individual. I no longer had any desire to conform. My size already set me apart and I made a virtue of being different. When it came to what I wore, I wanted to look totally different from everyone else.

One day when I was thirteen, I was sitting in the cafe bar at Oldham Theatre Workshop when a boy in my year group came up and asked, 'Why on earth have you got banana skins on your feet?' It was Antony Cotton, one of the stars at Workshop. A total princess, Antony had amazing presence and you always knew when he was in the room, so it was nice to be noticed by him. It was a bit like being selected to be a Pink Lady in *Grease*. He vividly remembers the shiny yellow patent boots I was wearing the day we first got chatting. I suppose they were unforgettable, as were the pink vest, tangerine orange cardigan and multi-coloured stripy leggings I was also wearing. (Yes, I'd finally found a pair that fitted!) The other thing Antony remembers is the cheeky twinkle in my eye.

Until then, I'd always felt on the edge of Antony's group. It was the cool, kooky set that included Gemma Wardle, Lucy Hallard, Michelle Kelly, Sarah Jones (better known now as Suranne Jones) and David and Martin Doherty, as well as Marsha Thomason, Natalie Casey and her sister Anna Jane. Of course, chatting to Antony in the cafe didn't get me into the group, but it was a start. You had to earn your stripes and I began to worm my way in slowly. It was just like *Glee*!

There were a few distinct groups at Workshop. Top of the pile were the people who got the parts. Casting directors looking for child actors made a point of coming to Workshop performances, so if David cast you in the lead roles in the shows and plays, it tended to follow that you'd get called up to TV and theatre auditions. I felt frustrated that David kept giving me small ensemble roles in the Christmas and summer shows. What about me? I thought. I believed in my abilities, so I didn't like being lumped together with the other ensemble actors. It also meant that I wasn't getting called up to many of the TV and theatre auditions some of my peers were going to. People like Antony were constantly getting roles, as was Gemma Wardle. Anna Friel, another contemporary of mine at Workshop, was in demand too, although Anna didn't really hang out with a group. She was quite shy and kept herself to herself.

I took heart from watching what happened with Kieran O'Brien, who was an ensemble actor for ages until David clocked him and started casting him in bigger roles. Soon Kieran was being sent up for auditions and he went on to get regular work in *Coronation Street*, *Children's Ward* and *Cracker*.

You never know, the same could happen to me, I thought wistfully.

Children's Ward was a groundbreaking Granada Television children's drama which mainly used children from Workshop. Co-created and written by Paul Abbott and Kay Mellor, it was set in a fictitious hospital and included storylines that dealt with cancer, alcoholism, drug addiction, rape and teenage pregnancy. June West, the casting director at Granada, really liked me and I was constantly going up for parts that were perfect for me. Yet I never got them.

My audition feedback was always good, but it would generally include a comment like, 'She's very advanced, isn't she?' I was chatty and confident at auditions and the consensus was that I seemed too mature to fit in with the young cast. And not only was I old for my age mentally, but I was a porky size sixteen with boobs, so I also looked physically older than I was. Since there was a wariness about casting a young girl in the role of someone older, I ended up with no roles at all. It was incredibly frustrating.

The atmosphere wasn't obviously competitive at Workshop, but an element of bragging inevitably went on. People would always tell you when they'd been cast in a role and I was desperate to be able to say I had too, partly because it would affirm to me and the others that I was serious about acting. Sometimes I got the feeling that they thought I was just playing at it. I longed for acceptance.

Every now and then, casting directors and scouts would come

along to watch us doing improv. In this case, David tended not to warn us because he didn't want us to feel self-conscious. He'd put us into role-play situations and do the red, amber and green dot elimination sequence, without telling us what we were auditioning for. If you got through, one of the chaperones would say, 'Can you come back on Tuesday for a casting session?' and then the big suits would come along to watch you.

It was disappointing when I wasn't picked, but I had to roll with the punches. I kept believing in myself and Mum was incredibly supportive. But then something happened that totally shook me up. It made me question myself, my confidence and my direction in life.

It began with an audition at Workshop one Sunday. For once, David had warned us that someone important was coming along to watch us. I wasn't fazed. I just went ahead and did what I would have done anyway. I was pleased when the casting director asked me back for a second audition, but I didn't get my hopes up. Then she asked me back again. And again.

Eventually we were told that she was casting two films for Warner Brothers, who were remaking *Black Beauty* and *The Secret Garden*. Many of the *Black Beauty* kids were likely to come from Workshop and they were also looking for someone to play Martha, the maid in *The Secret Garden*. I had been singled out for Martha. 'They really, really like you,' David told me. 'They adore your acting.'

My hopes soared. In the period dramas I'd watched, the cooks and maids always tended to be bigger girls, so I pictured the maid in *The Secret Garden* as pale-skinned and a little bit chubby, dressed all in white with a mop cap on. I'm perfect for this role,

I thought. I'm going to be in a film! At last I'll be accepted at Workshop.

I absolutely believed that I was going to get the part. I remember telling friends at school about it. 'Yeah, whatever!' they said.

'No, really,' I said. 'I think I'm going to be in a movie.'

But it didn't happen. I didn't get the part. Someone else from Workshop got it – a girl called Laura Crossley. I was in tatters when I heard. I went home and broke down to Mum, sobbing my heart out. 'Why didn't I get it?' I kept saying. 'David said the people from Warner Brothers loved my acting. So why did Laura get it instead of me?'

Laura was a pretty brunette with brown eyes and olive skin. She was also a lot smaller than me. For the first time it dawned on me that maybe my acting wasn't enough. It had never occurred to me before, but now it suddenly struck me that your look has a lot to do with the roles you are cast in. So, where did that leave me, if I was going to act for the rest of my life? Is this how it's always going to be? I thought miserably.

'Am I not going to get the roles I want because I'm fatter than the other kids?' I asked Mum between great gulping sobs. 'Do you have to be a dinky to get on?'

'No, there are roles for everybody!' she said vehemently. 'Pam Ferris isn't skinny.' She adored Pam Ferris's work.

But no matter what Mum said to make me feel better, I was devastated and my confidence plummeted. I had thought that I would be great for the maid's part in every way, including my look, and when I realised that wasn't the case, I decided to change my look. The following day, I demanded that Mum took me to a dietitian. I didn't relish being different any more. In fact, for the first time in my life I wished I wasn't different. I had never had any desire to lose weight before and in my heart I still didn't want to lose weight, but I was prepared to do it if I had to be thin to be an actor. I desperately wanted to work.

In today's world, I might even have begged Mum for a gastric band. I've read loads recently about teenage kids having gastric bands fitted, which sounds crazy, but perhaps it's the only thing that works if you're really big. I wasn't that big, though. It was just that my self-image had been knocked out of proportion.

I had three sessions with the dietitian. Weirdly, her regime was all about carbs and she said nothing about portion control or nutrition. She told me that I had to stick to a diet of Weetabix, brown bread and brown rice every day. She was basically saying, 'Eat fibre and go and have a poo!' Well, you don't tell a teenager that. She made me feel like an old man with piles. Anyway, rules weren't going to change me. I'm a bit like my mum in that I don't do rules.

Instead, I went on a diet without knowing the first thing about how to plan a balanced weight-loss programme. The dietitian hadn't helped and, having seen breakfast TV presenters talk about dieting while their weight yo-yoed, I knew I wasn't going the 'grapefruit and one slice of toast, thinly buttered' route. I needed something that worked. Self-enforced starvation seemed the only way. So, I'd have a bowl of cereal in the morning and then try to go the rest of the day without eating. If I felt hunger pangs, I'd drink a beaker of water.

I soon learnt how to dodge meals. When I was at a friend's

house and someone offered me some food, I'd automatically say, 'I'm not hungry!' It always came out a bit sharply, like when you say, 'I'm fine!' really quickly, although you're not fine. At home, I'd tell Mum that I'd eaten at a friend's house, or earlier while she was out. Or I'd call down from my room, 'I'm reading. I'll grab something later.'

After a week of living on one bowl of Frosties a day, I began to feel sluggish. It was terrible. What can I do? I thought, determined not to start eating again. I started pepping myself up with little cartons of Ribena. The sugar hit helped to keep me going, but I started to look gaunt and my energy levels kept dipping. I hated the way not eating affected me. Being tired all the time took my pizazz away. I looked like I'd not slept for a month and I wasn't giddy any more. I was losing my zest for life – and my boobs appeared to be shrinking too. No one told me that the weight comes off your chest first!

Mum soon realised that something was amiss. 'Is anything wrong?' she kept asking. 'Are you sleeping OK?' Then she noticed that I wasn't putting any pots in the dishwasher. The penny dropped immediately. She's stopped eating! she thought, totally horrified. This is not right in any shape or form.

'What the hell are you doing, Lisa?' she asked me anxiously. 'You're not yourself.' She was really scared, because a friend of hers was anorexic and she knew how damaging it could be. 'This has got to stop right now.'

4

Back where I belong

My first and last diet was over. Once Mum was on my case, I couldn't go on starving myself and, to be honest, I was relieved to be out of it. I wanted to be me again, full of life and sparkle. I wanted to jump out of bed in the morning, rather than sink back into the mattress feeling weak and pathetic when my alarm clock went off. That was so much more important to me than losing a ripple of fat.

I'd also hated the deceit, the constant lies about what I was or wasn't eating. I didn't go straight back to pie and chips, though. I was more aware of what I was eating, so I took it easy. Before the diet, if we were in the car and pulled up for petrol, the old me would have asked Dad for a packet of Opal Fruits. That stopped, because I realised that I didn't need sweets. It was just a habit I'd got into and it was easy to break.

My energy soon returned, but my confidence didn't follow. I was happier in myself but my dream of being an actor was slipping out of reach. I was still getting a lot of encouragement at school and Mr Keating was constantly telling me how talented I was, but David Johnson wasn't giving me the parts that showed me he believed in me and professionally I was going nowhere. It wasn't only *Children's Ward* and *The Secret Garden*, it was everything. I wasn't getting *Corrie*, *Brookside*, *Cracker* or *Prime Suspect*. All the kids in those programmes were coming out of Workshop, but nothing was happening for me.

I couldn't understand it. If *Children's Ward* were looking for a scruffy, Salford-born, fourteen-year-old girl from a broken home, living in a council flat in Salford, why didn't they choose me? Why didn't I get it? I started to think, Can I do it? Am I good enough?

I started to doubt my abilities. I felt torn between David and Mr Keating. They had different approaches to teaching drama and trying to please both of them was confusing. When they both gave me the Nurse's speech from *Romeo and Juliet* to work on, it felt like cheating to do it the same way, so I tried to do two different interpretations instead of just searching for the character in my heart. It was good in the sense that it broadened my mind, but it didn't do much for my confidence, because I made a mess of both attempts. I felt I had let my teachers and myself down. The same thing happened when they asked me to do the Donkey speech from *Midsummer Night's Dream*. I wanted to bring out all the comedy of it, to be witty and humorous, but I felt like I was under a mushroom. I can't do this! I thought. I can't work for more than one drama teacher.

Everything came to a head in my final year at St Gabriel's when Mr Keating gave me a monologue to learn as part of my

GCSE drama course and I found I couldn't learn it. Narrated by an unborn baby who was pleading not to be aborted (well, I was at a Catholic school!) it was a powerful piece of writing that I would normally have found easy to memorise. I took it home and started reading it over, but the words wouldn't stick in my mind. I tried and tried, but I couldn't even remember the first line.

What's wrong? I asked myself, feeling seriously worried. Why can't I learn it?

It triggered a real crisis of confidence. Do I really want to be an actor, or am I playing at it? I wondered.

I was constantly mucking around at school now. Boys were on the scene and I felt restless and distracted. Nothing seemed to be going my way. My friends were starting to get proper boyfriends, but I was still just snogging lads. I was the one the lads wanted to have a giggly time with, but I wasn't the twiglet blondie they wanted to go out with. It didn't seem fair.

Am I just the class clown, the jester? I thought. Is that my only role?

Around this time, my teacher said to Mum, 'Lisa should forget all her ideas about becoming an actor. She won't amount to anything.' Mum couldn't believe it. He could have said, 'It's all very well, Mrs Riley, but the acting world is precarious. She should have something to fall back on.' But he chose to be anything but polite.

Every term, I got naughtier. While Sam and Kate and several of the other girls I'd known at Holly Mount were in the top set at St Gabriel's, I was in Set Two for a lot of subjects, so in those classes

I made other friends, including a girl called Helen. People called the pair of us 'Naughty and Naughtier' and I was 'Naughtier'. We weren't good for each other. We were partners in crime for years and Helen blames me to this day for not getting her degree. We laugh about it all the time.

At school, we were constantly giving each other dares. 'Lisa, light a cigarette in class,' she said once.

I refused point blank, but she kept on at me. 'Go on! I dare you.'

So I lit one up in the back of the chemistry lab and was immediately sent to Mr Hopkins. It's incredible that I wasn't suspended or expelled.

That wasn't the worst thing I did, either. I got myself into even more trouble one afternoon when we were all padded up for hockey. Suddenly it started raining, so we were told to play in the gym instead. It felt horribly claustrophobic and I'm not good at being hemmed in. 'I don't want to play hockey inside,' I complained to a couple of mates. 'I can't be bothered.'

'What are you going to do about it?' they said, shrugging.

That sounded like a dare to me and what I did next was purely for attention. Without thinking about the consequences, I started singing 'The Only Way Is Up' by Yazz and whacked my hockey stick into the fire alarm on the wall. I thought it would only set the gym building off but, no, the entire school – nine hundred children – had to be evacuated. Three fire engines turned up and the school had to pay out loads for creating a false alarm. I felt incredibly guilty. Worst of all, my crush of all crushes, Pete Macanamy, was in the queue of the line-up, while I stood there in my gym kit and hockey pads, not looking too hot! It was the second time in one day that I wanted the earth to swallow me up and it certainly didn't do much for my relationship with him.

Pete was a friend of Kate's brother Matthew, who was in the year above, which was kind of cool. Although he looked a bit weedy, I was completely obsessed with Pete in every way, especially after I snogged him at a party. It was one of those brilliant house parties where the parents are abroad and there are teenagers snogging in every corner. Pete and I went at it in the kitchen and did a little bit of first-base malarkey, too. After that, I was like a woman possessed. Pete was my be-all and end-all.

Just before Valentine's Day, we had a snog and a fumble at another party. That was the year I got a card from twin boys in the year below me at school. It was signed from the pair of them, which I thought was kind of weird at the time. Obviously I sent one to Pete. I was desperate for one in return and I totally and utterly believed it would arrive. On the morning of Valentine's Day, I even said to my friends, 'He must be planning to put it in my school bag. He knows where I leave it during break.' But the card never came.

Soon afterwards, I found out that Pete was arguing with a lad at school and I decided it would be good to challenge the other guy. 'How dare you have a go at him? He's lovely!' I said. I was really pleased when I heard the lad had backed off and was leaving Pete in peace.

I imagined Pete thinking, Wow, she saved my life!

Only he wasn't thinking that, as I later found out. Instead, it rubbed salt into the wound to have a girl sort his rows for him, which was something that hadn't even occurred to me. In my head and my heart, I'd thought I was doing the right thing. I'd assumed it would make him fancy me more.

A few days later, Kate and Matthew's mum went out and we had a bit of a party round at Kate's house. I'll never forget Kate bounding into the room and saying, 'Matthew's bringing all his mates back!'

My heart missed several beats. Giddy with excitement, we ran up to Kate's bedroom and gave ourselves a full make-over. Please, please, please let Pete come too! I thought, as I crimped my hair and plastered on foundation that was about nine shades too orange, leaving a lovely tide mark around my hairline. I had no idea about make-up back then, but I was the queen of crimp. I hadn't discovered hair mousse, and hair straighteners weren't in the shops, so the only things that would take the frizz out of my huge natural curls were BaByliss crimpers. Samantha and I both had our hair cut into sharp bobs – we were really into Betty Boo, who had the best bob ever – and we'd do a straight fringe and then crimp the rest, so we ended up with triangle heads.

Finally Matthew came back and, joy of joys, Pete was with him. From the moment he walked in the door, I was like a little doll in a window, staring at him with fixed shining eyes. About an hour later, my every wish came true when we slipped away to snog in a side room. Meanwhile, Sam pulled one of Matthew's mates. It was turning out to be a brilliant party.

I decided to go for it and tell Pete how I felt. 'I really fancy you,' I told him, looking shyly at him through mascara-laden lashes.

'Oh,' he said, looking down. There was a long pause.

My heart plunged. Oh God, he wasn't going to ask me out!

After an awkward silence, we went back to find the others.

School on the Monday was mortifying for me. I was crestfallen, absolutely gutted. I'd blatantly told Pete that I had feelings for him, but nothing had come of it. Why doesn't he feel the same? I kept wondering.

I picked myself up, but not in the right way, because after that I went on a minx-athon. I craved male attention and snogged a different bloke at every party I went to, making it known at school every time so that it would get back to Pete. Evidently he wasn't bothered, though. Snogging lads left, right and centre didn't have the desired effect of making him declare his undying love to me. The upside was that I had a lot of fun trying to make him jealous, so it wasn't all bad!

All this was going on and I still hadn't got to grips with Mr Keating's GCSE monologue about the baby in the womb. By now I was really fretting. Although I had lots of friends, I wasn't doing well at school and I didn't have a boyfriend. I felt I needed to shine at something.

'I can't learn it,' I told Mr Keating. 'I don't know why.'

'Can't means won't, Lisa,' he said crossly. 'But you can do it and you will.'

At home, Mum did her best to help me. We went through the piece together loads, but it still wouldn't go in. Mum was concerned, because she could see how much it was upsetting me. She was also perceptive enough to realise that not being able to learn my lines was a symptom of my insecurity about acting. She could tell that it was still eating away at me that I hadn't got the role of Martha in *The Secret Garden*. It didn't help that Andy Knott, a dear friend of mine, had been cast in one of the movie's lead roles. Then Gemma Wardle got *Les Misérables* and became the youngest Eponine in history. Don't get me wrong, I was happy for people like Andy and Gemma. I was just disappointed that it wasn't happening for me.

Dad, however, couldn't understand what the fuss was about. Wanting to be an actor was slightly *Billy Elliot* in my dad's book. He saw it as a hobby. I was just messing around and having fun on stage, wasn't I? Doing a little song and dance? Playtime dressing up? Since most things in the family were drawn on gender lines and Dad was always off with Liam doing sports, he didn't see how I was developing as an actor. Everything he did was for Liam. In his eyes, drama wasn't a proper subject and he couldn't take it seriously as a GCSE.

'What does it matter?' he said, shrugging. 'It's not like you're really going to be an actor.'

'What do you mean? You know I want to be an actor,' I screamed.

Dad wasn't fazed. 'But what's your proper job going to be?' he asked, infuriatingly.

'F*** off!' I yelled. It was the first and only time in my life that I swore at him.

I stormed off to my bedroom, where I picked up a tape recorder and determinedly spoke the monologue into it. I'll show you, I thought, silently fuming at Dad. I *will* be an actor. I will be an actor till the day I die! I must have played back the tape a hundred times, repeating the lines again and again. By the end of the evening, I was word perfect.

Dad had given me the jab I needed to pull my socks up. He spurred me on. In later life, it became a natural reaction to kick and scramble against negativity, and I always wonder if my attitude dates back to that moment. When people tell me I can't do something, I think, I'll show you! I've spent my life trying to prove myself. Whereas some people get discouraged by negative feedback, I find it fuels me and makes me more determined to believe in myself.

Something clicked in me that night. I *am* an actress! I thought. I just need to stay determined. After that, I got back to thinking, Take me as I am or not at all. It was the next step on the path to self-acceptance.

I started working harder than ever for Mr Keating and David. I made peace with the fact that my size is integral to who I am as a person and an actor. For ages, me and my mates had idolised Helena Christensen, the Versace supermodel. She was the epitome of completely perfect. We so wanted to look like her. Then something within me said, 'I'm me. And I ain't that bad, thanks ever so much!' I knew I was good fun to be around and I became less bothered about what people thought of me.

This moment of acceptance coincided with another huge turning point in my life, when David Johnson cast me in my first major role at Workshop, playing Brown Owl in the summer musical *Worzel Gummidge*. At last, at last, at last! To me, it was the biggest thing ever. Whenever I'm asked what my big breakthrough role was, I say it was Brown Owl, even though it wasn't a professional role. I hero-worshipped David Johnson and being recognised by him meant everything to me.

I had spent nearly five years working my arse off and trying to make my mark. I'd spent so long thinking, What do you do to get David to tick the box? Now he had finally singled me out, which meant that I would be in with a much bigger chance of getting work in the real world. I felt I could hold my head high and say I really was going to be an actress. I knew then that I would act for the rest of my life. I had reached self-acceptance and now I could combine it with self-belief.

Antony was cast as Worzel and we started spending all our time together in rehearsal. We got on like a house on fire and it wasn't long before I was part of his gang. Even better, the show went down a storm. Words can't express the elation I felt up on stage, especially when I got the laughs I was going for. At one point, we had to pass a basket across the stage and something told me it would be funny if I dropped it. I don't know how I knew. It's not something you can learn. Perhaps all those hours of watching Morecambe and Wise and Ronnie Barker had taught me something. Anyway, I dropped it and got a huge laugh from the audience. A rush of pleasure swept through me. I can do this! I thought. This is what I want to do: make people laugh like this. It was a real tick-the-box moment for me and I felt completely fulfilled. Afterwards, I was swamped by people telling me how good I'd been. I'd finally made it within Workshop.

By now, me and Antony were inseparable. Then our mums realised that we were from the same area and they started a car pool with another girl's mum. Workshop was fourteen miles from home, along the treacherous M62 motorway. Sharing the driving made things much easier for our parents, especially as David had a rule that you could not be a single minute late to his class. He never faltered from that rule.

Woe betide anyone who was late to class at Workshop. The way David saw it, if you are playing the National Theatre and you arrive one minute after 'the half', which is thirty-five minutes before curtain up, you ain't going on that night.

One Sunday morning, there was a huge smash on the M62, which delayed our journey by fifteen minutes. Workshop had started when Antony, Emma and I arrived. The register had been taken and the class were well into doing improvs.

'David, I'm so sorry we're late,' I said.

'And so am I!' he roared. 'Leave!'

'But we've got nowhere to go,' said Emma. 'Our lift has gone.'

'If you were in a play at the National, you wouldn't be going on stage. Now, leave!'

So the three of us sat on the staircase in the hall until we were picked up that evening. We weren't even allowed into the room to watch the others. It was a lesson I've never forgotten to this day.

David put the fear of God into you. I was the ultimate jester at school, but I never messed around at Workshop. If you even moved your elbow during the register, he'd call out, 'Why are you moving, child?' The discipline he instilled in us included precise timekeeping and respect for your fellow actors, especially your elder actors. You stand up if someone walks in the room. You open the door for people. He was a stickler for all that and I'm grateful for everything he taught me.

The autumn after I played Brown Owl in *Worzel Gummidge*, he cast Suranne Jones and me in the lead roles in the Christmas pantomime, *Snow White*, which also starred Anna Friel's brother Michael. I got a lot of praise for my performance again. Anna bounded up and said, 'Oh my God, you were so funny, Lise!' I valued her opinion, so I was really chuffed.

It confirmed to me that I was on the map. I had found myself within Workshop and I was doing well in drama at St Gabriel's, too. Neil Jaworski and I played Hansel and Gretel in the school production of a musical called *The Dracula Spectacula*, which was a real wow moment. It was a bit like a kids' *Rocky Horror Picture Show*, without the naughtiness, and everyone said that it was impossible to take your eyes off me and Neil, who is now living in London, writing movies.

I would have liked a boyfriend, but it didn't seem to matter all that much. I had lots of great mates and we were always meeting new people, so I never felt left out. There was no 'Woe is me!' because I was content with what I had. For some girls, having a boyfriend was the be-all and end-all – and still is now – but it wasn't like that for me. I would have loved the boys at school to fancy me, but I was so caught up in Workshop that I wasn't seriously bothered. I used to get bored with all the trivia, the constant, 'He said, she said,' and all that malarkey. I was an old romantic and I dreamt about New Kids On The Block and film stars more than real boys. Anyway, to my schoolmates I was the one with the giddy, exciting life. I was off doing plays at Work-shop and I had friends from outside Bury, which many of them didn't, so I didn't feel like I was missing out.

My first childhood crush was Andy, a boy from another school in Bury. I met him through a friend at St Gabriel's and we just clicked. It was the first time a boy had liked me for me. He didn't want me to look like Helena Christensen. Meanwhile, I looked at him like he was Michael Hutchence. To me, he was the best thing since sliced bread. He played the drums for Besses Boys Band, a second section brass band that's been going since the 1940s. I love that music. I'm an incurable romantic and it made me feel like we were in the movie *Brassed Off*. Based in Whitefield, just outside Manchester, the band used to play at Whitefield Civic Hall and I always went to watch Andy play. I was very supportive of his musical ambitions and I don't know if he'd experienced that before. 'If you want to be a drummer, you should go for it,' I'd say.

People in Bury don't tend to think that way. The attitude there is more conventional. 'What's being a musician? You must get a career.' In London, no one would have blinked an eye, but up there, it wasn't done. Still, I always said to him, 'You absolutely could be a musician.'

Although we had a brilliant time together, it irritated Andy that my first priority was always my acting. This has been a major hiccup all my life, because acting comes first and it always has, which means that dating has to be on my terms. Even when I was sixteen, I'd find myself saying to Andy, 'I can't see you on Thursday because I'm rehearsing for the show,' or 'I can't see you this weekend, because I'll be at Workshop all weekend.' I was determined to work as hard as I could to be an actress, but he didn't get it. They never do.

Frustratingly, I had to cut Workshop back to just the weekends while I did my GCSEs. I went on to get As in English literature and drama, then a couple of Cs and the rest were Ds, Es and Unclassifieds. I could have done a lot better, but I didn't try hard enough. For instance, I was good at Spanish and probably could have done well in the exam. I loved exaggerating the lisp and getting my lips round sayings like, 'Grande bananath! Muthath pethetath!'

Yet when it came to the GCSE Spanish oral, rather than go for it, I messed around in order to get a laugh. During the exam, I sat at a table with four other girls and answered questions into a tape recorder. It wasn't long before I started ad libbing and saying things like, 'You love my belly button,' in a stupid Spanish accent. I was quite able to give the proper responses to the questions, but I preferred getting the laugh and ended up with a D. It was stupid of me to throw it away like that and I'm not proud of myself, but all I cared about was my acting, even then.

I constantly had tonsillitis around this time, so I was often poorly. Eventually, the GP said to my mum, 'Cath, she's got to have an extraction.'

Another hiccup! But I wasn't going to let it get me down. I went to the hospital to be admitted for the tonsillectomy during the break for study leave before we took our GCSEs. On the section of the form that asked for your occupation, I wrote, 'Actress'. I was still only fifteen.

'You're a college student?' the administrator asked.

'No, I'm an actress,' I said firmly.

Granddad Sam was with me that day, because Mum had started a job at the travel company Airtours and was at work. Granddad has never forgotten that day. 'There was such determination in your eyes,' he says.

After our GCSEs finished, everybody left school. Most of my mates were going on to Holy Cross College, but they didn't do the right kind of drama there for me. 'Well, what do you want to do?' Mum asked. She had done some research and discovered that I could do a Performing Arts Diploma at Stand College in Whitefield. 'Do you want to go? They'll give you allowances for Workshop, because they know that you're heavily involved there.'

On paper, it seemed brilliant and I loved it when I actually turned up. But during the first term, I often bunked off and went to Andy's house, where we messed around and he taught me to play the drums, which I thought was really cool. We had a seriously strong connection. Life was rosy. I had Andy. Things were going well at Workshop and I was hopeful of getting work. I felt I had turned a corner, Everything seemed to fit. Everything, that is, except Stand College. It wasn't what I wanted. They were teaching me the theory when all I wanted was to get up and act. You can be taught every aspect of Shakespeare – and I've learnt all about that in my own time – but spending a whole year at drama school poring over the nuances of a certain word seems like a waste of time to me.

One day I looked up and said to Mum, 'I'm not going in tomorrow.'

'Why not?' she asked.

'I'm sick of learning. I want to start acting for real.'

Mum, being Mum, completely backed me up. She understood my point of view. After all, it was pretty simple in my book. If you can't act, you can't act. And if you can, get out there and do it.

5

Mingle with a Dingle

It was all well and good telling people I was an actress, but I hadn't actually had any proper work yet. Meanwhile, people were getting jobs all around me. Anna Friel had been cast in *Brookside* and was everywhere in the press, which was brilliant. Gemma Wardle was about move to London to play Eponine in *Les Misérables* in the West End, after a sell-out stint in Manchester. We were desperately proud of Gemma. It was the biggest thing ever when she moved to London. Our friend was going to the smoke!

I believed things would start happening for me too. In my eyes, it was only a matter of time. June West, the casting director at Granada TV, was still calling me up for auditions. She organised some extra work for me as a supermarket girl in *Corrie* and I was also an extra in *Brookie*. In the meantime, I devoted myself to Workshop, which inevitably meant that my relationship with Andy faded out. That wasn't the last I saw of Andy though. More of him later.

Mum and Dad started getting a bit irritated with me. I'd blithely left college with high hopes for the future, but I wasn't working or earning. All I was doing was spending their money. Like a typical selfish teenager, I was expecting to be driven everywhere, to Workshop and auditions, I spent hours on the phone when I was at home and I was out partying whenever I could. You can see why they found it annoying.

Now my mates were off at college and I wasn't seeing so much of Andy, my social life revolved around my Workshop mates. All the gay boys at Workshop stuck to me like Velcro and a group of us started going clubbing, to the Paradise Factory and the Hacienda. Michelle and Lucy used to come out too, as did Martin and David. After Andy, I went out with Martin for a bit. Michelle did too. That was before he came out, ha! Martin was Mr Cool at Workshop, the John Travolta of the group. He was incredibly good looking and everyone fancied him. I remember snogging him behind the Oldham Coliseum Theatre once, when a group of us went to see a matinee there. This is what it feels like to be Sandy in *Grease*! I thought happily.

The Hacienda was our favourite club. It was my idea of heaven, because I'd grown up hearing stories about this amazing nightclub where Madonna had played before she was even signed, and where Kylie had done a secret gig. Even my mum had partied there, back when it was the Twisted Wheel. It was the pride of Manchester.

Standing in the queue was always tense. Will I get in? Do I look old enough? Will I be able to find someone in Salford to sell me a fake passport?

The moment I walked past the bouncer my heart would soar. Yes! And I didn't even need a fake ID.

One night, Robbie from Take That was at the club, which was desperately exciting. I didn't want to kiss him; I just wanted to say, 'I think you're brilliant!' As it happened, Marc Owen from Take That had been a Workshop regular. He was one of the shy bunch who mainly got the ensemble roles.

I was having a fine old time, but Mum and Dad weren't impressed. Finally they said, 'You need to earn some money!'

So I started part-time behind the bar at the Bull's Head in Bury, which was near to where I lived. Antony got a job there too. It was perfect, because the landlords were happy to give us time off to go to auditions, as long as we worked our shifts around them. Even better, one of my duties was to oversee the puddings. What a fabulous perk that was! The chef's homemade cakes were out of this world.

Working at the Bull's Head gave us our fun money for the weekend and some left over for other bits and pieces. Having said that, I spent every single penny of my first wage packet – a full fifty-nine quid – on a yellow Vivienne Westwood T-shirt with the orb emblem in the corner. Vivienne Westwood was my idol. I'd go into her shop in Manchester and dream in my little romantic head that I'd work there one day. You had to be kooky to work in Westwood. I didn't think I was kooky enough, but I was going to try.

I never got to work in Westwood, but I did wear my new T-shirt to audition for a two-part BBC television drama called *Blood and Peaches*, a gritty tale about growing up in Bradford that tackles racism head on. I was auditioning for the lead lad's girlfriend, which was a great part, really raw. My character appeared in around nine scenes, mostly at the party her boyfriend has when his parents go away and leave him in charge of the house. Mayhem!

I was called up to the audition by a casting director called Michelle Smith who had spotted me at Workshop. She sent me three scenes from the main script to read beforehand. I wasn't supposed to learn them because you're not expected to give a full performance. That comes later, after you've got the part. But, being me, I worked hard to prepare and learnt the dialogue by heart. I was desperate for this role. If I could get a job in a TV drama, I could say truthfully that I was a professional actress. I'd finally have something to put on my CV. I'd have the telly stamp of approval.

I felt intimidated when I arrived for the audition at BBC Manchester. My eyes grew wider as I entered the building. I was like a kid in Disneyland for the first time. This was where they made the news I watched in the evening! I so wanted to be a part of it.

But I'm far too common to work for the BBC, I thought. I talk with a Northern accent.

I wasn't thinking straight, obviously. I was auditioning for a Northern drama, so of course they were going to want someone with a Northern accent.

There were four plastic chairs outside the casting room. Two of them were occupied by girls the same age as me. Are they going up for the same role? I wondered. If so, why is one of them blonde and the other one thin?

Just then, a girl with red hair in a bob turned up and sat in the last free chair. I started to panic. I don't look like any of them! I'm not going to get this job.

In later life you learn that at these auditions you're probably not going for the same role at all. The casting department sees loads of people for loads of different roles. But I knew nothing back then. When I got into the casting room, my motormouth went ahead of me and I started nattering away, nineteen to the dozen, totally overcompensating for my nerves. I didn't realise that I only had a ten-minute slot and they had a hundred other people to see. Before we knew it, ten minutes had gone by and I hadn't even started reading. Fortunately, they found it endearing and I went on to read the scenes, trying to make it look like I hadn't learnt them.

I had to wait just over a week before I heard whether I'd got it or not. That week felt like three months. By the second day, I was convinced they didn't want me. I didn't take into consideration that my audition tape had to be sent to London and viewed by a bunch of execs, and then by another bunch of execs. I still haven't got used to that wait. If they don't make the decision there and then, I always assume I haven't got it. I think a lot of actors are the same – and it doesn't get better with experience.

Mum was hovering beside me when the phone eventually rang. I was a bag of nerves. She was a bag of nerves. She probably wanted it for me more than anybody.

'You got the part,' Michelle Smith said.

I nearly screamed. 'What? You're joking, aren't you?' I said. Mum was frowning hard at me, trying to gauge what my reaction meant. I flashed a grin at her and did a thumbs up and she immediately leapt into the air, whooping for joy.

'I'm not joking,' Michelle said. 'You impressed the director. Well done!'

Waves of happiness swept over me. The feeling of being accepted was phenomenal. At last I could tell everyone at Workshop that I had a job, and what's more that I would be working with Jason Done, who was known for being a talented young actor. Years later I'd work with Jason on *Waterloo Road*.

I spent three brilliant weeks filming *Blood and Peaches* in Bradford. It was so exciting. The entire cast and crew stayed at the Victoria Hotel, so I was surrounded by experienced industry people day and night, listening to their anecdotes about other jobs and famous actors and directors. All of a sudden, I was an insider. I felt like a kid in a candy shop. I loved the work and the feedback from the set was one billion per cent positive. I couldn't have been happier. At the end of the day I'd have a glass of wine in the bar, brimming with laughter and confidence. The whole experience was pure fun to me.

There's a scene in *Blood and Peaches* where my character is drunk and hanging out of a window, laughing. Michelle Smith told me that when she watched it with the director, he pointed at me and said, 'She's special.' I couldn't believe it when she told me. I went round in a daze for about a week afterwards. Then it occurred to me that maybe she'd muddled me up with someone else. I kept wanting to ring her up and say, 'Are you sure it was me he was talking about?' But of course I didn't dare.

At least my granddad Sam didn't have any doubts that it was

me. 'That laugh! You stole the scene with your laugh,' he said proudly.

Before long, I was taken on by Laine Management in Manchester, which was closely affiliated with Oldham Theatre Workshop. Michelle Smith started calling me in for regular auditions and the next thing I knew, I had a part in *Flight*, a four-hour BBC2 drama split into two parts. I was over the moon.

At last, Dad started believing in me. He finally realised that my acting wasn't just a hobby. She's pulling it off, he thought. She's actually getting roles.

Soon afterwards, I had a call from Laine Management saying that I had to go to BBC Manchester for a fitting. 'Brilliant,' I said enthusiastically. 'I'll be there.'

'Mum, what's a fitting?' I asked, the moment I got off the phone. Being young and innocent, I had no idea they meant a costume fitting.

Like *Blood and Peaches*, *Flight* depicted racial discrimination in Bradford, but this time the lead was a young Pakistani girl who flees an arranged marriage and moves to London. I played Kelly, her best school friend, a naughty, party-going teenager who leads her astray. It was a wonderful experience for me – and I knew all about being a naughty schoolgirl!

Hot on the heels of *Flight* came four episodes of *Hetty Wainthropp Investigates*, which was billed as a Northern *Miss Marple* and starred Patricia Routledge as Hetty, with Dominic Monaghan as her sidekick.

I remember Mum saying, 'I can't see Patricia Routledge being Miss Marple, can you?'

Yet the series did brilliantly and Patricia Routledge was

excellent as a Mother Hen type who always seems to be present when there's a murder in her village. It was a bit like *Midsomer Murders* in that you wouldn't want to live in that village! The murder mystery I was in involved the killing of yet another villager. Me and Rebecca Callard played best friends who are obsessed with witchcraft, form a coven and try to re-enact the activities of the Lancashire Pendle Witches from four hundred years ago.

I hit it off straight away with Rebecca and we had a ball. We were naughty and giddy and there was lots of Northern banter between us. We were both totally in awe of Patricia Routledge, who had the aura of a strict headmistress. I was never fearful of my teachers at school, but I would definitely have been scared of her if she'd been my teacher. Me and Rebecca used to laugh about like crazy when she wasn't there, but the moment she came on set, we stood up straight and behaved. She had a huge presence – and a massive Winnebago to match. When it rained, she'd be whisked off to her über-caravan while me and Rebecca had to huddle in a tent, feeling a bit resentful. But, of course, there was nothing wrong with the way she was treated, because Patricia Routledge was the star. One day, I hoped, I'd be a star too, with my own runner and a great big Winnebago.

I'm not sure what kind of role I was hoping for next, so I was quite happy to play a dippy, innocent girl called Danielle who gets murdered by a psychotic lesbian serial killer, in a film called *Butterfly Kiss*. It was so exciting to be cast in a movie. I met up with Michael Winterbottom, the director, without having any idea of what a genius he is. Luckily, that suited him fine. He was looking for the rawness and naivety that he recognised in me and I got the part. I was totally bowled over.

Wow, I'm on a film set! I thought on the first day. This is where magic happens. It's totally fairy tale.

It turned out to be a bit dull, though. It took me ages to get used to the pace of working and I couldn't believe how long it took to shoot a few lines of dialogue. In TV, the turnaround is really quick, whereas on *Butterfly Kiss* we'd rehearse a scene with the director and director of photography and then sit in our caravans for hours and hours before we came out to shoot three or four lines. I'd had no idea that this was how film worked and I found it devastatingly boring.

One day I was in the caravan with quite a few of the cast. They were a lot older than me and a damn sight wiser, so they laughed wearily when I jumped out of my chair and said, 'Do you realise that we rehearsed at eight o'clock this morning and it's now lunch break and we've not shot anything?'

I was completely bored. I'm a doer and I'd had enough of sitting there listening to all these actors hold forth about their last theatre piece. 'The intensity of the role!' they'd drawl. 'I couldn't find it. Oh God, I dug so deep to find the core of this role.'

Everyone would nod sagely. Then I'd chip in, 'Anyone see *Graham Norton* last night?' (Believe me, I haven't changed.)

Still, I loved the acting, when I finally got to do some. I had about eight scenes, which was brilliant, and I took juvenile pleasure in dressing up for my role as a service station checkout girl. Even now, I adore the dressing up aspect of my job. Michael Winterbottom is an incredible director and I was at a point in my life when I desperately needed to experience different directors' perspectives so that I could develop. He was totally involved with every role and what each actor was doing, so it was great working for him.

To my delight, one of the crew paid me a lot of attention while we were filming. He was a lot older than me – I was seventeen and I couldn't help but be flattered. On my last evening a bunch of us were in the bar of the Novotel in Preston and he wrote his room number on my packet of Regal cigarettes. Shall I? I thought. Why not? A little later I went and knocked on his door.

I look back and think, Was that really me? I wouldn't do that nowadays! It was all part of being in the fairy-tale film world and I remember it being loads of fun.

I enjoyed telling everyone about my movie experiences, but secretly I was glad to get back to Workshop. In early 1994, we had started working towards the upcoming summer showcase at the Oldham Coliseum Theatre. It was set to be a special show, because it was celebrating the twenty-fifth anniversary of musicals at Workshop and David had decided to do an amalgamation of all the previous shows, with fifteen pieces in Act One and ten pieces in Act Two. I was lucky enough to be cast as the music hall star in *Oh! What a Lovely War*, the part Maggie Smith plays in the film and which Anne Kirkbride played in the original Workshop production.

The song was about luring men to join the army, promising them sex if they did, and my performance was very camp, full of saucy innuendo and knowing winks. I studied the musical and the era it was depicting, then I went out and hammed it up. 'We need recruits!' I sang. 'On Saturday I'm willing … to make a man of any one of you.'

*

Unbeknown to me, there were several important casting directors in the audience, including the head of casting for Yorkshire Television, Sue Jackson, although it wasn't until about six months later that I heard from her. In the meantime, I kept going for auditions and hoping the next thing would come along, although I wasn't too bothered when I went to an audition and didn't get it. I felt I was an actress now, tried and tested, and I was prepared for the peaks and troughs of life in the industry. Don't get me wrong, I was always desperate for work. I went the extra mile at every audition I went to, but I also had to accept that I was in a profession that calls for a lot of resilience.

I went back to working in the Bull's Head and partying with Antony, Michelle, Lucy, Martin, David and various others. By now Martin had come out of the closet, as had his brother David. They had a flat near the gay village in Manchester and I often stayed there after a night out. One night, Marsha Thomason came out with us, bringing a guy called Darren with her. Marsha was doing some part-time modelling at the time and she'd met Darren at the model agency.

Darren was fantastic and we hit it off straight away. Funny and gorgeous, with more than a passing resemblance to David Beckham, he was shy with a lot of people, but with me he was exuberant and always laughing. Suddenly he was joining us all the time, which may have put Marsha's nose slightly out of joint because she had introduced him to the group. Meanwhile, Antony took an instant dislike to him. It's well known that gay men are territorial over their fag hags – and Antony had been out forever and I was most definitely a gay magnet – but I think there was more to it than that. Antony smelt a rat. He was suspicious of Darren but I took no notice. Darren could do no wrong in my eyes.

In February 1995, I had a call from Laine Management saying that Sue Jackson from Yorkshire TV wanted to see me. Apparently I'd made quite an impression on her when I'd camped it up for the summer showcase, so she'd immediately thought of me when she was asked to line up some possibles for the part of Mandy Dingle in *Emmerdale*. Mandy was a cousin of the infamous *Emmerdale* Dingles, who were renowned for adding comedy to the soap opera. She was being introduced for one episode only, as part of a huge storyline around Tina Dingle's wedding. Everyone was expecting a comedic wedding, but the writers flipped it and Tina jilts her groom at the altar. As for Mandy, well, she turns up and causes Dingle mayhem; a total minx, she flirts with everybody.

My gran's eyes grew wide as saucers when she heard I was going for a meeting at Yorkshire TV about a role in *Emmerdale*. She had watched the very first episode when it aired as *Emmerdale Farm* in 1972 and she'd been watching it ever since. 'A Dingle!' she kept saying with wonder in her voice. 'Our Lisa, on *Emmerdale*.'

'Don't jinx me, Gran,' I said, wishing my mum hadn't told her. I desperately wanted to get the part, even if it was only for one episode. *Emmerdale* was practically a national institution and almost everybody I knew watched it. I was a quaking wreck when I went to the meeting, knowing how special it would be for my family if I played Mandy Dingle. I would have loved to appear cool, calm and collected in front of the producers, but I'm a chatterbox when I'm nervous and I rattled on about anything and everything.

'I didn't get it,' I told Mum when I got home. 'I talked too much.' She just smiled and went on preparing tea.

Elaine at Laine Management phoned two days later. 'Congratulations, Mandy!' she said. I nearly exploded with excitement. I'd been watching *Emmerdale* all my life and now I was going to be in it, one of the UK's biggest soap operas! I was so thrilled that I didn't know what to do with myself, so I danced around the kitchen singing the *Emmerdale* theme tune until Mum started throwing biscuits at me.

All my elation counted as nothing on my first day on the set, though. I was desperately nervous, totally consumed by fear. I couldn't breathe. I felt sick. I had that churning feeling that I call 'washing-machine belly'. It was horrible.

The producers had warned my agent that the turnaround is very quick on *Emmerdale*, as it is on most soaps. That means that there isn't time to fluff your lines and do them again. They were more or less saying, 'Make sure she knows the dialogue.'

Well, if there's one thing I pride myself on, it's learning my dialogue, but I always have this terrible fear that I don't actually know it. Oh God, I've forgotten it! I kept thinking, and I went over it again and again. It was awful. Experience has since taught me that sometimes the more you go over it, the faster it leaves your mind. I was all over the place. It didn't help that I was completely in awe of the rest of the cast. Cy Chadwick, Malandra Burrows and Ian Kelsey were all lovely to me, but I didn't really mix with anyone else.

Things moved very quickly that first day. Being a newbie, I had no idea what was and wasn't acceptable behaviour and practice on set. Am I allowed to say that I wasn't quite happy with the last take? I wondered. The director said he was happy, but was he really?

Everything was done so speedily that sometimes I didn't feel a hundred per cent confident about what I'd just delivered. But I also didn't have the confidence to say, 'Gosh, can we go again?'

Still, I worked hard and tried to make my mark. I remembered one of David Johnson's pieces of advice: 'Make an impact on Day 1 and you'll be there on Day 101.' So many Workshop kids had gone into *Corrie* that he knew how it worked. The writers bring in new characters and test them, to see if they will be viable in the long term.

What's next for me? I wondered when it was over. Filming *Emmerdale* had been scary, but exciting. I knew I'd jump at the chance of more soap work, but now it was time to wait and see. Meanwhile, me and Darren went on holiday to Palma in Majorca for ten days. We were really good mates now. We got on like a house on fire and had the best fun wherever we went.

Mum was still with the tour operator Airtours. She worked in the complaints department, dealing with dissatisfied customers. Unofficially she was also the company's in-house therapist and everyone went to her with their emotional dilemmas and problems. People were drawn to her because she was fun and bubbly, but she was also a great listener. I've got mates who describe her as 'the mum I never had'. The door was always open and she never judged anyone, no matter what kind of trouble they were in. 'You walk with your own heart and shoulders in life,' she'd say.

As well as being sympathetic, she had a way of spurring people on with her positive attitude. 'When the chips are down, you cook more,' she often said. I love that.

It was lucky for me that Mum was so well liked at Airtours, because if she hadn't been, my future might have been very different. While I was in Majorca, my agent rang home, urgently needing to speak to me. We didn't have mobiles then, so it was much harder to contact people than it is now. Thankfully, Mum knew which hotel I was staying in and she was able to fax the Airtours rep at the resort. 'Can you please get Lisa to phone home, like, yesterday!'

On the third night of the holiday, the rep knocked on my bedroom door. 'I've had a message from your lovely mum,' she said. 'She needs you to ring home right this minute,' she said.

I started panicking. I thought, Oh my God, something awful has happened! I ran to the lobby and dialled home. 'Mum?' I said breathlessly, when she picked up the phone.

'Laine Management have been on the phone,' she said, just as breathlessly. 'The people at *Emmerdale* want you back for three episodes! You're to fly home as soon as you can, because filming starts next Wednesday.'

'What?' I could barely take it in. 'When?'

'Leave it to me, darling,' she said. 'I'll sort everything out this end.'

Mum arranged flights for me and Darren. We flew back on the Monday and I started shooting on the Wednesday.

Poppa and his brother-in-law, Uncle Bert, drove me to Leeds the day before I started. Me and Mum called them the alternative Thelma and Louise. Only, they didn't want to speed along the motorway. It was a beautiful day in early September and they wanted to take the scenic route.

'That's all well and good, Poppa, but we need to get there. The scenic route takes time,' I said fretfully.

'Oh, but it's beautiful over the top!' he said.

'I appreciate that, but we have to get there. In television, you can't be late!'

Of course, Poppa, being Poppa, had his own way and we took the leisurely route to Leeds, thankfully arriving in good time for my meeting with the producers.

It was great being back on the show. I was part of the 'Home Farm Siege' storyline, which is now seen as a classic in *Emmerdale*'s history. It was brilliant and I had a ball. Basically, the Dingles call on Mandy to come and help them fight off Frank Tate, who is claiming that their land is rightfully his. In fear of losing everything, their home, their farm and all the animals, they form a barricade to protect what's theirs. Mandy's involvement in the ensuing siege ends when she is arrested and thrown into jail. Little did I know that this was going to be the first of many arrests for Mandy.

Because I was doing three episodes this time, I began to make friends with some of the cast. Jacqueline Pirie (Tina) and I hit it off straight away, and I got on really well with James Hooton (Sam), Steve Halliwell (Zak) and Paul Loughran (Butch). I felt very grateful to them for the way they looked after me. I think they must have guessed that I was going to be on the show for a lot longer than three more episodes, because they went out of their way to show me the ropes. They took me to see all the dressing rooms, the green room and the canteen; they showed me round the offices and pointed out the pigeon-holes for mail; they explained how everything worked and where to pick up the latest scripts and schedules. They made it clear from the start that I could lean on them, which was very reassuring. Whenever I passed any of them in the corridor, they'd say, 'Are you OK? Do you know where you're going?'

Back then, all the internal scenes were filmed at a huge old five-storey mill building in Farsley. Later, we moved to pur-pose-built studios in Burley Road in the centre of Leeds and the old mill became the *Heartbeat* set. While *Emmerdale* was in Farsley, the different interior sets – the inside of all the different characters' homes – were housed on the first four floors of the building. The green room and dressing rooms were on the fifth floor. It was such an old building that everything creaked, so when they were filming on the fourth floor, you had to stop in your tracks if you were on the floor above. A red light would go on and you weren't allowed to take a step until it went off. It reminded me of the scene in *Mary Poppins* where the household comes to a standstill when the old admiral blasts his cannon from the rooftop. 'Posts, everybody!'

Every day was non-stop and there was a lot to learn. I discov-ered early on that a quick change meant you had to leg it upstairs to your dressing room and leg it back down again. You really had to get a move on if you didn't want to keep everyone waiting, which of course I didn't. I was desperate to make a good impres-sion. It was the same with the dialogue. There was no room for mistakes. You did a take and quickly moved on to the next set-up. Often, lunch break barely happened. I'd get my tray of food from the canteen, wolf it down in the green room or my dressing room and before I knew it I'd be back in make-up having checks for the afternoon. It was never-ending and I loved it.

Before a replica village was built on the Harewood Estate in 1998, the exterior scenes were filmed in a real village called Esholt. The problem there was that the public could come and watch and you'd have to stop for babies crying or planes flying overhead. It used to drive the sound operators crazy. The Woolpack was a real pub that carried on business as usual when we weren't filming, as did the village post office and the church on the corner.

On the last day of filming, I told Steve Halliwell about how I'd been in Palma and nearly missed my chance of doing the Home Farm Siege episodes. 'I was lucky,' I said.

'Oh, you'll be back again,' he said. 'They love you.'

'What?' I said, my heart thumping. 'Don't be daft!'

'Lisa, they love you,' he said, in all seriousness.

His words were chewing in my head by the time I got home. Why would he say that? I thought. Come on, I'm not going to be a regular in the third biggest soap in the country! No way.

I was eager to tell Mum, but I didn't want to jinx it. So I tried to suppress my excitement by thinking about something else. As the minutes ticked by, I began to feel like an unexploded firecracker. It was no good. I had to ring her.

'Mum, I don't want to tempt fate, but Steve Halliwell said something and I've got to tell you about it.'

'Darling, I don't have any doubt in my mind,' Mum said, after

I'd blurted it out. 'After all, why would they get you back so quickly after the wedding episode?'

'The thing is, Mandy's been sent to prison,' I said. 'They can't get her out now!'

Mum was her usual reassuring self. 'It'll be fine, darling. Don't worry about it.'

In the end, I went over it so much in my head that I had to put a stop to it. I had to put it to bed and forget about it. I've had two bites of the cherry, I thought. It's been gorgeous and I've thoroughly enjoyed it, but I can't expect any more. Not being familiar with the workings of soap world, I wasn't aware that the storylines are written eleven weeks in advance and filmed five weeks before they're transmitted. I didn't know about script conferences and how a character's future gets decided. And I certainly didn't realise that the writers can do anything they like with a prison sentence. You can get nine years and be out within a month. They simply say, 'Your sentence has been slashed,' and you're out. And that's exactly what they did with Mandy, after the writers and producers had been to a script conference and decided to include her as a regular character.

Lo and behold, five weeks later I got a call offering me a year's regular work in *Emmerdale*. When I got off the phone, I jumped up and down so hard that I nearly did myself an injury. 'Mum!' I screamed. 'Can you believe it?' I could not have been happier.

'I said it would happen,' she said, smiling her great big smile. 'I know talent when I see it. Don't you remember how I spotted Robson Green when he was that porter with three lines in *Casualty*? Just look at him now! I said it first!'

I remembered it well, not least because she had never let me or anyone else forget it. 'Mum, you should become a casting director,' I said. 'Then you could put Pam Ferris opposite Robson Green in a British version of *The Graduate*.'

Me and Mum fell about in fits, laughing hysterically. After all, it was no more far-fetched than the idea of me becoming a regular in *Emmerdale*.

6

All right, Mandy?

Standing completely still, paralysed with shock, I gaped at the vast magazine rack in front of me. Staring back at me were ten or more magazines with my face on the cover. *TV Times*, *TV Choice* and *TV Quick*; every TV, soap and weekly magazine had a picture of me on the front. I couldn't believe my eyes. It was overwhelming. It felt like I was having an out-of-body experience.

All of a sudden I felt claustrophobic and I burst out crying. This is my life now, I thought, and it's completely and utterly out of control.

I was in Asda in Pudsey, Leeds, doing my weekly shop with Darren. A few people had already said, 'All right, Mandy,' on our way in. I'd said hi back, dipping my head and feeling self-conscious. I was still getting used to being recognised and I'd found that I didn't like being famous.

David Johnson had warned me that my life would change

dramatically the moment I entered *Emmerdale*, but I wasn't pre-pared for a whole rack of magazine covers with my image on them. It was scary beyond belief, especially as every cover had Mandy written beneath my photograph. Who is Mandy Dingle? Who is she? I thought. She's a character in a story. She's not real. Yet everywhere I go, people call me Mandy. It's not my name! It was so confusing. I was doing a job I adored, but I loathed the fame.

Everywhere I went strangers were tapping me on the arm. 'Is it you? Is it you?'

'Is *what* me?'

People were always whispering around me. Sometimes it felt like I was hearing voices in my head, only I wasn't, because the air really was filled with the sound of whispers. Sometimes they'd speak loudly as they walked past me, so that I would turn my head. Often I'd look up to see someone pointing and laughing at me. For a split second I'd think I must have pen on my face or something, but then I'd hear them saying, 'Look, it's her. It's Mandy!'

'What on earth is the matter?' Darren asked when he came back to find me in front of the magazine rack.

'I've got to go,' I said, tears streaming down my cheeks. I left my trolley where it was and hurried out of the shop without buying a thing.

Back at the flat, I sat on the sofa and cried my heart out. Everything in my life had changed so much, so quickly. I was missing Mum, Dad, Gran and home like crazy. I was living away from home, filming all day every day, and unable to go anywhere without being recognised. The whole country seemed to know who I was. I should be happy, I thought. This is my dream; I'm doing what I've always wanted to do. And yet I felt scared and intimidated by it all.

Darren brought me over a cup of tea. 'There you go, love,' he said gently. He sat down beside me and put his arm round my shoulders.

For the hundredth time I wondered where I would be without him. Darren had turned into the best friend anyone could have and I felt I needed him more than I'd ever needed anyone before. Not only did we get on brilliantly, but he had a way of looking after me that felt very reassuring. I was so thankful that he had agreed to share a flat with me.

At first I'd lived in a B&B, in the same building where Jacqueline Pirie had an apartment. Then, when I realised that I was going to be in the show for a long time, I decided that I would need my own apartment in Leeds. 'Will you help me look for a flat?' I asked Darren.

Suddenly I had to be independent. I had to set up home for myself. I had to go to Ikea and buy four beakers, four cups, four plates and a whole load of cutlery. Yet I was a teenager. Most of my best friends were at college, smoking weed and eating pot noodle, while I was working all hours and setting up a home. It felt weird.

I hated the idea of living alone. 'It's a two-bedroom flat. Do you want to move in?' I asked Darren. I felt safe with him. My family adored him and to this day Liam calls him the older brother he never had. This could work, I thought. Why not? We had a wonderful friendship. Thankfully, he agreed to move in and he helped me sort everything out. In no time, I was relying on his support.

I suppose I should have known that the storylines I was in-volved in on *Emmerdale* would attract a lot of attention, but I was totally innocent back then. The producers would say things like, 'You'll be going to London with this storyline.'

'All right, OK,' I'd say confidently, but I'd be thinking, Go to London for what? I didn't ask, because I didn't want to look like I had no idea what they were talking about. I soon learnt that they meant I'd be going to London to do a publicity day and TV interviews on *GMTV* and *This Morning*.

In my first episodes, the writers set up a situation that would be the source of comedy and pathos for years to come. It all starts the moment Mandy sees Dave Glover, the village heart throb played by Ian Kelsey, and becomes obsessed with him, bless her. She spends three years trying to win Dave over, but he just thinks she's the local slapper. Mandy's unrequited love, which was drawn out into a series of connecting storylines, became hugely popular with the viewers.

I always said that Mandy was based on a girl I used to see at the bus stop on my way home from school. This girl went to one of the not-so-good schools in Bury, where the kids acted a bit rough and cool and the girls tried so hard to get it right on the fashion front that they got it desperately wrong. That's how I saw Mandy. I had a very strong sense of how she should look. From the very start I had a vision of her as a tart with a heart. Outwardly, she's a bolshy semi-ladette, but inside she's vulner-able and innocent, a broken little biscuit who just wants to be heard. I wanted her to have bunches, so that you could see she was a bit juvenile and could forgive her for making mistakes. The wardrobe department was brilliant and the collaboration of make-up, wardrobe and great writers produced a character that really worked.

I'm desperately proud of what I did with Mandy. We didn't see the writers much, but when we did they always told me, 'You're a joy to write for.' They said that my portrayal of Mandy made it possible for her to make mistake after mistake, which in a soap is pure telly gold. One writer who had previously written for *Coronation Street* told me that she had incorporated elements of the wonderful, disaster-prone Raquel Watts (played by Sarah Lancashire) into Mandy Dingle. That made sense to me. Mandy and Raquel share a vulnerability.

The storyline that catapulted me onto all the magazine covers I'd seen in Asda revolved around the possibility that hunky Dave Glover would ask Mandy out on a date. Will he ask her? Is Mandy going to get the date? There was a frenzy of speculation about it.

It isn't long before Dave does ask her out. Desperately excited, Mandy gets herself all dolled up for him, only to overhear him saying that he's only doing it for a bet. It's all been a joke. Poor Mandy is devastated.

The writing was stunning and I threw myself into the emotional scenes that show Mandy's hurt pride and disappointment when Dave dumps her. She collapses in a phone box and cries bitter tears that make her mascara run down her face. The costume and make-up departments made me looked like I'd been raped, and that's exactly what Mandy's cousin Butch assumes has happened when he comes to her rescue. Butch has been in love with Mandy all along, but she still doesn't want him.

We filmed the scene at night, so at three in the morning I was sitting on the cold floor, wearing a feather boa, having to cry and cry again, in take after take. Luckily, I don't find it hard to bring tears to my eyes. Often I genuinely feel the emotion and the tears follow naturally, but if I'm doing loads of takes I might put my headphones on and listen to a song that will instantly make me cry. Some actors use a tear stick, which contains menthol and camphor to make your eyes water, but I can't bear it. I'm really lucky in that way. It is easy for me to find a way to trigger the emotion.

'This one will do it for you,' the director told me after we wrapped the shoot. I wasn't sure what he meant, but I knew I had hit on the raw emotion of the scene. I was beginning to feel the same confidence about the emotional scenes as I felt about the comedic scenes.

A few months later, I won Most Popular Newcomer in the 1996 National Television Awards for my work within that storyline. That meant so much to me, because the awards are decided by public vote. Back then, before the internet, a lot of people voted by post, which is hard to imagine now. It's like looking back on the Dark Ages.

I was there on the night. It was too exciting and I felt so glamorous. I wore a beautiful Harrods black dress with diamanté spaghetti straps and had my hair and make-up done. But I was a bag of nerves too. My tummy was in knots when Trevor McDonald said, 'After the break, we will be announcing this year's Most Popular Newcomer.'

I thought Paul Nicholls from *EastEnders* was going to win. I knew Paul from Bolton. He was a heart throb, a great actor and *EastEnders* had higher viewing figures than we did. So when my name was announced, it didn't immediately register. It took about three seconds to go in and then I jumped out of my seat with joy. It was incredible! Everyone was so desperately pleased for me. It was a wonderful, celebratory evening.

The next day at Heathrow, as we were all about to board our plane to Leeds, one of the check-in staff pointed at my award and said, 'Miss Riley, that's going to have to go in your case.'

I hugged it to my chest. 'No, I'm taking it on the plane with me!'

He smiled. 'But it looks like a weapon,' he said. 'I'm afraid ...'

'It's not going in the hold! Please let me have it on the plane, please, please, please!'

He relented. As soon as we were up in the air and the seatbelt sign went off, I pulled down my table, gently put down my beautiful award and spent the rest of the flight staring at it. That's mine, that! I kept thinking.

Back in the *Emmerdale* reception area, I had to fight my way through bouquets from friends, cast members, ITV execs and people from home. It looked like a branch of Interflora. I was very touched and felt terrible that I had to give most of the flowers away, because there wasn't room for them in my flat.

I couldn't wait to get home to Bury with my award. Mum was proud beyond belief. Everyone was. When I showed it to Gran, she took it in her arms and held it like a baby. It was beautiful to see. She was glowing with pride. She'd watched *Emmerdale* since the day it first aired and now her granddaughter was one of the show's stars. 'You've done all you set out to do, come wind, come storm, come everything,' she said, her lip trembling. In her mind, I'd hit the dizziest heights.

'Gran, can I have my award back now?' I said eventually, and we burst into giggles.

Soon after that, I won Personality of the Year at the York-shire Young Achievers Awards, which was ace. After winning, I received an invitation to an open house at Buckingham Palace. Zoë Ball and Denise Van Outen were also there. Denise was all over the papers afterwards for nicking a toilet roll that day.

It was amazing to be there, a real wow. It was brilliant to meet the Queen, even if it was only for a second or two. My only disappointment was that I didn't get introduced to Harry. I wanted to meet him more than anything in the world, although it's probably a good thing that I didn't, because I would have kept hold of his hand until I was prised away by footmen!

When I was introduced to Prince Charles, someone had obviously told him I worked on *Emmerdale*. 'So, you work on the land of Lord Harewood?' he said.

'Oh yeah!' I replied chirpily.

Listen to yourself, I thought crossly, you sound so common! My mind was whirring. There was too much to think about. Have I held his hand for too long? Has he asked me a question? Can I speak now?

'It's stunning countryside. It's very rural up there,' Prince Charles said.

'Yeah, you love a field, don't you?' I trilled. 'You love your great outdoors. Anyway, where's Harry?' And I wonder why I haven't been asked back.

It was all very well to win awards, but once the *Emmerdale* writers realised that Mandy was such a great character, my life became completely insane. My average day, Monday to Friday, would be: 7 a.m. in make-up, 8 a.m. on camera, get back to the flat at 7.20 p.m., get straight into the bath and learn the following day's script in the bath, followed by a bit of telly and bed.

We were shooting three or four episodes a week and the pressure was intense. The fear of forgetting my lines never went away. I could be scheduled to do seventeen scenes in The Woolpack pub in Emmerdale village, filming from 8 a.m. to 8 p.m. – then suddenly I'd hear that another member of the cast was poorly and all the scenes were being rewritten. That meant I'd be learning full scenes again in the make-up chair on the morning of the shoot. It was nerve wracking.

Things are always changing in a soap and I had to programme myself to learn the script in a certain way. At any moment the story editor can come downstairs and say, 'We've realised in transmission that we've got a loophole here. So, can you add this sentence, to make it right?' Then they'll slot another bit of dialogue into the script for you.

Your brain has to get used to that way of working and learn how to adjust at the last minute. During filming, you have to try and get it right for the first take. The schedule is so packed that you're lucky to get a third take, unless you've got a big, emotional storyline going on. Over time, I got better at pulling it out of the bag first go.

In a soap opera, you can have as many as ten different directors in a month. Often, they don't have time to do more than set up each shot. They trust you to know your character and to do it your way, so you end up almost directing yourself. I found that my experience of having had two drama teachers with their different perspectives was valuable. You learn to believe in yourself, your character, your own voice and your own way of doing things.

I became completely dependent on Darren. Throughout the madness of this time he was there when I got up in the morning and when I got home from work. He stocked the fridge, picked up my dry cleaning and sorted out our bills. We spent every weekend together. He was still modelling and doing brilliantly, but his work schedule gave him a lot of flexibility. We became incredibly close, beyond brother and sister. We were each other's rock and I'll be forever grateful to him for the strength and encouragement he gave me.

In a roundabout way he was like a boyfriend. We were desperately tactile and we'd cuddle up on the couch and watch *Friends* when I got in from work. Nothing else happened because I assumed he didn't fancy me. I fancied him like crazy, of course. He looked like David Beckham!

One boozy night about six months after we moved in, we got together. It felt awkward at first. What are we doing? we thought. Yet somehow it was right. We never sat down and said, 'We are a couple.' But things would happen from time to time. Originally it would be after we'd had a few drinks. Then it became more frequent, although it was never predictable. Some nights we would and some nights we wouldn't; I had my room and he had his room. It was friends with benefits and the benefits were fab, but I always wanted more.

Still, I loved the work and my buddies on *Emmerdale*. Me

and Steve Halliwell, James Hooton, Paul Loughran, Jacqueline Pirie and Jane Cox (Lisa Dingle) were so tight. I'm proud of how hard we worked to get the most from our scripts. The writers were genius, but we always tried to put our own stamp on what we did. While some of the other members of the cast might sit and watch *GMTV* in the green room, we would gather around a table and go through the script, looking for places where we could add extra laughs and visual gags.

The Dingles were slobs, a dysfunctional, common family, and we tried to squeeze every drop of comedy out of them. It was desperately important to us. Steve had this amazing instinct for knowing when to make a noise, at just the right comic moment. Then I might decide to speak with my mouth full of egg. Even though it wasn't in the stage directions, comedically it worked brilliantly and was exactly the sort of thing Mandy would do, in the same way that a family meal could easily end up with everyone throwing their tea at each other, because that's the kind of family the Dingles were. We were always thinking about how our characters would behave.

A wonderful camaraderie grew up between us and I knew I was making friends for life. It was so exciting to be doing something that really worked, with committed actors who wanted to make their performances the best they could be. We realised how popular we were in the show and we all wanted to continue making great comedy drama. We ate, slept and breathed each other on and off set. Not a day went by when I didn't see Steve Halliwell or Paul Loughran, so it was lucky we got on so well. It wasn't just the Dingles. I made brilliant friendships with

Ian Kelsey, Dominic Brunt (Paddy Kirk) and Adele Silva (Kelly Windsor).

I had some fantastic storylines in the years that followed. After Dave Glover is killed in a fire, Mandy falls in love with the new village vet Paddy Kirk, but ends up marrying her cousin Butch for money. All kinds of things happen before she and Paddy finally get together and tie the knot. The *Emmerdale* producers even flew a bunch of us out to Australia for eight weeks to film a spin-off video, *The Dingles Down Under*, which was a phenomenal, incredible experience. I was so lucky. I look back and I pinch myself.

One morning, one of the actors came up to me and said, 'I must congratulate you, Lisa. They'll never write a line for you like, "Can I have a gin and tonic, please?"'

'What do you mean?' I asked.

'Trust me,' he said.

I realised later that the writers have a list of the characters they are contractually obliged to include in a scene, even if they're not connected with the current storylines. In that case, they'll put the character in the pub and get him or her to say, 'Can I have a gin and tonic, please?' Job done.

My popularity didn't go down well with everyone. I was new on the block, and yet I was getting a lot of the limelight, both at work and in the press. There were storylines that didn't affect our family, yet the writers would want to slip Mandy in, often to provide light relief within a very serious section that dealt with a subject like rape or domestic abuse. There were certain cast members whose noses were put out of joint by this. 'Hold on a minute!' they'd complain. 'She's had her own storylines and now she's involved in other people's storylines.' The eight-week trip to Australia to film *The Dingles Down Under* was also chalked up as preferential treatment.

What could I do? I was simply learning my lines, tipping up to work and doing my job. Aware of all the crosscurrents, I had to toughen up but it was difficult to deal with all the backbiting. I was still a teenager. I didn't have enough experience of life to understand so I just tried to ignore it.

During the first couple of years, when Mandy was at her height of popularity, I'd do two or three public appearances (PAs) at the weekends. It was so easy: I'd turn up, sign autographs and get paid three and a half grand. How crazy is that? Fortunately, it was always in a controlled environment, with enough security to make sure nothing got out of hand, so it didn't make me feel nervous or panicked like a trip to the shops could. What's more, I could do a bingo hall PA at lunchtime on Saturday, a nightclub PA for an hour later that evening and then another bingo hall at five o'clock on the Sunday. I was earning a phenomenal amount of money for a teenager and the money definitely turned my head. Thankfully, *Emmerdale* sorted me out with a financial adviser straight away and I was careful about putting a percentage aside for tax. I had some great advice, and Mum also helped me to be organised and sensible about saving.

I bought a car and Darren started driving me everywhere, to PAs, to see my friends in Manchester and back home to see Mum, Dad and Liam, who regarded him as a winning streak in my life. In turn, Darren loved my lust for life. Things hadn't been all that easy for him when he was a kid and he appreciated being around someone who was gutsy and full of fun. He was beside me every step of the way in those early days of fame.

Mum knew what the situation was between us and understood how much I needed him, but I think everyone else thought we were a couple, including my friends at *Emmerdale*. Darren came to clubs, parties and awards ceremonies with me. I loved having him on my arm because he was so fit. He was like a tailor's dummy – 'peachy keen', as Rizzo says in *Grease*. We even did an 'At Home' together for a magazine. It was horrid on every level and makes me cringe now, but at the time I was swept away by the power of Mandy Dingle. Was it right? Was it wrong? I didn't know. All I knew was that I was being paid masses for it.

I prided myself on being mature for my age, but I was just a kid. On the one hand, I was freaked out that people kept mistaking me for a fictional character. No one can know what it's like until they experience it. When you're in a soap opera, sections of the public think they own you. They wanted me to be someone who blunders around hilariously thumping blokes, but I wasn't that person. We're all human and there are days when everybody feels down, but I'd be accused of being stuck up if I didn't look delighted when strangers came up to me. Sometimes you want to go into a shop, buy a pint of milk and leave without having to chat, but nobody seemed to understand that.

On the other hand, a part of me bought into the hype surrounding soaps and actors on soaps. There was always a PA or a glamorous bash to rush off to. People greeted me like a long lost friend at every party I walked into. There was no reality. I thought it was all part of the job and I had to go along with it if I didn't want to fall off the bandwagon, but I also loved being the centre of attention. I threw myself into what I call 'the fake fame game' and on one level I enjoyed it. I knew no better. It makes me squirm to remember.

The friendships you make along the way are so false. The people you hook up with aren't your friends. They just want to string along with you because you get them into a club for free. If my best mates from home had met some of the people I was hanging out with, they would have said, 'Lise, they're all knobs.' Sadly, I wouldn't have wanted their advice, or listened to it. On the other hand, I couldn't put a foot wrong with Darren. He was very loyal and never criticised me or my lifestyle.

To the day she died, my mum would say, 'You don't regret anything in life.'

'But I do, Mum,' I'd say. 'I really do. I regret that time in my life more than anything.'

Antony says I became seriously weird. It got to the point where he thought, Where's Lisa gone? He barely recognised me. His happy, laughing, bubbly mate had been replaced by someone else. He couldn't understand it. What he didn't realise was that the pressure of work, intense media attention and homesickness was making me feel scarily out of control. I was losing my sense of who I was and I didn't know how I was supposed to be. My confidence and identity were slipping away from me. It felt like the world had gone crazy.

Like most kids, I had practised writing my autograph, with different swirls on the L of Lisa, yet I'd had no idea what fame meant. My dream was about getting lead roles and recognition for doing my job well. I never imagined I'd be faced by magazine racks with my face on them, or people constantly tapping my arm. The more it happened, the more I hated it.

One day I arranged to go shopping with Antony at the Manchester Arndale Centre. I turned up with sunglasses on, even though it wasn't very sunny outside. When we walked inside and I still didn't take them off, he felt he had to say something. 'What the hell have you got sunglasses on for?'

'I can't stand the pressure,' I told him.

He didn't say anything, because he thought I wouldn't get it, but he thought I was behaving like an absolute idiot. In his opinion, I was lost in showbiz and needed a good sniff of reality. In actual fact, I was suffering. Over time, I felt more and more anxious about going out. Shopping became particularly difficult. When the Trafford Centre was built in Manchester, it was the biggest shopping centre in Europe. It's wow, it's mega, it's got everything you want under one roof, but although I loved it the first time I went, with my mum and gran, I found it scarily busy. All the exits seemed to lead to the car park and I didn't like the idea of not being able to get outside into the open. Everyone was looking at me, which made it worse. My legs buckled under me and I started to feel short of breath. 'Can we get out of here?' I said to Mum. By the time we reached the car park, I was having a panic attack.

I felt suffocated by the attention I attracted wherever I went. It made everything unpredictable. The people who randomly approached me in public weren't always Mandy's fans. Often they'd tell me off for something Mandy had done wrong, shaking their heads and wagging their fingers. It was like being told off at school for something you hadn't done. 'You need to speak to the show's writers about that,' I'd say. 'They're the ones controlling what Mandy does, not me.'

Unlike at personal appearances, where everything was ordered and controlled, when I was out and about I never knew what would happen next. Would someone shout at me for something Mandy had done? Would they lunge at me or try to hit me? I was constantly saying, 'I'm not Mandy Dingle, I'm Lisa Riley.' But nobody took any notice.

I began to feel uneasy a lot of the time. I had nights when I didn't sleep at all. I'd lie in bed and start to worry that I was going to panic. That would trigger a panic attack and I'd be overwhelmed with the sensation of not being able to breathe, which would make the panic worse. Then I'd think I was about to have a heart attack. It was so, so awful. I wouldn't wish a panic attack on my worst enemy. When it got particularly bad, Darren would ring Mum and ask her to drive over. She was the only person who could calm me down and soothe me, and she always dropped everything to be with me when I needed her.

I had work, I had money and I had fame, but I was feeling increasingly wobbly. My life was a whirlwind of hard work and constant socialising. I developed a terrible fear that I was missing out on 'normal life'. Losing touch with my best friends in Bury didn't help. During this time, I barely spoke to my bezzies Kate, Sam and Nicola, aka 'Flossie', because they were all doing 'normal things' and I was constantly being referred to as a 'soap icon' in the press. Kate was at uni, Sam was pregnant and settling down and Flossie was training to be an air steward. Our worlds seemed miles apart. When I did speak to them, they kept telling me how lucky I was. My life was brilliant, they said. I was in a soap, acting for a living, with the money coming in week after week. What more could I want? Everyone was proud of me, but I felt something was missing.

When I voiced my doubts, they dismissed them. 'People would kill for the chance to be doing what you're doing,' they told me. 'Just enjoy it while it lasts.'

After a while, I stopped ringing my friends in Bury. When they rang, I'd say, 'I'm busy, I'm really busy!' But I should have made time for them, especially Sam, who had given up her dream of going to uni when she found out she was pregnant with Jack.

When Antony came over from Manchester, Darren usually went to stay at his Mum's, because they were both aware that there was no love lost there. At the same time, they knew I needed them both. They were a bit like divorced parents who had to be civilised for the kid!

Antony would want to go clubbing or to different wine bars, but every time I saw him I insisted on going to this one restaurant called Fat Franco's, where we'd have dinner and then go straight back to the flat. 'God, we do the same thing every time I see her!' Antony used to complain to his partner at the time. He didn't understand that I wanted to forget that I was 'Lisa from the telly' and just be myself with my best friend. It makes sense to him now he's in *Coronation Street*, but at the time he found it boring. But I couldn't be myself at wine bars. There would always be too much attention from strangers.

I felt I couldn't go anywhere or be me any more. Instead of

letting my hair down at a club on a Saturday night, I'd stay in the flat with four friends and neck endless bottles of wine and Jack Daniels chasers until the early hours. Trapped in a claustrophobic bubble, I began to feel desperately unhappy.

7

The penny drops

The anxiety got worse. What can I do to make myself feel better? I thought.

I got a credit card and began to spend, spend, spend. I'd nip out between scenes, get a cab to Harvey Nichols in Leeds and squander two grand on bags and shoes in a couple of hours. It was ridiculous. With my designer sunglasses on and ten Harvey Nichols bags hanging off my arm, for one *Pretty Woman* moment I'd feel like Julia Roberts. It was briefly comforting, but it didn't make me feel better in the long run.

Being caught up in the fake fame game meant I thought I had to have Louis Vuitton luggage and a Versace handbag. If I didn't have Dior sunglasses and a Chanel watch I was going wrong. I focused on accessories because none of the designer clothes fitted me. After Jacqueline Pirie left *Emmerdale* in 1996, I started to become closer to Adele Silva. She was my best friend at work and she looked great in the latest Donna Karan dress. But it wouldn't fit me, so I'd buy two pairs of shoes instead. Shoes were my designer stamp, along with handbags, jewellery and luggage.

I was always being asked to go on chat shows and Darren would come with me when I went to London. On the way back to the station after one show, I suddenly got it into my fairy-tale mind that I wanted to go to Tiffany's. I wanted to stand there and think I was Holly Golightly, but I ended up buying a £900 bracelet that I didn't need or particularly want. It meant nothing, nothing at all. It was just so I could have something I'd bought in Tiffany's.

I started lavishing people with presents, as a way of making them stay close to me. I took great joy in buying Liam not one but three pairs of Dolce & Gabbana jeans, none of which he needed. I'd get my mum a Louis Vuitton handbag and scarf, amazing shoes and jewellery. I suffocated Darren with designer clothes. He paid his rent and we shared the bills, but I ruined him with gifts. 'I don't want another Westwood jumper,' he'd say. 'I really don't.' I took him on extravagant holidays around Europe.

It was my way of saying, 'You will stay, won't you? Because I won't be able to cope if I'm left alone in the flat.'

I tried to control him because he was the one thing keeping me anchored. I was also deeply in love with him and desperate to please him. He loved video games and I was convinced that if I went out and bought a PlayStation and eighteen games – not one, but *eighteen* games – it would make him happy. I was prepared to do anything to ensure he stayed. I needed the stability and comfort he gave me – someone to come home to, someone always there – because I couldn't cope alone with living in a crazy 'You've now become Mandy Dingle' world.

Sometimes Liam came to stay. Although he got a bit of flak for it at school, he loved the fact that his sister was on *Emmerdale*. It was only later that he began to find it difficult. Mum and Dad would let him stay the whole weekend with me and Darren and we'd usually take him round Leeds shopping on the Saturday. One day we came back from the shops with a wheel for the Sega video games console, which I'd bought so that Darren and Liam could play a new driving game. Liam couldn't tear himself away from that wheel. His eyes didn't leave the screen when Darren served him up a steak and he was so engrossed in the game that he forgot to chew the meat after he bit into it. A piece of steak got stuck in his throat and he began to choke. As he struggled to breathe, he went red in the face. Then he went white. Then he started to go blue.

Eventually, Darren grabbed him and did the Heimlich manoeuvre on him. Meanwhile I was hysterical with terror. Thankfully the meat dislodged and came flying out of his mouth. My brother could have choked to death there and then, but Darren saved his life. It was so scary and we were all shaken up afterwards. Liam hero-worshipped Darren after that and it confirmed to me that I needed him more than anything.

On paper, I had it all. I had a great career. Everyone loved my character and I was doing every chat show going. I knew I should feel lucky, because everyone kept telling me how lucky I was. Yet I had a constant nagging feeling that something was missing, I was having fretful, sleepless nights and I felt anxious a lot of the time. I was desperately unhappy. The real Lisa was struggling against the fake Lisa, against overwork, media pressure, Mandy Dingle, the frustration of having an almost-boyfriend and isolation from my real friends. I was desperately lonely living away from home. I wouldn't admit that my relationship with Darren was unsatisfying.

One afternoon, me, Darren, Mum and Auntie Joyce went shopping in Bolton. When we got back, Darren went off to do something upstairs and Joyce said, 'What's the deal here?'

'What do you mean?' I said, playing dumb.

'With Darren,' she said. 'Is he your boyfriend or isn't he?'

'What can I say? We're closer than close.'

'Really?' She gave me a quizzical look and left.

To celebrate my twenty-first birthday, *Now* magazine decided they wanted exclusive pictures of me on a family holiday. Where would I like to go? they asked. I was spoilt for choice, but I chose Limassol in Cyprus because it seemed like the perfect place to have a beach holiday and enjoy some amazing sights. I've always loved visiting ancient ruins. Obviously I took Darren with me. The magazine flew me and Darren out there for two weeks, and Mum, Dad and Liam joined us for a week, also at *Now*'s expense.

I had a lovely week alone with Darren, but afterwards I began thinking that I needed a proper boyfriend, not this fake relationship that we had innocently developed. I realised that the casual sex thing had to stop, because he was my friend, not my boyfriend. The sex was now only happening when there was a bottle of wine involved, so there was no reality or relationship there and I wanted a relationship, a boyfriend. The problem was, I didn't want to lose Darren. I was between a rock and a hard place.

We talked about it and agreed to stick to friendship only. But I sensed that Darren was starting to feel the need to reclaim his life and identity. He began going out in Leeds without me and that panicked me. My control over him was wavering.

One night, we drove to Manchester for Antony's birthday. At the end of the evening, my car was no longer in the car park, and two days later, the police found it burnt out in Bolton. On complete impulse, I bought a BMW to replace it, even though I still couldn't drive. Antony went mad. He thought Darren was fuelling my crazy spending, but he wasn't. It was all me.

'Why have you bought a BMW?' Antony asked me a couple of weeks later, after we'd been out for a lovely supper. We were back in my flat having another bottle of wine and the truth began spilling out.

'I'm doing all these PAs. I need to be safe. So I've got to have a nice car,' I said defensively.

'You had a VW. What was wrong with that?'

'I want a flash car,' I said.

'Was it Darren's idea?'

'No. Lay off Darren. He's been the most brilliant friend to me.'

'Do you think he's gay?'

I practically choked on my wine. 'What, Darren? No.'

'Well, I do.'

'Don't be silly,' I said. I just thought it was Antony being catty.

Not long afterwards, Martin and David came over to see me. 'There's no easy way to say this, but we think we saw Darren kissing a man in a club,' David said tentatively, as I poured them a drink.

'Don't be ridiculous,' I snapped.

I hated the idea, not because Darren had been seen kissing a man, but because he was mine. I would have hated it if someone had seen him kissing a woman. He was the only thing in my entire mayhem life that I considered to be mine and I wanted him to remain mine. Even though there was no longer any sex or romance in our friendship and he was free to see someone else if he wanted, I couldn't bear the idea that he might leave me. I lived in fear of him moving out. The bottom line was that I loved him.

But now that three of my dearest gay friends had said they thought he was gay, a part of me had to accept that he might be. What the hell was I going to do? I knew it would be the end of everything if he got a boyfriend – or worse, if he brought someone back to the flat. Even though I knew he couldn't be mine, it would break my heart to see him with someone else.

But my friends were saying, 'Lisa, you look a fool, wake up and smell the roses,' and deep down I knew they were right.

Eventually I faced up to it and admitted to myself that I was being an idiot. 'Look, the boys have made this accusation …' I said to him. My heart sank when he freely admitted that it was true, but it wasn't unexpected. He had snogged a man in a club. He also said that he'd had a short relationship with a guy in the past.

'That's fine,' I said. After all, I told myself, he was a young, good-looking model. It was natural to experiment. I think a lot of men have tried it. A couple of instances didn't stamp him as a homosexual. It didn't matter anyway. All that mattered was that he didn't get a boyfriend or a girlfriend, because it would totally change the dynamic of the relationship. I refused to admit that I was still in love with him. I was in complete denial.

Nothing seemed to make me feel happy any more. I was lost in so many ways. Spending money was only a temporary solution, so I started drinking more. Instead of going back to Darren at the end of the day – or more likely to an empty flat – I'd go into Yeadon in Leeds with a few of my *Emmerdale* mates and get plastered in a pub. There was also a pub across the road from the studio in Farsley and sometimes we'd go in there straight from work.

I'd start with a bottle of wine, because I knew it would kick in quickly. Wine tends to hit me like a ton of bricks. Then I'd have a sambuca shot or two to enhance the kick, followed by G&Ts for the rest of the night, and maybe some more wine when I got home. It was a shock to the system for someone who had been a social drinker until then. I was used to having the odd glass of wine in the week and the occasional weekend blowout, but I was always careful not to go too far because I needed to be fresh for work. Being in control was important to me. Yet now I was drinking to the point of no return.

The hangovers were worse than awful, but I was prepared to put up with them if it meant I could have a few hours off the constant tension and anxiety. Getting drunk was a way of letting off steam. The pressure at work was as intense as ever. The days were long and I had lines to learn almost every evening. I didn't have a boyfriend and I was terrified that Darren would abandon me. I felt isolated from my family and friends in Bury, and there was the fame thing too. It became too much. I needed an outlet and I found it in drink.

Around this time, Darren started working as a booker at his model agency, so he was out all day, every day, and often wasn't at home when I got in. He no longer had time to play housekeeper or personal assistant.

'There's no milk in the fridge,' I'd complain.

'Well, go and get some, then,' he'd say.

He made loads of new friends and started going out in Leeds with them. He never wanted to be a part of my drinking sessions. He'd have a drink, but he didn't want to be downing shots until the wee hours, like I did. 'Come on, Lise,' he'd say, gently trying to cajole me to go to bed.

'I'm fine!' I'd snap.

Over time, I began to feel threatened by his new friends, who mainly seemed to be guys. I made jokes about him being gay yet I refused to take the conversation further, even though I sensed he wanted to talk about it. I danced around the idea that he could be gay. It was a painful time for me. I could sense that he was starting to break away.

In the midst of all this, my friend Martin dropped a bombshell. It landed early one Sunday morning when someone from my management company rang up at a shockingly unsociable hour while I was flat out asleep. The phone kept ringing and ringing until I finally picked up.

'Yes?' I said groggily. 'What is it?'

'You need to go and buy the *News of the World*.'

'Really, why?' I said, blinking innocently. Everything about me in the press had been very positive until this time. The media loved Mandy.

'I'm sorry, but Martin Doherty has sold a story on you and you need to see it.'

'What?!!' It had to be a joke.

I shook my head to clear away the cobwebs. Had I heard right? Surely it was a mistake. Although I hadn't seen Martin for a while, we were the best of friends, weren't we?

I got out of bed and glugged down a pint of water. Frowning, I had to admit that a slight distance had grown between me and Martin in recent months, as it had between me and Antony and David, who were now sharing a flat in Manchester. The antagonism between Antony and Darren had led me to keep Antony at arm's length while I desperately tried to hang on to Darren. Avoiding Antony had meant avoiding David and Martin too, although looking back I realised that Martin hadn't been around for some time. I'd been too wrapped up in my own life to notice it.

Darren went to the Co-op and brought back a copy of the newspaper for me. I gasped in horror when I saw it. I couldn't believe my eyes. The big, black, bold headline on the front page said something like REAL LIFE FARM GIRL SHAGGER and the text beneath it said I was just like the character I played in *Emmerdale*. The double page spread inside went into very personal detail about the sex me and Martin had when we were briefly together during our teens. It was awful. There was a raunchy description of us romping in a barn in Glossop, the next village along from Denton, where Martin was from. The wording was extremely graphic and there was all this abhorrent stuff about me being very sexual and loving sex. It cut me to the quick as I read it. I was torn apart and I felt hurt like I'd never felt before.

Why would you do this? I thought. You were my best friend. What have I ever done to you? It was wrong in every way, a betrayal beyond belief.

Left: Thank God Mum went from geek to chic. Here she is aged 11.

Right: Fashion has never been Daddy's strong point, even at 7 (far right).

Left: Proud as punch. Poppa, Mum and her bridesmaids on Mummy's special day, 1974.

Below: Mum's trendy and Dad's . . . just Dad, 1979.

Left: Me as a baby with my very proud Daddy, 1976.

Right: Butter wouldn't melt!
This is me, aged 2.

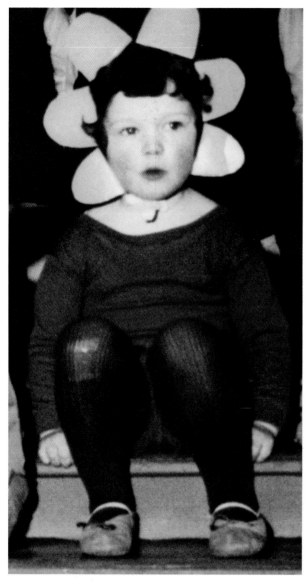

Left: Debut performance of
Lisa Riley, aged 4.

Below: Britain's next top
model? Strike a pose . . . aged 7.

Left: Fancy a jog
Gran? No, let's
pose. Bevel, bevel,
aged 7.

Right: Time to
lounge with
my Poppa, in
Canada, 1983.

Right: 'I did everything they told me not to . . .' In uniform, aged 14.

Below: A toast to the best smile ever, my mum, Christmas 1993.

Right: See, I knew him before he was a Hobbit. Dominic Monaghan and me, aged 16.

Left: Mandy does have eyes, boys. With my great mates James Hooton and Paul Loughran, 1995.

Below: Mandy has been knocked about a bit; but it's OK, it's only makeup. This was taken for makeup continuity, 1996.

Mandy Dingle Emmerdale

YORKSHIRE TELEVISION

Above: Mandy Dingle and hair.

Right: Aunty Joyce's pride when I brought the Best Newcomer Award home, 1996.

Left: Don't want to play sport, just want to sponsor it. Liam and that LJR strip, 1997.

Below: We were never going to be librarians. Antony Cotton, my GBF, 1998.

Before and after. Could my hair be any bigger? Thank the Lord for hair straighteners!

Left: Trouble and Troubler – my guiding light, 2000.

Right: My spotlight picture, time to be a Fat Friend, 2002.

Above: My Favourite *Fat Friends* Fotoshoot, 2003.

Right: Me and Ruth call wrap on a *Fat Friends* Day, Series 3, 2003.

Above: Liam Gladiator, Lisa Winslet,
Mum and Dad . . . really?! Where's
the dressing up box for the Rileys?

Left: I want to be the Statue of
Liberty! Mum's 50th in New York.

Below: Mum and Dad at the top
of the Empire State Building,
always tactile, the way I like it.

And you wonder where I get my smile from?! With Mum and Dad, 2005.

Giddy days with Mum and Antony. Mum was always the life and soul of the party – it wasn't one for the road, it was four, 2006.

Worst of all in my mind was the thought of my gran seeing it. Gran had the *News of the World* delivered every Sunday for the crossword. Jesus Christ! I thought. She's reading every intimate line about what we got up to. How will she face all her friends at bingo next Saturday? I imagined the entire bingo hall silently mee-mawing behind her back. I hated to think of her pride being dented.

I knew my mum would be fine. I knew she'd say, 'What the hell is that?' because Mum hated the red tops. She was a *Guardian* reader. I rang her in tears. 'I'm not even going to look at it,' she said disgustedly. Neither Mum nor Dad read it, which I respect them for.

I wept like a baby for most of the morning. I rang Antony in pure disbelief. 'I'm sorry I haven't been a good friend to you recently,' I sobbed.

'Darling, I love you and I will always love you,' he soothed. I was so grateful for his friendship and reassurance in that moment.

We talked about the possibility of David Johnson hearing about it. Horror of horrors! It was a mortifying thought. I was sure that David wouldn't have been seen dead reading the *News of the World*, but there was a chance one of his kids would see it and tell him about it. Oh God, someone had sold a story on me! And it wasn't just anyone, it was my dear friend Martin. It was like Joey from *Friends* selling a story on Phoebe.

I hated going into work the next day and facing all those raised eyebrows. I could tell that some people were secretly glad that it had happened. All my true friends were stunning about it, though. 'Lisa, it's chip paper. It's part of what we do.'

Their kindness brought me to tears again. 'Is it? Because I don't like it,' I said.

My friends rallied round and showed me the most incredible loyalty. Martin was ostracised. Almost everyone cut him out of their lives. Michelle is the only one who speaks to him now, which is fine. I don't have a problem with that. I just wish he hadn't done it. More than anything, I felt sad to lose him.

I spoke to him only once after that Sunday. I had Antony with me for support and phoned him and asked him, 'Why?'

One person told me that he'd been paid five grand. Someone else said it was seventy grand. I don't know if he was paid for the story but people usually are. If he was, I don't know how he could have accepted it. It's beyond me how somebody could take money for talking about having sex with their friend. How could you spend that money? Wouldn't it burn your fingers?

'They kept following me and asking questions,' he replied weakly.

'Put the phone down!' Antony whispered. And I did. I've never spoken to Martin since, nor would I.

It was my first taste of being betrayed in the press. Until then, I knew nothing about the world of kiss and tell. I've never been interested in that kind of thing. I turn the page when I come to an article about someone's sex life. I don't care! Everyone has sex. It's like going for a poo. It's the most normal thing in the world. To this day I can't understand how my sex life could be of any interest to people. What's the big deal? You're in a soap and you have sex. Wow!

The whole thing knocked me off balance. I felt I had no control over my image or identity any more, which was torture for a control freak like me. It drove me to party harder and drink more. We'd film Monday to Friday and the second I left the set I'd be at Morrison's buying shitloads of wine. Drinking was my great escape. It whisked me away from reality. I didn't know who I was any more, but I did know that when I was absolutely blind drunk, I was louder, funnier and happier. I was always the drunkest person at the *Emmerdale* dos, the centre of attention for all the wrong reasons.

For a while I shut out everyone except my *Emmerdale* mates, even my mum. When she rang, I'd say, 'Yeah, everything's fine!' She knew how much I was drinking and it worried her.

Thankfully, I never turned into a moody, finger-pointing grotbag. I'd drink myself giddy and then get giddier. Still, sometimes I got so drunk that I became reckless and put myself in dangerous situations. I remember distinctly being in a pub in Farsley where we all used to drink. I'd gone there straight from work with a couple of mates and when they left, I stayed on. I got chatting to four lads, painter-decorators, and I was loving it. It was all about me, all the attention was focused on me, and of course I bought all the drinks all night, which they loved. I was so drunk, oh my God, I was out of the game. They were absolutely leathered as well and we ended up going clubbing in Leeds. I shudder to think of it now: me on my own with four strangers in the night. I couldn't even walk, I was that plastered.

Liam was furious when he heard about it. We're a social family and my mum and dad always loved a drink, but not like I did. I was always the drunkest. One weekend, I took home a pair of big Buffalo trainers like the ones the Spice Girls wore. We'd incorporated them into Mandy's wardrobe because she wanted to be like a Spice Girl – she had a Union Jack dress and everything. On the Friday night I got leathered at the local pub, came home and put on Mandy's massive trainers, sang 'Wannabe' about a hundred times and danced around Mum and Dad's living room doing the whole Spice Girls routine. I was so wobbly that I fell over several times and could easily have broken my leg.

'Lisa, look at the state of you,' Liam said when he watched me staggering about. My baby brother was telling me off and he was only a kid of fourteen or fifteen!

Me and Mum always found something to laugh about, but she was aware that I wasn't happy deep down. I was still spending money like water. I'd go out and blow a thousand pounds on clothes for Liam, all designer, all Ralph Lauren, Moschino and Dolce & Gabbana. He'd be thrilled, but he never seemed to hang on to any of it for long. 'Where's that jersey gone?' I'd say, a few months later. 'Remember that jersey I got you? I've not seen it for ages.'

I bought him a beautiful Ralph Lauren sleeveless puffa that cost me a demi-fortune and it just disappeared. Later I found out that he had given it away. It turned out that he was giving most of the clothes I gave him to his mates at school, who are still his best mates now. That's Liam all over. He's so good. I didn't know it then, but people were constantly having a pop at him for having me as a sister. I think some cruel things were said and it really cut him up.

He was – and still is – a wonderful cricketer and he was playing for a team in the Bolton League at the time. He could probably have made it as a cricketer if he had the Pepper drive, but instead he's got more of the Riley chill, so it didn't happen. Either way, he used to hate me going down to watch him play, because the opposition would shout jibes at him when he was going in to bat, to put him off. 'Your sister's this, your sister's that, she's a fat bitch!'

At every match, someone would sponsor the ball and the money would go to the upkeep of the cricket club. 'Come on, will you sponsor our lad?' Dad would ask me.

'Yeah, of course I will. It's for Liam.'

When you sponsor the ball, your name goes up on a plaque beneath the scoreboard. It used to make Dad so proud that his daughter's name was up there, but it made Liam cringe, because it fuelled his opponents' insults. I thought I was doing the right thing by sponsoring him and coming along to support him, but it was entirely the wrong thing to do.

I was oblivious, partly because when I wasn't drunk, I was hungover. Some nights I'd get so drunk that I was sick, but it didn't bother me because it would sober me up for a bit and I could carry on. The battery kept on going. My face never fell in the soup.

Dominic Brunt often came out with me. By the end of the night he'd be saying, 'Stop singing!'

Me and Dominic became inseparable almost from the first day he joined the cast of *Emmerdale* in 1997. He couldn't believe how much energy I had. He called me a firecracker from the start and was always telling me to shush. 'Lisa, just be quiet, just for a little minute, please,' he'd say.

I loved it that he had the cheek to say that to me, even though we hardly knew each other. He never pandered to anyone. 'No, Lise, it's lunch break, just stop, please.'

'No, but …' I'd begin.

'SHUT UP!' he'd yell, and we'd both collapse into giggles.

As I became closer to Adele Silva off set, her character Kelly and my character Mandy started to become good mates on screen. So we spent more time than ever together and we always had a laugh. Adele is such good fun. One day we did an end-of-episode scene, which can be one of the hardest scenes because you have to hold your final expression for longer than usual while the music plays and the credits roll. It feels so wrong, let me tell you! In this particular scene, Kelly comes into Mandy's bedroom with a pregnancy test and shows it to Mandy. I had to say, 'So, who's the father?' and stay serious as the music started and credits rolled. Well, we couldn't do it for laughing because it felt so eggy. We lost it over and over again, to the point that the director became really cross and shouted, 'Girls, get it together!' That made us giggle even more. It was terrible.

I made friends behind the scenes too. Linda, one of the make-up artists, became like a second mum to me and I often confided in her. Then there was the amazing receptionist, Jules, who everyone called 'Mrs Emmerdale' because we relied on her so much. Jules has the most incredibly sexy, gravelly voice and she knew everything, from each individual weekly roster to any press we were doing. She really looked after me, especially in the early days.

I may have been making friends at work, but at the same time I was losing my best friend in the world. Me and Darren finally had 'the conversation' and he told me he was gay. It took us ages to get there. Loads of guys had come out to me over the years and so I was well aware of what he was trying to tell me, but I kept heading him off. In the end, he just said it.

I couldn't accept it. I wouldn't accept it. 'It's probably just a phase you're going through,' I said. I didn't mention it to Mum and I told Mum everything. Deep down, I still had strong feelings for him. My vision still went swirly when I looked into his gorgeous eyes.

'I think I'd better move out,' he said gently.

'No!' I yelled. 'You're not going.' I went mad. I turned into Veruca Salt from *Charlie and the Chocolate Factory* and had a full-on tantrum. The thought of coming home to an empty flat terrified me.

'This isn't right,' Darren said. 'I love you so much that I've got to let go.' He had to think of himself too. In helping me to live my life, he'd nearly lost his own identity. Now he was growing up. We were both becoming adults, but I didn't understand that.

'I'm doing it as much for your sake as mine,' he went on. 'You've got to stop the partying.'

Oh yeah? I thought. I'll show you, and I went out and partied more than ever.

Not long afterwards, the inevitable happened and Darren got himself a boyfriend. I didn't want to meet him. Instead I went away on a family holiday and tried not to think about it. But there was a surprise in store for me when I got back to the flat and found Darren on the sofa with his arm around this bloke. There was no getting away from it then. It was there in front of my eyes and I couldn't pretend otherwise. At first I felt shocked and outraged. Then I realised that Darren was entitled to his own life. He didn't love me in the way I loved him. It was time for us to go our separate ways.

8

In the frame

We're friends again now, but after Darren left, I cut him off for a long time. I wouldn't reply to his texts or phone calls. You go off and be you now, I thought bitterly. You've broken our happiness. Don't expect me to be there for you.

Of course, what I called happiness wasn't happiness at all. The only thing Darren had broken was our unhealthy dependence on one another, but I didn't see it that way at the time. In my fake Mandy Dingle world, I got everything I wanted, so why couldn't I have Darren? I sulked like a spoilt child. I drank like an old lush. Lonely and lost, I longed for a boyfriend.

I felt vulnerable after what had happened with Darren. It didn't help that I was constantly referred to as 'Lardy Lisa' and 'Roly-poly' in the papers. I don't think the journalists were doing it nastily – in fact, they always wrote nice pieces about me and probably thought they were using such terms affection-ately, as a way of describing me. It's a given that women are described in terms of their appearance in the press. Their age is always mentioned too, whereas a man's age often isn't referred to. I have a laugh with my friends about it. We joke that journalists always describe me these days as, 'Lisa Riley, 37... stone.'

I was 'Lardy Lisa' from the moment I started playing Mandy Dingle, but around this time I became a little more sensitive about it. I was single and the papers were basically calling me 'Fatty'. It didn't do much for my self-esteem – and then one newspaper ran a photo of me in a swimsuit with the headline 'Emmerwhale!' That wasn't pleasant. It didn't make me want to change myself. I liked the way I was. But it's not nice to be called names. It's a bit bullying.

I knew there were men out there who loved bigger girls, because I was always being propositioned by guys in clubs and pubs and I'd even gone home with a couple of them. Yet the situation was never right, for one reason or another. Sometimes I got the feeling that they were more interested in getting with Mandy Dingle than Lisa Riley. Or they wanted to experiment, to see what it was like to go with a big girl. I didn't meet anyone who convinced me they wanted me for me and liked me for me. It was all a bit soul destroying. I just wanted a stable relationship with someone I loved.

Then something really depressing happened in a nightclub in Leeds, when a few of us from *Emmerdale* went out to celebrate James Hooton's (who plays Sam Dingle) birthday. We were having a few drinks in the VIP area, which was slightly raised up from the rest of the club, when a guy came over to chat. He was funny, friendly and good looking. As he flirted with me, I thought, I'm in here! I was genuinely excited. When you're single and looking, you can't help but wonder, Could this be him?

After about thirty minutes of chatting and flirting, we had a bit of a snog. Just then, I happened to glance down into the club and saw a group of nine or ten lads pointing and laughing at us. What's going on? I thought. This doesn't seem right.

They turned out to be his mates. 'We bet him to go and talk to you!' they told me, roaring with laughter. 'He was supposed to pull you and then tell you to get lost!'

My heart plummeted. 'Really?' I said. '*Really?*' I couldn't see what was funny about it.

The guy I'd been chatting to shrugged his shoulders and smirked. His mates started patting him on the back. 'Well done, lad! Good work!' It was horrible on every level and I turned and left the club to go back to my empty flat, alone. Am I just one big laugh, that comedy fat bird from the TV? I thought miserably. Will I never have the fairy-tale love that everyone else seems to find?

I tried staying on in the flat on my own, but I couldn't handle it for long. Fortunately, there was a room going at the White House, a house in Yeadon where a bunch of the *Emmerdale* boys were living, including Dominic, Mark Charnock, Nicky Evans and Tim Vincent. Knowing that I wasn't in a good place, they asked me to move in. I jumped at the chance and got rid of the flat as soon as I could. I loved living at the White House. It was amazing being with all the lads and I had the company I craved at the end of the day. I can't go home to nothing. It's not in my nature.

I looked around for new things to do. Sam Joyce, an old family friend who had also been at St Gabriel's, was working as head barman at a smart restaurant-bar on the King's Road in Chelsea. I'd seen him on and off back at home. Now I rang him and said, 'What are you up to?'

'Come down and see for yourself,' he said.

I had a blast down in London with Sam and his friends and I started to go every weekend. After I finished filming at around seven on the Friday, I'd get on the eight-fifteen flight to London from Leeds Bradford airport. Then I'd fly home on the eight o'clock flight on Sunday night in time to start filming on the Monday. Flossie often came with me. We'd get a hotel and stay up late drinking. We had brilliant, crazy times, but there were consequences.

Inevitably, all the late nights started to affect my work. I had always prided myself on my professionalism and being on time, but now when the driver arrived to pick me up in the morning, I'd have missed my alarm because I was so hungover. I wouldn't have learnt my lines the night before, because I'd been out partying, and I'd try to cram the script as I sat in the make-up chair each morning. It was bad. It was hideous. Sometimes when we were filming at The Woolpack, I'd find a little crevice round the back and go to sleep until they said, 'Right, we're ready to record.' Then I'd jump up and go straight into action.

Fortunately, by then we had moved to the purpose-built village on the Harewood Estate, so there were no members of the public around to see me napping! I loved the new village. It was so realistic, an almost exact replica of Esholt. I'll never forget the first day I went there. It was beyond giddy. It took twelve minutes to get there along a track in the middle of nowhere and I felt like

I'd suddenly landed in the middle of a *Mission Impossible* film.

In the past I hadn't let any of the hundreds of *Emmerdale* make-up people do my hair or make-up, because I knew they'd make Mandy look too pretty. When people have been in a soap for a long time, they can end up looking a bit over-polished and the character they're playing becomes less believable, so I always did my own hair and make-up because I wanted Mandy to look dishevelled and unfinished, a bit kooky. But waking up at six in the morning after a mega-night began to take its toll and I started letting Linda do the odd touch up every now and then. 'Are you sure you're not overdoing it?' she'd ask worriedly.

Finally I was called into the office at *Emmerdale*. 'So, you were photographed coming out of Brown's nightclub in London with Ian Kelsey.'

'Er, yeah,' I said. I knew exactly which photo they were talking about. It was the one that made me look like I was lurching around drunkenly, when in fact my heel had got stuck in a grate and I'd lost balance. I'm not saying I wasn't tipsy that night, but I wasn't as all over the place as the picture made me look, so it was a bit unfair. The media were starting to paint a picture of me as a tart with a heart, but it wasn't really me, it was Mandy.

'Are you all right?' they asked.

'I'm fine!' I said quickly, like you do when you're not fine at all.

On the surface, things looked good for me. They started looking even better when I had a call from Nigel Hall, the executive producer on *You've Been Framed*, asking if I would do a screen test. Never in my wildest dreams had I thought about hosting, but Nigel had seen me on loads of chat shows and thought I had the right mix of warmth, charisma and humour for the role of *You've Been Framed* host. Jeremy Beadle, the outgoing presenter, had run his course with the show. The viewing figures weren't all that good and the producers wanted a new look for the programme.

I didn't hear anything for ages after I'd screen tested, so I assumed it had gone away. I wasn't bothered, because it wasn't an acting job. I didn't think of hosting as performing, although of course it is. You definitely have to turn things up a notch to be a good presenter.

Then I was called in again. 'We'd like you to take over from Jeremy,' Nigel said. He went on to explain that, if I agreed to do it, *Emmerdale* were happy to write me out of the show for a few weeks to give me enough time to shoot a series.

I said yes there and then. I was made up. It was very exciting, a new chapter to my life, and I particularly liked the idea of having a break from *Emmerdale* because the relentless schedule was starting to exhaust me.

A meeting was set up for me to meet the show's costume designers. I needed sixty-seven different outfits, so they took me to Harrods and sat me down in a private area. Wow, I felt special. What's little old me from Bury doing here? I thought, as I was presented with dress after dress. The price tags were ridiculous – we're talking a hell of a lot of dough – and some of them looked a bit ghastly. But I just kept thinking, I'm in Harrods, they must be fine!

After a while I felt like Churchill the nodding dog. 'Yeah, I'll wear that,' I kept saying.

'How about this tapered trouser suit?'

'Yeah, I'll wear that,' I said. What was I thinking? The clothes I wore on the show ended up being awful. I either looked like a Christmas tree or the mother of the bride. They certainly didn't dress me in the kind of stuff someone in their twenties would wear. It was rotten. It wasn't me.

Later, when we were filming, the hair and make-up people would ask, 'Is it OK with you if we set your hair in tight curls?'

No, it wasn't OK, because it made me look about fifty! But I didn't like to seem difficult or vain, so I said, 'Yeah, you can do anything you want.' I was like a Girls' World doll. It was crackers.

I had a few doubts about whether I'd be any good, but I had a week and a half of intense preparation with the producers before we started recording, which was helpful. They talked me through the whole process and I threw myself into it. I got the hang of the autocue quite quickly and rattled off the scripts. For me, the best thing about doing the show was having a bit of banter with the live audience every week. I loved having that live interaction. I don't think I would have felt so at home in an empty studio.

Amazingly, while I was presenting, the viewing figures rose to thirteen and a half million, the highest ever for the series. It was insanity. When I went back into Granada to do extra voiceovers for the programme, people rushed up to me and said things like, 'Riley, you're hot property!' I was incredulous. I didn't know about viewing figures, although I was aware that *Corrie*, *East-Enders* and *Emmerdale* were always the top three. Now *You've Been Framed* was consistently in the top ten and it put people's antlers up within the industry. All of a sudden, the offers were flooding in.

ITV decided they wanted to make a British version of *E News* covering celebrities, pop and film. Called *OK TV* and linked with *OK!* magazine, it included segments showing behind the scenes at celebrities' weddings as well. I was proper giddy when I was asked to go out and do a six-week stint in Los Angeles. It was so exciting. They wanted me to be their red carpet grabber, go to premieres and do one-on-one interviews with film stars. 'Wow, how fantastic!' I said, thinking of all the Hollywood films I'd loved as a kid. I was going to Universal Studios! But it turned out to be one of the worst gigs I've ever had in my life. The content of the job was soulless.

I was beside myself with excitement when I was told I was booked in at the Beverly Wilshire Hotel. Oh my God, I'm staying at the *Pretty Woman* hotel! I thought. It's where Julia Roberts and Richard Gere got hot and steamy on the piano! I vowed to re-enact the scene while I was there. I love *Pretty Woman* to the point of obsession.

I flew out to LA with my cameraman and researcher. When we arrived at the hotel, I could see the car pool where Richard Gere dropped off his sports car, and there was a smart, uniformed concierge, just like in the film. But when we got inside, I didn't recognise anything. 'This doesn't look right,' I said to the concierge. 'Have you had a refurb?'

'No, ma'am,' he said.

At the check-in desk, the clerk told me all about how they were putting me in a really good room because I was staying a while. 'Can I look at the penthouse while I'm here?' I asked.

'Of course, whenever you want. But we're sorry, we can't put you up there, ma'am.'

'Don't worry! I just want to see it.'

A few days later, I was escorted upstairs for my tour, only to find it was nothing like the penthouse Julia Roberts stayed in. 'Have you had a refurb?' I asked again. 'Because it's nothing like it was in *Pretty Woman*.'

My guide smiled condescendingly 'Ma'am, that was a set. They only used the outside of the hotel in the film.'

I felt so stupid! I'd worked in TV all my life and yet I was foolish enough to think they'd taken over the whole hotel for the film.

I was also distraught. I had really wanted to act out *Pretty Woman* in my spare time. I was desperate to say to some old man in reception, 'Fifty bucks, Grandpa. For seventy-five, the wife can watch.'

The job was OK, initially. I was feeling my way for the first week or so. Wherever you go in LA with a camera crew, people want to talk to you. It's utterly fake. The moment they saw the camera, they pounced. It was animalistic. Everyone wanted a piece of me. You could tell they were thinking, Can you get me to where I want to be? People were pushy even when I didn't have the cameras with me. I'd go to a cocktail bar and the barman would say, 'So, are you here on vacation?'

'No, I'm filming.'

'Oh my God! What are you filming?' Suddenly I'd be surrounded by a flock of people.

'I'm just working on a silly programme called *OK TV* back in England. That's it!'

I'd heard that LA was all about being a size six, with blonde hair and fake boobs, but I'd wondered if it was really true. Oh my God, it's beyond true! You could see people looking at me as

I did a piece to camera on Rodeo Drive, as if to say, 'Look at the size of her! What's she doing in front of a camera? Who the hell gave her a job?' They found it bewildering. I didn't conform to the norms there. The teeth, the Botox, it's chronic. We are so far removed from that over here.

Hardly anything about the job came up to my expectations. Interviewing the stars wasn't much fun because they all had these massive entourages. When you do a one-to-one with a star, a lawyer comes in, a publicist comes in; everyone is jumpy and controlling.

I even had their hair and make-up people coming in to check on me. 'Are you OK?'

'I've got my own hair and make-up, thanks. I'm fine.'

The lawyer and publicist would warn, 'You can't say this, that or the other.'

After a while, I started thinking, Oh, for God's sake, this is ridiculous. Let these people be!

Some of the stars were unbelievably fussy. I remember one big celebrity asking for a can of Pepsi, with one straw. Just one straw, mind. It was sent away when it arrived with two straws. God, I thought. Use a glass!

It started winding me up, which of course brought out my rebellious streak. I couldn't help myself, although I probably should have been more professional and risen above it. One evening, I grabbed John Travolta on the red carpet at the premiere of a movie in which he was starring with Lisa Kudrow. On camera, I said, 'John, are you staying alive?'

'What?' he said, looking perplexed.

'Go on, do a dance move for me, John!' I demanded. He

laughed weakly. Actually, I'm amazed he could even move his face, because his make-up was that thick it must have been applied with a cement trowel. 'We're live to England,' I said, although we weren't really. I just wanted to stir things up a bit.

'No, we're not!' my researcher barked in my earpiece. 'What are you doing? You're messing this up!'

'While we're at it, John,' I went on, 'can I just say – and I hope you don't think I'm being rude – that you are wearing more make-up than I am, and I'm a girl!'

Well, of course it *was* very rude of me to suggest such a thing and his team went crazy. 'Cut that out! Are you really live? Oh my God!' I couldn't help chuckling. They were behaving as if I'd murdered somebody.

'We're going to send out the legal team if you don't agree to cut that section,' they insisted. I think they were worried I was the new Dennis Pennis or something. Like everyone else, they couldn't work me out. A fat presenter? It must be some kind of joke.

Every morning I was given a roster listing all the stars I'd be interviewing. I'd get up and think, Who have I got today? Oh, someone from *ER*. I wanted to be funny with these people, as much for their benefit as mine, but I wasn't allowed to be myself, so I didn't enjoy it.

Having said that, I had a wonderful time interviewing Noah Wyle from *ER*, who was Mr McSexy incarnate. He was absolutely phenomenal and I could hardly get my questions out because I was melting with desire. I think he thought I was a bit crazy, but I found him really lovely.

All the same, I started feeling homesick and unhappy. The

highlight of my day was ringing Mum every night when I got back from work, although I was often in tears as I spoke to her. Knowing that I had to come back to the room in between interviews to have my hair and make-up done, she began sending me faxes to cheer me up. 'You're very popular, ma'am!' the concierge said, 'I am up and down to your room like a yo-yo.'

I'd get back to find seven yellow envelopes from Mum waiting for me. Sometimes they would just say, 'I love you, my darling,' or 'Keep your chin up (or in your case, chins! ha ha).' One fax had a drawing of a donkey on it. It really made me laugh, because it was so silly. That's what I needed. Mum's faxes kept me going.

I loved doing the touristy things in LA. My best moment was having my picture taken next to Barbra Streisand's star on the Walk of Fame. That was mega, because I'm a massive Barbra fan, like my mum was. And one day I did a *Beaches* sketch, where I played the Bette Midler role. 'Believe me, I don't need a script. I know every single word,' I told my crew. They couldn't believe it when they realised I meant it literally. And I had a brilliant time when I visited the lot where Judy Garland and Mickey Rooney made their films. All of that was great, but the star interviews generally drove me crackers, because they were so restrictive.

I was relieved when the job ended and I got home again. I don't think I've ever hugged Mum harder than when I arrived back in Bury. I was offered more hosting work, but first and foremost I am an actor, and I was glad to get back to playing Mandy. By now, Mandy was having an affair with Paddy Kirk, the village vet, behind her husband Butch's back. The ongoing saga of Mandy and Paddy's secret love for each other was a rich source of storylines, because it was beset with obstacles. Eventually, Mandy divorces Butch, leaving her free to get together with Paddy.

'Please don't marry Mandy off,' I used to say to the producers.

However, she loved Paddy, Paddy loved her and the whole country wanted them to get together, so they had to get married eventually. That was a turning point for me, because where was the comedy if Mandy was blissfully happy? If she couldn't blunder about making mistakes any more, she wasn't any fun to play.

Mandy and Paddy honeymooned in Venice and in the summer of 1999 a gang of us went on location to film a special honeymoon video, *Don't Look Now: The Dingles in Venice*. The weather was amazing and we stayed in the most beautiful hotel overlooking the Grand Canal, but I didn't make the most of it, because all I was interested in was getting drunk and behaving badly.

We usually wrapped around six in the evening, after filming all day in the scorching heat. 'Quick change, meet downstairs in the lobby bar,' a few of us agreed on our second night. It was a gorgeous evening, perfect for sitting on the terrace and drinking a few glasses of wine. Soon the drinks were flowing like nobody's business and I was hammered.

'Do you dare me to throw an ashtray into the canal?' I said, my arm dangling over the canal. Ha ha. Plop! The ashtray went into the water.

From there, it was a race to top the comedy. Someone else threw an empty bottle over the railings. Ha ha. Plop! The bad behaviour escalated and soon a plastic chair had gone in. Wahay!

Splash! Things went from terrible to even worse – or became even more hysterical and hilarious, depending on your point of view and how much wine you'd drunk – and I was the driving force behind it. I behaved like a complete brat. At one point I pulled a fire extinguisher off the wall of the hotel and squirted it in Paul's ear. It was extremely dangerous. His ear quadrupled in size because of the expanding foam inside, but we were so leathered we just laughed. I can't bear to think about it now. It was scarily awful.

The following morning, the hotel presented us with a bill for all the damage we'd done, and rightly so. The list included broken glasses, the missing chair and the empty fire extinguisher. I hung my head in shame as I remembered the mayhem we had created. Who did I think I was? Noel Gallagher? What an idiot.

Get a grip, girl, I told myself.

That night at dinner, I turned to Steve Halliwell and said, 'I'm leaving *Emmerdale*.'

'You're not,' he said with a laugh.

'I am, I'm going,' I said firmly. 'I can't stay. I've had enough.'

He still didn't take me seriously. 'You and Claire King are the most popular people in this soap opera. Believe me, they will not let you go.'

But I knew it was the right decision. I loved doing the show. It was brilliant in every way, yet I wouldn't have stayed even if I'd been offered £500,000 a year. Nothing would have kept me there. Finally, I'd realised that I couldn't give what I wanted to give to the job, because I was completely and utterly lost. I needed my friends. I needed my family. I needed to find me again. It was time to go home.

9

Love is blind

I started feeling better the moment I decided to leave *Emmerdale*. And then I fell in love, which sent my happiness levels up to gas mark 10. After the frustration and uncertainty of my on-off years with Darren, at last I had a proper boyfriend.

Lee Cooper was the assistant maitre d' at the restaurant-bar in London where my mate Sam Joyce worked. We really hit it off on my weekends down in London with Flossie. We had a proper laugh together and there was a strong attraction there too. I was thrilled beyond belief the night we got together.

'You're amazing,' he said, as he went to kiss me for the first time. 'I've fancied you since the moment I met you.'

Lee had everything I wanted in a boyfriend. Gorgeous and charismatic, he had velvety brown eyes, hair like one of the brothers from Spandau Ballet and a smile that made me melt. He was very dapper and always beautifully turned out in designer clothes. I didn't stop to question how a guy on a waiter's salary could afford Gucci shoes. All I knew was that I was in love. It was wonderful. I enjoyed every blissful moment I spent with Lee and when we were apart we spent all day texting and phoning.

For once, the man on my arm at soap awards and nightclub bashes was actually my boyfriend, someone who wanted to be with me. Why did I waste so much time with Darren? I thought. I could have had this all along! This is what was missing. This is what I wanted.

Everything was perfect and fabulous with Lee, including the sex. He loved my curves. He wanted me to be a bigger girl. It turned him on, which was wonderful. He was the first person who made me feel really sexy. Being in love with a closet gay man who didn't really find me attractive had seriously dented my sense of self, as had the few unsatisfying flings I'd had. Now my confidence soared.

My drinking tapered off, although I was still the life and soul of the party. Me, Lee, Flossie, Sam and their Australian mate Gavin often went out drinking in a gang and we had a lot of fun, but I never went too far, partly because I didn't want to risk being photographed pissed any more. Lee didn't always understand the pressures of being in the public eye. 'Come on,' he'd say. 'Let's stay out and have a few more.' But I wasn't just thinking about my image. I wanted to be sober for when Lee and I got back to my hotel. Getting drunk had lost its appeal. Love had taken over.

Lee shared a flat in London with Sam and Gavin. His father owned a successful old people's home in Leicester and he took me home to meet his dad and his dad's girlfriend. They were lovely and welcoming. He showed me round the home and all the staff were gorgeous to me. One of the night sisters, Rose, was especially fun and friendly. It was touching to see how much Lee adored her. Sadly his mother had only recently passed and he was still in a very bad way about it. She'd been dead about seven months and he was missing her really badly, because they'd had a wonderful relationship. I shuddered to think how I'd feel in his place and I did my best to comfort him.

I still had it in my head that I wanted to move home to Bury. I knew I needed the security of having my own place. Now seemed the right time, because when I eventually left *Emmerdale* I wouldn't have to be based in Leeds any more, and *You've Been Framed* was filmed at the Granada studios in Manchester. So, when I was on my way up to Mum and Dad's one Sunday and saw a billboard advertising a new development of four-bedroom houses, I thought, Right, I really am going to come home. It felt like it was meant to be.

Thanks to *Emmerdale* and *You've Been Framed,* I was lucky to have enough money saved to pay for the house and it felt like the right time to stop partying and settle down. In the back of my mind, I was hoping that Lee might be a part of the future I was planning. I couldn't help dreaming about moving in with him, living together, maybe even getting married.

The housing development was two minutes in the car from Mum and Dad's, which felt just right. I had missed my family beyond belief over the last five years. At times, it had been hard living apart from them, because my family are my world. Ask any of my friends and they'll tell you how important my family are to me. My mates mean everything and I'm passionate about my work, but my family are my life's heart and soul.

The houses on the development were still being built and I

chose a corner plot, with a nice double garage and a sweeping drive. I hired interior designers to help me plan the bathrooms and kitchen and the house looked amazing as the designs started to take shape. Amazing and quite kooky, which was how I wanted it, because I hadn't lost my quirky tastes.

This was a happy time for me. Everything felt like it was finally fitting into place. And being happy helped me to relax, which meant I started opening up again. If I was moving back to Bury, I realised, I needed to rekindle my friendships back home, something I'd been longing to do for ages. So I waved the white flag at Samantha and Katie and all my other friends and I'll always be grateful that they welcomed me back with open arms. They were gorgeous to me.

When I went round to see Sam, there wasn't a moment of awkwardness between us, even though we'd hardly seen each other in four or five years. It felt really normal to be round her house having a cup of tea. Our friendship clicked back into place and we instantly felt like bezzies again. There was so much to tell each other. It was wonderful.

I felt a lot of guilt about not having been there for Sam when she'd had Jack. We talked everything through and I explained how I'd been swept away by work and unhappiness. 'I should have been around more,' I said, bursting into tears. Sam was really understanding. Soon afterwards, she asked me to be godmum to her second child Sophie. That's how lovely Samantha is.

I started going home a lot at weekends, taking Lee with me. Everyone adored him. Everyone, that is, except Liam. 'I don't know about him,' he said to Mum the day he met him. He never warmed to him.

I wasn't bothered when Mum told me what Liam had said. I assumed that it was because he was missing Darren. He still worshipped the ground Darren walked on. He'd grown up with him. His teenage years had been characterised by having a famous sister with a mayhem life and Darren as the kind of gentle, stable, big brother type that most boys yearn for. I couldn't blame him for wishing Darren was still around.

'But I think Lee's fabulous,' Mum said reassuringly. She loved his personality.

One Saturday, Samantha rang and asked if we could go round to her house in the evening. 'I want to ask you something,' she said.

There were a few people there when we arrived, including a journalist from the *Manchester Evening News* called Amanda. I'd never met her before, but we instantly hit it off and she's one of my best friends now. Sam had us round because she wanted to ask us to be bridesmaids at her wedding to her partner Simon in a couple of months' time. Since she already had nine bridesmaids, I said no! We agreed that I'd do a reading instead.

Lee took baby Sophie outside to push her on the swing in the garden. Me and Samantha sat in the bay window of her lounge watching them. 'I think he's the one,' I said dreamily. 'I've never in my life been more happy. Everyone adores him.'

'Do you know what? I really like him,' Sam said. I felt myself flush with pleasure. Samantha was the epitome of the protective friend. My other friends would say things like, 'Just as long as you're happy.' But Sam was always wary of people, so it was brilliant to hear her give Lee the thumbs up.

Sam and Simon's wedding was fantastic. I took Lee and we had the most wonderful time together. I was desperately, desperately happy that day, sitting next to the person I loved, surrounded by my best friends in the world. I was exactly where I wanted to be. We sat on the same table as Antony, who instantly adored Lee. To get Antony's seal of approval was amazing. It made the day even more special, if that was possible. I remember looking around the room at all my friends and thinking how lucky I was. After years of feeling anxious, lost and lonely, life was totally hunky-dory. At last my fairy tale was happening.

Lee came up to Leeds to stay with me whenever he could get time off work. All the boys at the White House adored him. From time to time, he went back to Leicester to see his dad. Obviously I didn't think twice about it, since I was very family oriented myself. It didn't occur to me that he could be hiding something from me. Why would it? Everything seemed fine and dandy.

After we'd been going out for about ten months, he came up to stay in Leeds when I had a few days off. I was so excited to see him that I didn't notice at first that he was a bit jittery.

I'd booked a nice restaurant for dinner. Halfway through our starter, Lee said, 'We need to chat.'

It was only then that I noticed he looked a bit pale and drawn. 'What's the matter?' I asked, reaching forward to take his hand.

He leaned towards me and lowered his voice. 'There's something I need to tell you. I've got a court case pending. I've been accused of something I haven't done.'

I didn't know how to react. It had come out of the blue and I wasn't prepared for it. 'Right, OK,' I said hesitantly. 'What have you been accused of?'

'Fraud,' he replied. 'At Dad's old people's home.'

A shiver went through me. Instinctively, I drew my hand away from his. 'I don't understand. Could you explain yourself?'

Taking a deep breath, he said that the families of two people with slight dementia in the home had accused him of manipulating their relatives and persuading them to change their wills in his favour. Someone else had accused him of taking their pension books and keeping the money for himself.

'But there's no truth in it, not at all,' he insisted. 'It's not my fault these people love me and want to show me how much they appreciate me.'

He denied stealing the pension books, but admitted that these people had put him in their wills. But he hadn't coerced them, he said, and I believed him one billion per cent. Why wouldn't someone put him in their will? I thought. He's brilliant.

I was thinking of a token amount, of course. A thousand pounds or something, not tens of thousands. Unaware of the amounts involved, I thought it made perfect sense. Lee made people happy wherever he went. He was the life and soul. It seemed perfectly natural that people would want to show how much they valued him. After all, I was constantly buying him presents as an expression of how much I loved and treasured him.

'I need to go to Leicester for a meeting with my legal team,' he went on, 'but I'll come straight back. I'll get the train there and back tomorrow.'

'Fine,' I said. It was disappointing that we wouldn't get to spend the day together, but I understood that this was something he needed to clear up as soon as possible. I was assuming the charges would be dismissed as being ridiculous. I had no idea how serious the situation was.

He left early the next day. 'Good luck,' I said as I kissed him goodbye. 'Ring me when you get there, to say you've arrived.'

'I will. Thanks for understanding.'

I didn't hear anything all day. Nothing. No call. I tried him but he wasn't picking up his phone. This is weird, I thought. What's going on? I left a message. 'It's me! Are you going to ring back?' Still nothing. I rang his dad's house line. No answer.

Feeling freaked out, I confided in Dominic. I told him everything that Lee had told me. Dom was very sympathetic. As far as he was concerned, Lee was great, so he had no reason not to believe his side of the story. But why wasn't he ringing me back? Dom agreed it was weird.

I got a bit upset. 'Why me, Dom?' I said tearfully. 'Why am I so unlucky in love?' After hankering after a closet gay guy for years and having a string of empty one-night stands, I had finally found someone who loved me and made me happy. 'Everything was going brilliantly and now this has happened,' I went on. 'Please say things will be all right.' I desperately wanted there to be a Cinderella ending to this story, but it was looking increasingly unlikely.

'Best sleep on it,' Dominic said, giving me a hug. 'I'll see you on the *Emmerdale* set tomorrow and we'll take it from there.'

I hardly slept that night. I tossed and turned, trying to make sense of what Lee had told me. Where was he? Why hadn't he rung? My mind filled up with nightmare scenarios. He was with another girl. Or lying in a ditch. He was on the run. Or in hospital, fighting for his life.

On my way to work, I tried him again. His phone kept going straight to voicemail. Maybe his battery has gone, I thought. Mobile batteries didn't last as long in 1999.

I couldn't concentrate at work. My mind kept going in a loop. Finally I confided in Linda, my second mum among the make-up artists at *Emmerdale*. 'I don't know what to do. Everything was going so brilliantly and it's just curve balled,' I told her. She did her best to comfort me, but I could see that she was at a loss for words. It was such an odd situation and there was no denying that the charges against Lee were disturbing.

Shortly after I'd got home that night, Lee finally rang. 'Where are you?' I said, not knowing whether to feel relieved or angry. 'I've been worried sick!'

'I'm coming over now,' he said. 'I'll explain everything.'

He arrived late that night. As he walked in the door, I said, 'Are you cheating on me?' I couldn't help it. The words tumbled out of my mouth.

He looked surprised and offended. 'Of course I'm not!'

'What's going on, then?' I asked.

He stretched out his arms and went to hug me, but I side-stepped him. I wanted to hear what he had to say first. He had put me through twenty-four hours of hell. I needed an explanation.

'Look, I'm sorry I didn't answer your calls,' he said, adding that he'd had some bad news. His legal team had said that the case against him wasn't looking good, he told me, hanging his head. He'd gone out and got completely pissed the night before, drowning his sorrows after an argument with his father.

Hanging in the air, unsaid, was the suggestion that he might have to do time in prison. I couldn't believe it. I was totally distraught. He'd seemed so certain that there was nothing to worry about when he'd first talked about it. Anyway, Lee was a good person. Everybody thought so. 'But it's going to be OK, isn't it?' I asked.

'Don't worry, it's going to be fine,' he kept saying. 'I trust my legal team.'

The next month was awful. Lee behaved like a different person. His phone was off a lot. He didn't call me as much; he didn't send me half as many texts, or reply to mine. It was a massive change. Before this, he had rung me every lunch break and when I got home. He'd sent me a text before bed saying, 'Night night, sweet dreams, my darling xxx.' When you're in love, you send silly messages all day, like, 'I saw a jar of Nescafé and I thought of you, cos you like it!' But all that stopped.

The distance between us seemed to grow wider by the day. 'I think he *must* be having an affair,' I said to Dominic, because I couldn't believe that his behaviour could be connected with the horrible things he'd been accused of – falsely, as far as I knew. But it wasn't only the lack of phone calls. It felt like he was trying to edge away from me emotionally.

It's all falling apart, I thought desolately. Here I go again. I'm never going to find lasting love. I could barely remember how wildly happy and secure in Lee's love I had felt just a month before. Everything had come crashing down and now I was scarcely managing to hold things together.

Eventually Lee told me he had a date for the court case, on the coming Monday. 'Everything is going to be fine,' he said again. 'I don't want you to worry.'

I only had his word for it, so I rang Sam Joyce in London, because I was starting to have serious doubts. 'Do you believe all this?' I asked him. 'Has he talked to you privately?'

Sam was quick to reassure me. He obviously believed Lee was innocent. 'It'll be fine,' he said. 'He'll definitely get off.'

Monday arrived. I wasn't shooting, thank God; I had the day off. I stayed up in my room at the White House while Mark Charnock pottered around downstairs. I hadn't confided in him, so he was totally unaware of the torture I was going through. Everyone else was at work. Lee had told me that the case was being heard at eleven o'clock and he'd sworn to ring me the moment it was over. Midday came and he hadn't rung. Oh my God, I thought. Something has gone wrong here. By two o'clock, I was frantic. The minutes crawled by. When my phone finally rang, it was near enough four o'clock and I was practically on my knees.

It was Rose from the old people's home. She sounded weary. 'You don't know me very well, but I thought I should ring to let you know that Lee's been sentenced to three and a half years, for fraud.'

My whole world fell apart with those words. Everything crumbled round me. This can't be happening, I thought. He was meant to be the one, my prince. Now it's over.

I burst into tears and rang Mum. 'Please, I need to speak to you!'

'Are you all right, darling? What is it?' Her first thought was that I was pregnant.

Great racking sobs started to shake my body. 'Can you drive over and see me right now? Please, Mum, I need you so much!'

She got straight in the car and drove to Leeds. Everything came flooding out the moment she wrapped me in her arms. 'Lee's been banged up, but I love him, Mum! I love him!'

'What's he done?' she asked gently.

'I don't know the ins and outs,' I sobbed. 'I've been drip-fed information. I don't even know if he's innocent or guilty.'

'Oh, darling,' Mum said, giving me the kind of all-enveloping cuddle only your mum can give you. She was the biggest comfort ever and I felt so thankful to have her there. I don't know how I would have got through that day and night without her.

Mum stayed the night with me and helped me to get some perspective on what had happened. She was amazing, as always. Whether he had done it or not, she said, it wasn't our place to judge him, especially as we didn't know the facts. 'Maybe you can get through this together,' she said, giving me a tiny shaft of hope in the midst of my dark despair.

Still, I was broken, suffering from a pain that I wouldn't inflict on my worst enemy. I spoke to Lee's dad briefly on the phone, but it was Lee I wanted to speak to. I needed to hear his voice. I needed him to say, 'It's all OK, darling.'

Later, as I lay in bed thinking about Lee in his prison cell, something dawned on me. The press would have a field day if they found out that my all-singing, all-dancing relationship had taken such a dramatic turn. What am I going to do? I thought. I've got to come up with some kind of story. I needed a quick fix that would work universally.

The next day I went to work and told everyone that Lee had

gone to Australia with his Aussie mate Gavin. I said he'd had a mad half hour and booked his flight on a whim. He was going for six months, but we were still together. Everything was fine between us.

I spoke to Rose again a few times in the days that followed. She was lovely to me. 'I need to speak to Lee!' I told her. 'How do I get hold of him?'

She gave me his address in prison and told me to send him a phone card, so that he could ring me. I went straight to the Post Office, bought five £10 phone cards and put them in an envelope addressed to him. I signed my letter and every letter I sent him after that with the words, 'all my love, LJ,' knowing that he was aware that the name on my birth certificate is Lisa-Jane Riley. I was very conscious of the need to be careful.

Lee rang and he was brilliant on the phone. 'We can get through this,' he said.

Hearing his voice made me feel a thousand times better. 'Yep,' I said. 'I'm going to stick by you. But you need to know that I've made up a story about what's happened. I've said you're in Australia and I need you to back me up. So you're not going to tell anyone who I am, are you?'

'Of course not!'

'God, I miss you so much,' I said.

'Are you going to come and see me?' he asked.

I frowned. Didn't he understand that would be impossible? 'That's the problem: I can't. It only takes one person to see me and the press will be on to it straight away.'

'Can't you pretend you're just a friend?' he said dejectedly.

He still didn't get it. 'But they know we're together, darling,' I said. 'I'm sorry, but it will have to be letters and phone calls only. Still, I'm willing to do this if you are.'

'I'll do anything to keep you,' he said. 'I don't want to live without you.'

I burst into tears and we said our goodbyes.

Over the next few months, I wrote to him in every spare moment I had. Sometimes I jotted down a quick note that would make him laugh; other times I'd pour my heart out onto the page, going into depth about how much I'd been thinking about him and how I missed him every moment of the day. The letters were to-ing and fro-ing between us. He wrote the sweetest notes back telling me how much he missed me. He said he was hoping to be let out in less than a year and a half, for good behaviour.

Fingers crossed, I thought. It was a long time to wait and I knew it would be difficult, but I loved him. I was determined to see it through. I blocked out any thoughts about the horrible crimes he was supposed to have committed. I refused to believe that he'd done wrong, even though a jury had convicted him. Love is blind, they say.

Meanwhile, I was gearing up to leave *Emmerdale* after nearly six years of being a regular. I knew it would be a wrench, but I was even more conscious that I needed a fresh start. I was still enjoying the work, but it was time to take on new challenges and play new characters. '*Emmerdale*'s been wonderful,' I kept telling people. 'It's been the best time in my life and there have been huge highs along the way. But there have also been quite a few lows. I feel I've done what I needed to do. It's time to get myself out there again and see what's in store for me.'

My house was nearly ready and I couldn't wait to move in. At last I would be close to my family and friends again, after years of living away. I could settle down and work on the next series of *You've Been Framed* while I waited for Lee to come out of prison. After that, well, I didn't know what would happen, but I had high hopes for the future. I just had to get through the next few months.

I'll never forget the phone call that changed everything. We were filming a storyline in which Kelly loses a baby. I was on set, in a hospital, when one of the runners said, 'Lisa, we've had three urgent messages for you to ring your management.'

Well, no one rings you when you're on set, so I knew it must be something serious. Five minutes later, I found out that the *Mirror* had some of my letters to Lee, which his cellmate had stolen from him. There was no point trying to deny they were mine, I was told. They'd done a handwriting match to prove they were.

Lee's first mistake had been to let his cellmate into the secret of who his girlfriend was. They had a telly in their room and one night when they were watching *Emmerdale*, it slipped out. 'Don't tell anyone, but that's my girlfriend,' he said, pointing at the screen. He trusted his cellmate and went on to show him some of my letters.

When this bloke was let out, a lot earlier than Lee, he went straight to the papers saying he had evidence that I was involved with a convicted prisoner. The *Mirror* ran the story the following day, which meant that I had to tell everyone that I'd lied about Lee going to Australia, to save face. They were gorgeous about it, but it was desperately embarrassing. The article implied that 'convicted fraudster' Lee Cooper was only ever with me for my money. Poor 'larger than life' Lisa! We wouldn't have thought you were that foolish! Such a sucker! I was gutted. My fans won't like me any more, I thought. They'll think I'm a bad girl, even though I'm not.

I was incredibly disappointed in Lee. I didn't understand why he'd shown his mate my letters. He was dating Lisa Riley and he knew what came with that. Unfortunately I do come with three suitcases, as does everyone in the public eye. We had often talked about what it meant. I had warned him about the papers countless times. Why would he take the risk? My friends thought that it was Lee who sold the story, using his cellmate as a cover, but I didn't and I still don't. What can I say? Love is blind and maybe I was being completely dumb.

'That's it now,' I said miserably, when I spoke to him. 'You know we can't be together.'

'I'm sorry,' he said simply. He didn't try to argue.

Weirdly, my agent was in talks about doing another series of *You've Been Framed* around this time. The irony was too much. You. Have. Been. Framed.

It broke my heart. I just wanted to be happy and in love, but it hadn't worked out. Whether he meant to or not, Lee had betrayed my trust and I didn't want to write or speak to him again, although I always sent him my love through Sam and Gavin when they went to see him. Doubt had crept into the relationship and once you start doubting, you can't go back.

To this day, I don't know what Lee did or didn't do, or why he went to prison. You hear about people doing the weirdest things in times of bereavement, so there's a part of me that thinks that his grief might have driven him to do something he wouldn't normally have done. Maybe he was searching for something and found comfort in these old women. I don't know. I've never found out and I don't want to. At the time, I didn't want him to be a badass and I didn't believe he could be. He was a good person. Everybody thought so.

I don't feel any hatred for him. I don't believe he sold a story on me and I will always love him for that. Far more importantly, he made me the happiest I've ever been in any relationship in my life. He made me feel beautiful and sexy. When I was with him I felt confident about myself in a womanly way, and that's such a good thing. I'm desperately grateful to him for that. Although the end of the relationship left me in tatters I don't harbour any negative feelings towards him. Still, I had to move on. By the time he finally got out, after fifteen months, we had been apart a long time.

I look back on our time together with fondness, but the memories are tinged with sadness and regret. If events had been different, we could have been married now. Who knows, we could have had children. Having said that, I might have always worried about the crimes he was convicted of. Either way, instead of marriage and children, I was left feeling I couldn't trust anyone. I became very guarded and I'm still guarded to this day. I started telling people, 'You can have the career, but you can never have it all.' I was seriously disillusioned.

10

Your fat friend

It was a Friday night and I was at Mum and Dad's. I had come over from Leeds to go out for a big family supper, which we often did on Fridays. Mum was in her en suite having a shower and I was sitting on her bed waiting for her, having a fag. As she came out of the bathroom, her towel slipped.

'What the hell is that?' I said, pointing to a shrivelled patch on one of her breasts. It looked like an inverted prune, sucking her breast inwards.

'Oh, that,' she said dismissively. 'I'm sure it's nothing to worry about.'

'Jesus, Mum! How long has it been like that?'

'Oh, about four months.'

Awareness about breast cancer in 2000 was nowhere near as high as it is now, but there's no question Mum was in denial about it. She couldn't bear the thought of telling me or Liam that she might have cancer. Fortunately, I knew enough about it to ring Mum's GP first thing the next morning. He saw her that day and recommended an urgent mammogram the following week. I went with Mum to see the GP, but she took Gran along with her to the hospital for the mammogram and diagnosis, which is something I still to this day don't understand, considering that they weren't exactly the best of mates.

Why didn't she take me or Auntie Joyce? I can only think it was to spare us the worry and pain. She knew that Gran wouldn't break down on the spot if the doctors told Mum she was going to die.

Mum being diagnosed with breast cancer at the age of forty-six came as a horrible shock to everyone. We were devastated. She was the most important person in all of our lives. Yet, knowing my mum and her strength of being – her personality, demeanour and everything – I never thought she could die. She had stage four breast cancer and it had gone to her lymph nodes as well, which caused lymphedema, which made her arm swell up horribly. So, when she had a mastectomy, they also took the lymph nodes away. This was followed by intense chemo and radiotherapy and she lost all her hair. It was awful. She had really bad times.

Mum, being Mum, was our guiding light through the ups and downs of her treatment and recovery. She used her warmth, humour and wisdom to keep us going. Typically, we laughed and took the mick through it all. 'Come on, Sinead O'Connor,' I'd say. Nothing was dour. Death was never mentioned. If we cried, we cried on our own, or I'd pull Liam to one side and say, 'Are you OK? It's going to be fine.' My dad was the king of the castle when it came to looking after her. He couldn't have been more brilliant through that time. He was a legend on every level, a wonder.

Mum didn't change a bit. She remained optimistic, positive, sympathetic and bolshy throughout. People still went to her with their problems when she was ill, and she was happy to listen and help. That was Mum all over. You had to take eighty hats off to her for the way she dealt with her cancer. 'I'm not going any-where,' she'd say, with steely determination. So, although it was a huge relief, it wasn't all that surprising when she went into remission. We all honestly believed she would get better, and she did.

There's a story I love from that time. When Mum went in for the mastectomy, she took two things with her. Along with a picture of me and Liam, she had a single book on the bedside table of her private room. When one of her friends from Airtours visited, she asked, 'What are you reading, Cath?' It was *Roget's Thesaurus*! That was my mum all over. She adored words. She had a massive vocabulary, but if she was ever unsure of the exact meaning of a word, she'd always go and look it up. She was so clever and bright.

Mum's cancer scare gave me even more reason to be glad I was moving back to Bury. And after six years in *Emmerdale*, I needed a break! I don't understand how people can stay in a soap for their whole working lives. I know why they do it, of course. It's continuous work and money in the bank every week. Yet it also consumes you totally. You live, eat and breathe your work and there isn't room for an awful lot else.

To this day, wherever I go, people say, 'Please go back to *Emmerdale*!' They think I'm mad not to, but I know I made the right decision to leave and not to go back.

Every soap actor has a story about the public getting them muddled with the character they play. My favourite example of this took place when Claire King and I were on the train back to Leeds one afternoon, after appearing on a chat show in London. On *Emmerdale* Claire played Kim Tate, a domineering mega-bitch who will do anything to get her own way. In the soap, our characters hated each other, but in real life, Claire and I were – and still are – really good friends, which must have been what confused the two nanas who came across us in the dining car.

We were laughing and joking and putting the world to rights when one of them walked straight up to Claire and bashed her with a brolly. 'Don't you dare be a bitch to Mandy!' they both yelled.

'She's my friend!' Claire protested, but they wouldn't have it.

I never got used to the attention. It always affected me the worst when I was on a plane, because flying already made me nervous, a hangover from I was a kid having nosebleeds at take-off and landing. I'm OK on airplanes now. I've been taught how to quash the panic. I carry a paper bag in my handbag, or rely on the sick bag if I need something to blow into, and I've learnt how to time my breathing. I know never to touch my pulse when I'm feeling panicked, because it will inevitably be going really fast and that will make me panic more.

My panic-calming measures go out of the window when some-one recognises me, though. So I have a strategy for flying now. I tend to get to the front of the queue, choose a window seat and put my head down and read a magazine. I'm usually very careful about planning my journeys, but occasionally I've messed it up.

The worst time was when I was on my way to Barcelona on my mate Katie's hen do. There were eleven girls and we got so carried away with the fun of being on a trip together that we forgot we were due to board our flight. We were in the departure lounge when an announcement came on the Tannoy urgently calling our names.

We legged it to the gate. An entire plane load of people were waiting for us and when they saw me, they started singing Barry Manilow's 'Mandy'. Oh my God, the embarrassment. Get me out of here, I thought. It was my worst airplane nightmare.

Luckily it was a quick flight, although it seemed a lot longer with all the tutting that went on around me. I think people thought I was boarding at the last minute because I'm on telly when that wasn't the case at all. It was just that it was my bezzie's hen weekend and we hadn't been watching the departures board.

Leaving *Emmerdale* didn't mean people would stop recognising me, but at least I had the sanctuary of my own home, now that it was ready to move into. It was such a wonderful feeling to walk in and think, This is mine! After all my hard work, after all the ups and downs I'd been through, I had somewhere that I could call home.

For months after I moved in, I hardly went out to clubs or wine bars. Instead I'd invite all my mates to come over in the evenings and enjoy the house. I was so proud of it. I felt safe there. It was a very homely time and I loved it.

Sometimes we'd go to the Italian restaurant near us. At the end of the meal everyone would say, 'Let's go back to Rilez's kitchen!' We'd have the best time back at the house, sitting and chatting over bottles of wine, me and my gay friends and girlfriends and their hubbies. I had missed doing that sort of thing. I was still feeling tender and bruised after what had happened with Lee, but there was no point in dwelling on what could have been. This is the new me now, I thought. I have to stand on my own two feet.

Moving home was a turning point for me. I grew up. I stopped going out and drinking myself into oblivion. Of course, there were a few nights when I went for it, but I wasn't going home to put my face down the toilet and be sick. My social life mainly revolved around my kitchen table, having a laugh with my mates. I had a karaoke machine and a dance mat, of course. We danced about to Five Star and New Kids On The Block and sang at the tops of our voices. 'I'm doing "I Will Survive"!' I'd yell.

'Not again,' they'd groan.

Fortunately, I had enough money in the bank to take a bit of time off. I didn't need to be working, working, working and I wanted to be choosy about my next project. After *Emmerdale*, ninety-five per cent of the scripts I was sent featured a busty barmaid dressed in leopard prints, but what people didn't understand was that I wouldn't have left the show if I'd wanted to go on playing that kind of role. 'I have to wait for the right script to come along,' I told my agent. He totally backed me up.

I got itchy feet as I waited. It was a weird feeling to turn work down, because it goes against the grain for an actor. Why am I saying no? I kept thinking. I hope no one thinks I'm too big for my boots. Still, I stuck to my guns. I didn't want to play the same part again. I wanted something that would make people sit up and reassess me as an actor.

If I'd closed my eyes and made the biggest wish, I would have asked for a Mike Leigh movie to come my way. Working with Mike Leigh is every actor's dream, because he encourages actors to create their own characters and make them real. I'd like to think that working for him would be a bit like working for David Johnson at Workshop. Either way, it would be my be-all and end-all as an actor.

Luckily, I had *You've Been Framed* to keep me going. I was originally signed for one series, but after the viewing figures soared, they contracted me to do three more series. Everything about the show was fun. I made some brilliant friends there and the figures went from strength to strength.

From the start I adored Nigel Hall, who was Head of Entertainment at Granada as well as being executive producer on the show. Now a big exec with Syco, Simon Cowell's company, Nigel is a gem of a person and I owe a lot to him. He believed in me and enjoyed dressing me up like a Girls' World doll.

Nigel livened up the studio sessions by making joke after joke into my earpiece. 'Check out the comedy jumper in row two,' he'd murmur. I'd burst out laughing, but the audience would have no idea what I was giggling at.

Me and Nigel went to Lapland together to shoot the *You've Been Framed* Christmas Day and Boxing Day specials and we had fun like I've never had before. The snow was three feet deep outside our log cabin and so we were forced to stay in after work. We spent our evenings playing gin rummy, drinking vodka, toasting marshmallows and role playing characters with ridiculous accents. The days were fabulous too. I shot links in every imaginable snowy situation, from a sledge on a husky trail in the ice to sitting on Santa's lap.

Another of my good friends on the show was Karl Lucas, one of the writers who also warmed up the studio audience before each show. *Stars In Their Eyes* was being shot in the studio next door, so every week Karl would raid their dressing-up cupboard and come out with a new outfit, just to make me laugh. One week he'd be Jean Valjean from *Les Mis* and the next he'd be a pumpkin. My mum used to come to the studio all the time and she'd sit on the desk with the lady who worked my teleprompter. One day Mum was feeling really cold and Karl, who was dressed as Harry Potter that week, wrapped her in his cape. I couldn't see what was happening, but I could hear all this hysterical screaming laughter though my earpiece. 'What is it?' I said into my mic.

Mum had her glasses on and Karl was yelling, 'Look, it's Cathy Potter!' It was fabulous, lovely.

We were lucky to have such a good team. Sometimes after work we'd go up to the apartment on top of the Granada building with all the crew, or we'd go across the road to the V&A hotel. We'd be there until two in the morning, downing bottles of wine, and it was always great fun. The wrap parties at the end of each series were brilliant. One time they hired a disco boat and we went up and down the Manchester canal. It was fancy dress and I went as Kate Winslet from *Titanic*, wearing a replica 'Heart of the Ocean' necklace and everything. A couple of hours into the party, after a few glasses of wine, I went down to the front of the boat and did the famous pose. It was ace.

All in all, *You've Been Framed* was a wonderfully positive

experience, even though I wasn't the best host. I was never sure that presenting was my forte, although the execs and public seemed very happy, which was the important thing. I was camp, I was jolly. I suppose I was right for the show at the time.

Whenever me and Nigel had a drink together, he'd say, 'I want you on *Stars In Their Eyes*, more than anything.'

'But there's no one I can be!' I would say, giggling at the idea. 'I'm not being Alison Moyet and all the other bigger girls are black.'

'How about Mama Cass?'

'No, I'm not being Mama Cass.'

'Well, Wilson Phillips, then.'

'Nigel, I know I'm fat, but I'm not three people!'

'But there's a bigger one. You could be her.'

'And what will you do about the other two? Superimpose them?'

I went home and told Mum about Nigel's latest suggestion. 'Wilson Phillips! Honestly, I'm not that big,' I said. '"Tonight, Matthew, I'm going to be three people!"'

Mum laughed. 'What about Stockard Channing?' she said.

I thought about it for a few moments. 'Yes, she could be perfect,' I said. 'She's not fat, but neither is she skinny. She's voluptuous, in a Marilyn Monroe way.'

I rang Nigel. 'You're not going to go for this, but Mum has come up with the idea of Stockard Channing.'

'I love it!' he yelled excitedly. 'You're going to be a Pink Lady, with the full outfit and everything.'

And that's how I ended up stepping through the dry ice on *Celebrity Stars In Their Eyes* dressed as Rizzo from *Grease* and singing, 'There are worse things I could do'. What can I say? It was one of those once-in-a-lifetime moments.

It was desperately nerve wracking, so I was grateful that Sally Lindsay was on the show with me. She was Dolly Parton and I was a Pink Lady. We looked abysmal, but we didn't care. We had to laugh about it. In fact, we didn't stop giggling, which was partly down to nerves. I remember Peter Kay was in the audience, because he's a friend of Sally's. Esther Rantzen was on the show doing Edith Piaf and when she came on to belt out, 'Je ne regrette rien' Peter was shouting, 'Go on, Esther, go on, you can do it, girl!' Me and Sally roared, which helped calm us down.

I did a short spell back in *Emmerdale* in 2001, because they couldn't carry on Dominic's storylines if Paddy didn't get a divorce from Mandy. It was only for four weeks and I loved working with Dominic again, but it confirmed to me that I'd made the right decision to leave the show. Doing seventeen scenes in one day instantly brought back to me how demanding it can be to work on a soap opera.

Meanwhile, when ITV started scaling down their children's programme commissioning, a weekday five o'clock half-hour kids slot became free. Granada pulled me in to discuss doing a more relaxed, child-friendly version of *You've Been Framed* that would go out every evening, Monday to Friday.

For the adult show, I shot three shows in succession in front of a studio audience. Now the plan was to get rid of the audience, place me in a beautiful, decorative garden and shoot fifteen links a day.

'Is that actually achievable?' I asked, thinking about how many costume changes it would involve.

'Don't worry, we'll hurtle through it,' they said.

And hurtle through it we did. 'And here's another person falling over ...' I'd say. 'Have you ever slipped on a banana?' Before I knew it, I'd shot a programme. It wasn't half as much fun as being in front of an audience and I didn't really feel at home.

I was on telly all the time, which in hindsight wasn't a good thing. I was on prime time on a Saturday night and every single day during the week. Subsequently I'd be asked to appear on *Jerry Springer*, *Phil and Fern*, *GMTV*, you name it. I think people got a little bit bored of me. To be honest, I got a little bit bored of myself.

Predictably, the press turned on me and started making jibes about my size. I could feel things cooling down at Granada. I was no longer the sunshine girl who couldn't put a foot wrong. People didn't call out, 'Hi, babes!' when I walked into the building any more. Execs no longer came out of their offices to greet me. I started to suspect that they were squirrelled away upstairs fretting about how they were going to break it to me that they wanted to change the concept of the show and get a new host.

Of course, it was no big cheese when they told me. I'll go and do something else, I thought.

They took me to The Ivy. 'Are you happy? You don't seem happy.'

'I'm happy,' I said, 'but I feel like a fool. I look like a Christmas tree and there are only so many times I can say, "And here's someone slipping on a banana," and make it sound cool or amusing. Since I'm getting the feeling that you want change, let's talk things over.'

We agreed that I would do another Saturday night series and that would be the end of it. I was completely happy with that. Jonathan Wilkes took over when I left and then they hit on the idea of replacing the host with a voiceover by Harry Hill and it worked brilliantly.

I still wasn't having any luck with finding my Mr Right. I was meeting people, but things often went pear-shaped quite quickly, perhaps because I was so independent, and also because I was completely committed to my work. I always seemed to be saying, 'I'm filming on Friday, I can't come out.'

I'd start a relationship and it would all be going well, and then he'd want to introduce me to his friends and I'd have to say, 'I can't come to that house party, because I'm filming.'

Then he'd think, Oh, you don't want to meet my friends!

I'd be up against that straight away and I seemed to hit a brick wall every time. It's been a major issue for me throughout my life. Still, I had a lot to be cheerful about, because when I finished *You've Been Framed*, a job came along that would make me fall in love with acting all over again. Completely out of the blue, my agent rang and said, 'Kay Mellor wants a meeting with you.'

'Pull the other one!' I said. But lo and behold it was true. I couldn't believe my luck. I had always loved Kay Mellor's work, especially *Band of Gold*, which I had watched avidly. Kay writes unbelievably well for women. I love her passion and her loyalty to Leeds. She has based everything she's written in Leeds, which I think is phenomenal.

I'd enjoyed the first series of her new drama, *Fat Friends*, which aired in 2000. I thought it was amazing. Set around a slimming club in Leeds, *Fat Friends* focuses on the lives of a group of over-weight people and explores a host of weight-related issues and problems, along with the absurdities of dieting today. The cast was stellar and included James Corden, Ruth Jones and Alison Steadman. I thought Janet Dibley, who played Carol, the club team leader, was perfect in the role of a neurotic, condescending woman trying to persuade everyone to follow her 'Super Slim-mers' diet. She was typical of someone from the slimming world, as I later discovered after some research.

I went to the meeting and met Kay and her daughter Yvonne Francas, the series producer. Also in the meeting was a writer called Lisa Holdsworth, who was working with Kay at the time. I look like you! I thought, as I sat down for a chat. Kay explained that each episode of *Fat Friends* focuses on one character, al-though there are lots of storylines woven through the series. She was planning to introduce a new family into the second series.

'We want you to play Rebecca Patterson, the daughter,' she said.

'Wow,' I mumbled. To say I was pleased and dumbfounded is an understatement.

I read some of the script and then I left. I later found out that Kay sometimes pulled in other writers to work on *Fat Friends* and Lisa Holdsworth was going to be writing Rebecca's sto-ryline. She had based elements of the character on her own life. Is it just a coincidence we look alike? I wondered.

A few days later, my agent rang and said, 'Kay definitely wants you to play Rebecca.' I was totally bowled over. I owe Kay a lot for believing in me as an actress. She trusted me to pull it off.

Two weeks after I got the part, I was called to a full casting day to find a mother for my character. When I looked down the list of actresses who were trying out, the name that jumped out at me was Lynda Baron, who had played Nurse Gladys Emmanuel in *Open All Hours*, one of my all-time favourite shows as a kid. I tried out with lots of actresses that day, but everyone agreed that me and Lynda were perfect together. She got the part and went on to play my mum.

My character in *Fat Friends* couldn't have been more different from me, except that we're both big girls. The manager of a garden centre in Leeds, Rebecca is very shy and timid. She's less than a wallflower. Blink and you'd miss her. Rebecca has bulimia. She overeats and self-harms, partly as a consequence of being bullied at school. Her mum is big, bolshy and dominant, always pecking on about her daughter's weight and desperately worried about her self-harming. Rebecca finds real sanctuary alone with her flowers in her greenhouse. No one can bully or nag her there. She fancies her co-worker, a little geek, who shares her love of flowers.

In my first series of *Fat Friends*, the girl who bullied Rebecca at school, played by the brilliant Sheridan Smith, reappears in her life when she gets a job as a till girl at the garden centre. History begins to repeat itself as Rebecca's quiet life is disrupted by this dolly girl bully, who tortures her by undermining her and saying horrible things to her. She calls her Fatty Patty and Fatty Patterson. Eventually, Sheridan's character tries to snare the boy Rebecca fancies, just to get at Rebecca. Wonderfully, he rejects her and declares his preference for Rebecca.

Kay knew that I loved the whole deglamorisation of my character. Of a morning, all the other girls would be in make-up for an hour – and I'd get five minutes. I'd have fake eyebrows applied and my hair would be doused in mane spray to make it look messy and dirty. Mane spray is normally used by balding men to fill in the baldy gaps on their head. When you spray it on hair like mine, it makes it look matted. After the mane spray I put on Rebecca's glasses and a little bit of Vaseline on my lips. That was it. My granddad struggled watching it, because he was never able to recognise me when I appeared on the screen. 'Don't worry, Granddad,' I said. 'One day you'll see me looking glamorous on the telly.' And he did, but it was a hell of a long wait.

Personally, I was thrilled by my transformation into Rebecca, because I had seen the person she was based on when I researched my part by going to various slimming clubs, and she was a scruff. I felt I had become her. I can't bear watching dramas where the actress wakes up with mascara on. It makes me want to scratch the telly. My attitude is, if you're going to do it, do it, or don't do it at all. We even tried putting train track braces on my teeth, but it affected my speech too much.

Of all the acting I've done, I'm proudest of *Fat Friends*. I feel I did it properly in every way. I wanted to prove myself as an actress and I think I did. All the feedback I had was mind blowing. I felt very fortunate to be working with a dream-come-true cast. I mean, Alison Steadman! She was married to Mike Leigh! Sometimes I'd look around me and think, God, I'm working with the greats here. I kept quoting lines from *Open All Hours* to Lynda and from *Abigail's Party* to Alison. I didn't want to be annoying, but I couldn't help myself. They had both influenced me so much.

I made brilliant friends with Ruth Jones and James Corden. After a few weeks of working together, James told me that he had been expecting me to be a bit of a tit after seeing me on *You've Been Framed*.

'Thanks!' I said. Don't judge a book by its cover, James.

Me and James were known for being like naughty little two-year-olds when we had a scene together. We had the best fun in the world. When recording stopped, we couldn't help messing around. Then, when I went for the next take, I had to retreat within myself to find Rebecca, because she was the opposite of who I am off camera.

Me and James were always inventing characters, making up songs and improvising silly sketches. There was one sketch in which me, James and Ruth pretended to be a fat version of the Brontës. Our Brontës weren't dainty and serious, always scribbling away with a quill. Instead, we had a vision of the sisters either merrily skipping through Haworth or staying at home eating, with their brother lying senseless on the floor beside them.

Among the silly characters we created were a group of psycho-fans who worked in the catering van on the sets of TV programmes. They took their fanaticism to the point that they would be able to predict what, say, David Jason liked to eat for breakfast as he approached the catering van. 'Two eggs, two sausage, one brown toast.' For some reason, that really made us laugh.

Fat Friends was a massive turning point in my career because suddenly people were saying, 'Frigging hell, this girl can act!' It was also my favourite and most rewarding acting job to date. I loved every minute I was in it. Because of my size, it was interesting for me to do a drama about people with weight problems. I had never been to a slimming group before – and haven't since – so it was fascinating to hear people talking about the diets they were on when I went to do my research. It's true that I like my Twix bars and biscuits but I also think that being big is in my genes. I come from a big family. Either way, I couldn't help taking a dim view of it when I was told that the ideal portion was the size of your fist. 'I definitely have more pasta than that,' I'd say. Then I'd think, Maybe that's the problem. But a fist? Come on! That's having a laugh.

I'm sure that a person's weight is a complex, individual issue that is far more dependent on metabolism than it is on portion size. Exercise is a huge factor in determining metabolism too, as I discovered nearly a decade later when I started training for a certain prime time dancing show. However, I'm no expert and I never will be, which is why I turned down the chance to make a fitness DVD off the back of *Fat Friends*, which was planned as a guide to doing housework and keeping active, a 'How to keep fit with Lisa around the house'. Can you imagine it? I'm an actress, not a personal trainer!

In early 2002, it became clear that Gran was very poorly. She had been diagnosed with lung cancer a few months before and she was obviously getting worse all the time. 'Your gran has joined the cancer club,' Mum told me, her eyes twinkling with humour. We took the mickey out of anything connected with cancer. We had to.

'Is that why you took her with you when you went to the hospital for your mammogram?' I asked her later. 'Were you having a cancer off, because you had a sixth sense that Gran had cancer too?'

I gave Kay Mellor the heads up that Gran was poorly, because no one knew how fast she would go downhill and I needed to warn Kay that I might be called away at any moment. The call came one night in February. It had been a long day of filming and after having something to eat with the rest of the cast, I usually went straight to bed. But, for some reason, on this particular night, me, James and Ruth had decided to have one glass of wine in the bar together. Then my phone rang. 'It could be tonight.'

'Right, I'll drive you,' James said, without a moment's hesitation.

'I'm coming too,' Ruth said.

The weather was terrible that night. I wouldn't have let a dog out in it. The wind was blowing savagely and the rain was pounding down. Already renowned for being treacherous, the M62 motorway from Leeds to Manchester was the worst I've ever known it. Ruth was squashed in the back of the car. James was driving. I was in a sort of trance, thinking, Will I make it? Will I get there in time?

Mum left a message on my phone warning me that there were loads of people at the hospital. When someone is dying, all kinds of people come out of the woodwork, some of whom you haven't seen for years! It freaked me out a little bit to think that there were people like that around my grandmother's bed and I wasn't there. Was someone trying to tell me that I wasn't supposed to see her pass?

When I arrived, Gran was in a coma. Dad said, 'Don't make a scene.' It made me cross, because I felt I had a right to say goodbye to Gran alone. Of course, Gran's sisters and children had every right to be there, but the presence of all the partners and husbands and wives and everyone else made it feel like there was a big wake going on, while Gran was still alive.

'Please, just go now, everyone!' I said. 'I need a few minutes with my gran.'

Some of them probably thought, 'Oh, here she is! Here's Lisa! She's arrived.' I didn't mean it to come across like that. I had something I needed to say to Gran.

I took her hand and held it. 'Thank you for being the best grandmother any child could ever wish for,' I said, my voice breaking with emotion. It was really hard.

A little later, I rang Kay to give her an update. 'Please take all the time you need,' she said. 'You can have emotional leave. We can rejig the schedule.'

I considered it, but then I thought about how much Gran thrived off all my tales about filming *Emmerdale* and *You've Been Framed*. She loved hearing about the people I'd met. She was beside herself once, when I showed her a photo of me with some of the cast of *Corrie*, people she'd grown up watching on the telly, like Barbara Knox.

Something in my head said, 'No, you've got to go back to work. Gran would want you to.'

So me and Dad stayed up with her through the night and it was decided that I would go back to work the following evening. Dad was adamant that he didn't want me to be on my own and Mum came with me. I agreed to go because I didn't think Gran would pass. I couldn't bear the idea of her dying.

Me and Mum left the hospital at about nine at night and

Gran passed a few hours later, with her boys around her bed: my granddad, my dad, his brother Graham and our Liam. Even though I was devastated that I wasn't with her, I found comfort in knowing that she had fallen asleep peacefully, surrounded by people who loved her.

11

Painted as a fool

I started doing pantomimes in 1999, when I played the fairy god-mother in *Cinderella* at the Victoria Theatre in Halifax. I haven't missed a year since. Christmas 2013 will be my fourteenth panto on the trot.

Initially, the producers were reluctant to cast me in evil roles. 'No, you're Lisa Riley. You're fun. You're camp. You can't be a baddie.'

'But I want to be!' I protested. I used to watch from the wings and think it looked much more fun to stir the audience into a frenzy of jeers than it was to hop around the stage trilling away in a high voice, being frightfully upbeat and good natured. And once I played a baddie, I never looked back.

Nothing beats being raucously hissed and booed by a crowd of overexcited kids as you creep malevolently behind the goodie on stage. I love that interaction with the audience. It's what panto is all about. Is it Ibsen? No, it's not. But it gets kids away from their computers and introduces them to the world of theatre.

Being in panto every year means that at Christmas I'm in a bubble for three and a half weeks. While everyone else is gearing up for and winding down from Christmas and New Year, I'm doing two shows a day, every day, except for Christmas Day.

When you're in the panto bubble, no one and nothing else exists, apart from the other cast members and crew. The Pope could die and you would have no idea. You're totally cut off from the world. That can be a good thing or a bad thing. In panto, I try to work with people I know and like because you work so closely that you're like a family. In the early days, my panto friends included Clive Webb and Danny Adams, a brilliant father and son duo of comedians, and Tiffany, a talented dancer I met while doing my second panto in Bradford, who went on to become a close friend. Tif is really good fun, a proper cockney girl from Islington. Her first child, Harrison, is one of my six godchildren.

Over Christmas 2002, I was at the Swansea Grand Theatre playing the Ring Mistress in *Goldilocks and the Three Bears*. Me, Clive, Danny and Tif rented a three-storey house on the beach in Swansea. Clive and Danny were on the top floor, I was in the middle and Tif was in the basement. Mum and Dad helped me pack up their car with the mountains of luggage I always take with me on my panto runs, and they drove me down to Swansea in time to start rehearsals.

The plot of this production of *Goldilocks* revolves around a touring circus that Goldilocks and the three bears are hoping to join. The Ring Mistress acts as the narrator. She's constantly on and off stage, so I never had the chance to go back to my dressing room during the show. While I was waiting to go back on, I'd sit in the wings and talk to the crew.

During rehearsals, I got chatting to a set painter called Nick Holly. He wasn't exactly an oil painting and he was nearly ten years older than me, but nevertheless there was something attractive about him. When he wasn't doing theatre work, he told me, he painted landscapes of Swansea. He played down his talent, but several people told me that his work was seriously good. 'He's known as the Welsh Lowry,' one of the crew said. This intrigued me, because I love Lowry. I'm proud that he was from Manchester and I know a lot about him. So I asked if Nick would bring some of his paintings into work so I could see them.

He brought a couple of Swansea landscapes along the next day and I was really impressed by them. They were fabulous. 'Do you have your own gallery?' I asked.

He seemed surprised at the question. It was as if he thought he wasn't good enough to have a gallery. It turned out that he used a room in his home as his studio and occasionally sold a few paintings from there. 'I sometimes wonder if it's worth the bother,' he said.

Sensing that he needed a boost, I tried to encourage him to aim higher. 'You've been given this talent and you should use it,' I said.

Like my mum, I'm always trying to motivate people to achieve their best. 'Don't be scared,' I say, 'even if you fall on the first hurdle. You might not get there till the fourth hurdle, but if you try to reach that fourth hurdle, you probably will get what you want.'

Me and Nick really hit it off after that. We would chat in the wings while I was waiting to go on and he soon opened up about his life and dreams. A lot of the time I just listened. I think he was flattered that I was interested in his work. I genuinely thought he was very talented. As the days passed, I could feel myself falling for him. Or, at least, I was falling for his talent. As for Nick, I don't think he'd met anyone like me before. Some parts of Swansea are quite traditional in that men and women have set roles, but I treat everyone the same. Nick thought I was fun and had a zest for life that he hadn't come across before.

We were well into the bubble when a notice went up on the board about a Mexican evening for the cast and crew in the crew room when the show finished at around half past nine. Themed evenings are always popular during pantomime runs and this one was all frozen tequilas and tortillas, Mexican hats and ponchos. It was seriously good fun. I spent most of the evening twizzling my fake moustache and speaking in a ridiculous Spanish accent.

Nick was by my side for the whole evening. He laughed at my jokes and told me how pretty I looked, despite the fact that I was got up like a Mexican *bandito*. Now I was the one who felt flattered. I couldn't help but revel in the attention he was paying me. He made me feel like I was the only girl in the room and I began to think that something was about to happen between us.

'I'll walk you home,' he said, when the party was over.

I laughed. 'I'm not walking! I'm getting a taxi,' I said. 'You can come back to mine if you want. Most of the cast are coming along.'

'OK, we can have a drink and a chat,' he said.

He came in and had one beer. As we talked, he mentioned that he was married with kids. 'Oh,' I said. I was surprised, because he'd definitely been flirting with me at the Mexican evening.

That's that, then, I thought with disappointment. Then he started saying that he wasn't very happy within his marriage. Did that mean his marriage was ending? I wasn't sure.

I saw him out. I shouldn't have done, but I did. The rain was torrential. As he stepped onto the doorstep, he pulled me out with him. The door slammed shut behind us and he wrapped me in his arms. As we kissed in the rain, I couldn't help thinking of Audrey Hepburn in *Breakfast at Tiffany's*. There goes my romantic mind again, I thought. Eventually we kissed goodbye. I went to bed feeling flushed and excited. But it was just a snog, I told myself. He's married. It can't go any further.

When you're in panto, you don't get up until eleven, but the following morning around eight, I was woken by my phone. It was Nick. 'Can I bring you breakfast?'

My heart started thumping. 'Are you sure that's a good idea? Everyone's here.'

'I don't care,' he said.

'OK. We can sit in my room.' He turned up with croissants and jam and little cartons of fresh orange. The rest is history. We stayed in my room until we had to go to work.

Things escalated from there. It was all very quick. He started coming round to my house nearly every morning. In between shows, we'd go into my dressing room and lock the door. After the show, we often went for a walk along the beach near the house. Soon we were spending all our time together. He was obviously lying to his wife about where he was, but I didn't ask questions. I'm ashamed to say that I found the situation a little bit naughty and exciting. As horrible as it sounds, I think I was swept away by the intrigue and adventure of it. Trapped in the panto bubble, dizzy with passion and caught up in the whirlwind of putting on two shows a day, I didn't stop to think about the possible consequences of what we were doing. Most of all, I think I was flattered by the attention he was giving me. I'd been deeply hurt in the past and now someone was telling me I was beautiful, that he was in love with me and couldn't resist me. And it wasn't just any man, it was an *artist*. I admired his talent so much,

I thought no one had noticed what was happening, but of course Tif knew something was up. 'What is going on?' she asked, one morning. 'You're not just friends.'

'We are. We just love talking.'

'No, Lisa Riley, you never close doors. But now your bedroom door is always shut.'

Anyone who knows me well knows that I can't bear closed doors. My mates call me the 'queen of wedges', because there's a wedge under every door in my house in Bury. It all stems back to my fear of confined spaces. When I have a shower at home, I leave the bathroom door open, no matter who is around, and if I'm in the house on my own after dark, I don't like having a shower or a bath at all. Obviously, I have to sometimes, because I'll be going out, but I find it difficult. For some reason, I feel like I'm going to drown. It's the weirdest thing.

Tif knew all about it. I was rumbled. 'I've been shutting the door because it's cold,' I said weakly.

She rolled her eyes. 'I've known you for two years, babe. Something is going on. You're famous in the industry for keeping your dressing room door open. Anyone can go in to see you normally, but now I can't even knock on the door and ask you if you want a butty from M&S.'

There was no point pretending any more, so I confided in her. 'He keeps saying how unhappy he is with his wife,' I said.

'Just be careful,' she warned.

By now, I was passionately in love, or thought I was. Nick had fallen for me too and was hinting that he wanted to leave his wife and be with me.

'You sound happy,' Mum said, when I rang her. 'Any particular reason?'

'Mum, I'm madly in love,' I gushed.

'That's wonderful, darling,' she said excitedly. 'Who is he?' After the heartbreak of Lee, Mum desperately wanted me to meet Mr Right and be happy. She knew how much I longed to find true love and settle down with someone. She also knew about the failed dates and flings I'd had since Lee. So, for a moment, her heart soared. Then I told her that Nick was married with children.

'Oh, no, Lisa!' she said. 'No, that's not right. Tell me it's not true.'

'But he's not happy in his marriage. I think he wants to leave his wife.'

'It doesn't matter,' she insisted. 'There are children involved.

It's wrong in every way to have anything to do with him. Your father will be appalled.'

'But, Mum …'

'No buts, Lisa,' she interrupted. 'You're being a bloody fool. Can't you see that? An affair like this is like a holiday romance. It's just a fling. It's never going to last. You must know that.'

I tried to argue, but she put the phone down. I felt stung. Mum had never hung up on me before, never ever. I rang her back, but she didn't pick up. I rang the house phone, but there was no answer. I felt really upset. She hadn't given me the chance to explain! She'd jumped to the wrong conclusion and cut me off. It was so unlike Mum.

I spoke to Dad a bit later that day. 'What's all this?' he said, sounding totally unlike his usual laid-back self. I explained that Nick had started saying that he wanted to leave his wife to be with me. 'How can you even think about breaking up someone's family?' Dad said angrily.

'Dad, I'm only telling you what he's telling me,' I said. He put the phone down on me.

Mum didn't speak to me for two days. It was the longest time I'd ever gone without speaking to her in my entire life. I tried to ring her but she didn't pick up. Dad didn't speak to me for six weeks.

I rang Liam. 'Why does everyone hate me?' I asked him.

'Because you're a dick,' he said, sounding surprisingly grown up and so out of his nature.

OK, I'll show you! I decided. I don't know what I was thinking. I should have listened to my family.

Mum buckled after forty-eight hours because she couldn't bear not to speak to me. But she made it clear how much she disapproved of me and Nick. 'Where the hell is your head at? You have really messed up here,' she said.

'Mum, you can't help who you fall for,' I said. I felt confused, though. I was so used to having my family's support.

That evening, Nick and I had a mega time together after the show. It was fantastic. But, as he left, I said, 'Don't come round in the morning. I'll see you at work.' I needed to think about what Mum had said. Maybe she was right and I was wrong.

Half an hour later, I was sitting in Tif's room when my phone went. It was Nick. 'Is everything OK?' he said. 'It upset me when you said you didn't want to see me in the morning.'

'I need some time to think,' I explained. I'd already told him about what Mum and Dad had said.

'I need to see you now,' he said urgently.

'Aren't you at home?'

'No, I'm at the church hall where the local drama society puts on its plays. I'm painting.'

He persuaded me to get a cab to meet him. It was insanity, but it was brilliant. 'Let's go for a walk on the beach tomorrow morning,' he said, as we left. 'We need to talk.'

I met him on the beach the next morning, around nine o'clock. It was one of those beautiful crisp winter days. The sky was vast and blue. The sea sparkled in the fresh January sunlight. Nick took my hand as we walked along. 'I can't let you go,' he said. 'We've only got a week left of the show. I spent all of last night thinking it through and I've made my mind up. I've decided to leave my wife. I want to be with you. I want to leave Swansea and start my life again with you in Bury.'

My God, I thought. This is it. It was so flattering to think he loved me enough to want to change his whole life. Standing on a long, empty beach with the sun in my eyes, holding hands with the man I loved, everything felt so right and so romantic.

'Are you sure?' I asked.

'I've never been as certain of anything,' he said.

I told him I needed time to think. Did I really want him to leave his family and come back to Bury with me? As I walked back to the house, I tried to imagine our future together. Perhaps it could work, I thought. I pictured myself coming home from a day's filming in Leeds to find Nick putting the finishing touches to his latest painting. It was a lovely idea. His children could come and stay at weekends. Perhaps they'd be wary of me at first, but I'd welcome them with open arms and win them round. Things didn't need to be complicated, I thought naively. Our love for each other would get us through.

I didn't think about Nick's wife and the potential fallout from their separation. I didn't know her. She wasn't real to me. None of it was real. I had no grasp of the seriousness of the issues involved. As Mum had pointed out, I was like a smitten tourist on holiday, trying to work out how to bring her waiter back home. I was in my pantomime bubble, dreaming. I should have known that Mum was right and the bubble would inevitably burst.

Yes, this is what I want, I thought. The passion and intensity of the situation had convinced me that Nick was Mr Right, even though I'd only known him for three weeks. No, let me correct that. Nick had persuaded me that he was Mr Right. He had driven everything that had happened. First, he had flirted with me. Then he'd said he wasn't happy with his wife. After we'd got together, he had declared his love and dropped hints that he wanted to leave his marriage. Finally, he'd said that he wanted to leave Swansea and be with me. I hadn't prompted any of it. I had simply been swept off my feet by all the attention, romance and flattery.

I tried Mum again. This time, she picked up the phone. 'So, it isn't what you think it is,' I said. 'It's serious. He's coming back to Bury with me.'

'What?' she spluttered.

'He wants to be with me, Mum, and I want to be with him. What we feel for each other is too strong to ignore. He's going to tell his wife.'

Mum sighed. 'OK, but you should know that your dad is beyond livid. He doesn't want anything to do with you because of those children.'

'Mum, I have to be an adult about this. On my shoulders be it, but this is what's happening.'

That was all well and good, but I was still expecting Mum and Dad to pick me up and bring me and all my luggage home to Bury, as they did every year at the end of my panto run, no matter where I was in the country. Mum had driven me everywhere all my life, because I still hadn't passed my test. She even used to pick me up from parties and clubs at three in the morning, because she hated the idea of me getting into a taxi late at night. But now she said, 'We're not picking you up. We're not bringing him home.'

It was my turn to splutter and say, 'What?'

'No.'

How will I get back from Swansea to Bury? I thought. It was a long way and I had loads of stuff. I spoke to Nick. 'Don't worry, we'll sort it,' he said, although like me, he couldn't drive.

He went ahead and told his wife he was leaving. Understandably, she was devastated. He told me that she flung every insult she could think of about me at him, but he stuck to his guns. 'This is what I want,' he said. I was unbelievably moved by the thought of what he was giving up for me.

On the last day of the pantomime, I booked into the Marriott Hotel across the road from the theatre. I waited in the room while Nick worked into the early hours, breaking down the set with the rest of the crew. I did everything I could think of to set the scene for a romantic night. I scattered the bed with fake rose petals, which I'd bought at Ann Summers earlier in the day, and I placed a bottle of chilled champagne beside the bed, ready for when he arrived.

When he eventually got to the hotel, Nick looked a bit vacant. At first I assumed he was tired after breaking down the set for hours. But it wasn't that. Instead, it was as if the penny had dropped and he had realised the enormity of what he was doing. Maybe someone from the crew had said something, I don't know, but I could tell he wasn't feeling himself.

I arranged for a driver from Manchester to come and pick us up the next day. Off we went to Bury. Mum was there to meet us when we arrived. She couldn't bear not to see me. She gave me a huge hug and told me how much she'd missed me. Then she turned to Nick. 'I don't know you,' she said, 'but

I don't like you. I hope, if this works, that I will grow to like you. However, my husband doesn't want anything to do with you.'

'I understand,' Nick said.

The following morning, Mum drove us to a paint shop so that Nick could buy the materials he needed to start painting. One of the reasons he had been attracted to me was that I encouraged him to work and be an artist, and he needed to start right away. In the afternoon, he went out scouting for views to paint while I moved everything out of my office so that he could turn it into his studio. He returned looking a bit crestfallen. Obviously, the Lancashire hills were nothing like the Swansea coastline. He felt slightly as if he had lost his muse.

Tiny doubts about our relationship began to creep into my mind, but I brushed them aside. It soon became blazingly obvious that we hardly knew each other. Now that we were out of the panto bubble and doing normal things like going to a supermarket, things weren't half as fun or exciting. I hadn't realised that Swansea was so much a part of him. His blood ran Swansea and all of a sudden he was on a relatively plush housing development, unable to drive, unfamiliar with the area and unable to paint views of his hometown.

More importantly, being apart from his children was killing him. I encouraged him to ring them all the time. As someone who needed to speak to her mum several times a day, even at the age of twenty-six, I understood how vital it was for him to stay in constant contact with his kids.

We'd been home about five days when the knock came at the door. Things were going all right, but they weren't brilliant. I was gearing up for a massive fundraiser I was organising in aid of The Christie Centre, the largest cancer centre in Europe. Nick knew how important it was to me. Meanwhile, I had managed to get his paintings accepted at a gallery in Bury, but probably only as a favour to me. I think he cottoned on to the fact that it wasn't necessarily his work that the gallery was interested in. That's not the person he was. It definitely rankled.

Anyway, I opened my front door to a find a woman standing on the doorstep. 'Hi, I'm from the *Sun*,' she said.

My heart sank. 'Yup,' I said.

'You're having an affair with Nick Holly. There's no point denying it because we've spoken to his wife and we've got photographic evidence of you both coming in and out of the house.'

'Yes, he's here,' I confirmed. 'Now, if you'll please excuse me, I've got things to do.' I shut the door.

Over the next few days, there were headlines like EMMER-DALE HOME WRECKER and DINGLE DISASTER. Nick's wife sold her story to *Closer* magazine, and said lots of horrible things she shouldn't have said. It was awful. Until then, I'd been squeaky clean in the press. I'd had my boozy woozy days, but in principle I was the girl next door and I hadn't put a foot wrong. Now, suddenly I was being portrayed as someone I didn't recognise, a heartless, predatory marriage wrecker. I found it hard to deal with, especially as all I longed for was a happy, stable relationship with someone I loved.

As soon as the story broke, opening my front door was like stepping into the scene in *Notting Hill* where Rhys Ifans is confronted by a crowd of paparazzi on the doorstep. Only this wasn't a comedy moment. I don't think I've ever been so scared in my entire life. At one point there were fourteen photographers outside the door and journalists parked all the way up my drive. We had to live with the curtains closed. It was surreal and horrible.

People were constantly knocking at the door. We just had to ignore it. The phone kept ringing. We didn't pick it up. I was advised to make no comment. Journalists continually hassled my management asking me to respond to the terrible things Nick's wife was saying about me in *Closer* magazine. Finally, I was approached by the *Mirror* to tell my side of the story and I agreed, because I wanted to put the record straight. 'I'm not a home wrecker,' I said. 'People have got hurt and that's not a good thing, but we want to be together more than anything. Still, our main concern is for Nick's children.'

'I don't want a penny for doing this,' I told the journalist. 'Please give the money you would pay me to Breakthrough Breast Cancer and credit it at the end of the interview.' Did they? No. So it looked like I'd been paid for doing an exclusive *Mirror* interview, which I couldn't bear, because I didn't get one bean for it and I didn't want to.

Nick and I tried to make it work, but it soon went pear-shaped. The crunch came on Valentine's Day, after only a few weeks of being together in Bury. Since he loved musical theatre, I booked tickets for us to see *My Fair Lady* starring Martine McCutcheon, which had just opened in the West End.

I cringe when I look back on that night. I'd booked a mega room at the Covent Garden Hotel and the best seats in the house for the show. But Nick didn't seem to be enjoying himself. I could tell he felt deeply uncomfortable that people were looking at us, and for all the wrong reasons. It wasn't a case of pointing out Lisa Riley. Everyone knew what was going on between us. We both felt exposed.

Back at the hotel, he didn't come near me. He didn't even give me a kiss. I can still picture him sitting on the end of the bed now. 'You're not right, are you?' I said.

He put his head in his hands. 'I'm sorry, I don't think I can do this,' he said.

I already knew in my heart that it wasn't going to work, but I felt crushed. The sacrifices hadn't all been on his side, after all. I had fallen out with my mother. I was plastered all over the papers as a home wrecker. Nick's wife didn't know me but was saying the most vitriolic things about me. Now the relationship was over.

I understood why, of course I did. He couldn't live without his children. 'Telephone them,' I kept saying. But obviously phone contact isn't the same as face-to-face.

We took the train back to Manchester from Euston the next day. It was the longest train journey of my life. Nick had tried to phone the kids at Euston, but he wasn't able to speak to them. He was silent for the entire journey. It was so awkward. It was horrid.

Back home, he said, 'I'm—'

'It's fine,' I broke in. 'I know what you're going to say.'

He rang a friend in Swansea who agreed to come and pick him up. This friend was a big Leeds United fan, so he killed two birds with one stone by bringing his kid up to see Leeds play and picking Nick up on the way. 'I need to see the kids, but I'll come back, don't worry,' Nick said as he left.

'Fine,' I said, believing him. We'd had a tough time with all the media attention and I thought it would be best for him to go and see his children. It was important to me that he did. I could see it was destroying him to be away from them. I wouldn't want that for anybody, whether I was with them or not. He went off with his mate, leaving behind quite a lot of stuff, including some clothes and all his art materials.

I tried to phone him the next morning. His wife picked up the phone. 'Don't ring this house again,' she said.

'I'm not ringing your house,' I said. 'I'm ringing Nick's mobile.'

I don't know whether she rang the *Sun* immediately after speaking to me, but the next day the *Sun* headline was, YOU'VE BEEN DUMPED! It was horrific. There was a picture of the two of them together. That struck me as odd, since he'd only been back a day. The next thing I knew, Nick had turned on a sixpence and started slagging me off in *Closer* and in the *Sun*. He was horrible about me and said I'd begged him to leave his wife and come back to Bury with me, which was totally untrue. His wife was even worse. She said I was 'just a fat cow' and claimed that I had not allowed him to speak to his children.

How either of them could sleep at night after that, I don't know. Say what you want about me: call me fat, call me anything, but don't tell lies about me.

The final straw came on the first Friday in March, when I was up a ladder stringing fairy lights across a massive ballroom at the Lowry Hotel in Manchester, where I was holding my fundraiser. The phone went. 'Hi Lisa, it's the *Sunday People*.'

Oh God, I thought. It's the Sundays now.

'Apparently you're bombarding Nick with phone calls all day, every day. His wife says you're hounding him. We have proof that you've rung him and we're going to run the story tomorrow. Do you have anything to say?'

I did everything I could not to cry. Would this nightmare ever end? Why were Nick and his wife doing this? I couldn't understand it. It hurt me beyond belief that this man, who had declared his love for me such a short time ago, was now being so incredibly callous and cruel. Still, I knew there was no point trying to dispute the story, even though it couldn't be further from the truth.

So, I was about to say my usual, 'No comment.'

But then I changed my mind. 'Do you know what, sweetheart?' I said. 'If you believe that, go ahead and print it. But, just so you know, tomorrow evening I'm co-ordinating a ball at the Lowry Hotel for six hundred people and we're going to raise thousands of pounds for people dying of cancer. There are fifteen of my best friends here with me now and we're all setting up this room to-gether. There's probably CCTV in this hotel that proves I haven't picked my phone up to ring Nick once, because I simply haven't had time. But go ahead and run the story. All I'm going to say is, It's bollocks.'

'We will be running the story.'

'OK, there's nothing more to say, but I know that I'm a good person and I know what I'm doing today and tomorrow night. Thank you very much. Goodbye.'

I may have sounded defiant, but I was desperately embarrassed. I was mortified. For the first time in my life I knew how it felt to have your pride really dented. I felt foolish beyond belief, an idiot, a mug, and I'd never experienced those emotions before.

What I'd done was bad. It was horrible and I shouldn't have done it. OK, it takes two to tango. I know a lot of people have done it. But it's totally and utterly wrong to go with a married man and I knew it. What killed me was I couldn't make it right. There was nothing I could do to change it.

That Sunday, it was all over the *People*. LEAVE ME ALONE! says Nick, above an interview about how I kept ringing him, begging him to come back to me. It was incredibly humiliating. I felt like a misunderstood baddie in a panto, with the whole country hissing and booing me. My only comfort was that we raised £78,000 at the fundraiser for Christie's, which was amazing. I was chuffed about that.

Nick and his wife must have made a packet from all the exclusives they sold. He went on to become a successful Swansea landscape artist, with his own gallery. Meanwhile, he left me brokenhearted. I only wish I'd listened to my mum when she told me what a fool I was to be with him.

12

Lift the curtain

My head was all over the place in the days that followed the article in the *People*. I felt confused, betrayed, hurt, foolish and, above all, desperately ashamed of myself. I was broken. To make things worse, I was sure everyone was pointing the finger at me. I didn't know how to deal with it. I wanted the earth to swallow me up.

As a result, I wasn't very responsive when my agent Phil Dale called to say that I'd been asked into the BBC for a meeting. It wasn't just any old meeting, either. It was a potentially life-changing meeting to talk about the possibility of playing the second lead in a brand new sitcom starring Paul O'Grady. Phil said that the role had my name written all over it, and he was right. It was the part from heaven. Paul O'Grady would be playing the manager of a bingo hall in Liverpool. My character – if I got the part – was the head of the bingo hall canteen, his sidekick.

'They absolutely want you, Lisa,' Phil said excitedly. 'There's no two ways about it. But first you need to go to the meeting and read for the part.'

'That's wonderful,' I replied, trying to sound enthusiastic. Normally I would have been over the moon to have a chance like this, but I was so caught up in my embarrassment and shame that I couldn't muster my usual zest and energy.

I was sent four scenes from the script to look over before the meeting. Although I was only expected to sight-read them, I would usually have learnt them off by heart. Now, though, I was feeling so fragile and lost that I couldn't focus. I tried to pull myself together and mentally prepare for the meeting, but I couldn't bring myself to read the scenes. I didn't even look at them. It was unheard of for me.

I'll read them on the train, I thought dejectedly, stuffing them in my bag.

I thought my heart was at its lowest ebb as I made my way to Manchester train station. But then I saw the latest copy of *Closer* magazine on the racks and somehow my spirits sank even further. On the cover, there was a teaser for yet another 'exclusive' instalment by Nick's wife about our affair. Only this time, Nick had also contributed his ha'pennyworth. I couldn't believe it. When he was with me, Nick had seemed shocked by his wife's eagerness to do a magazine deal and air her dirty laundry in public. Now he was joining in. I was appalled.

I shouldn't have bought a copy, but I couldn't help myself. I was on a one-way path to destruction. On the train down to London, instead of studying the sitcom script and getting myself prepared for the most important meeting ever, I read and reread a bunch of fabricated twaddle about myself in *Closer* magazine.

Left: Mum's last public appearance at the Bury Hospice Arts Day with the Mayor of Bury, Yvonne Creswell, 2012.

Below: My mum on her last day of treatment. Who'd have thought she'd just had her last dose? She's my hero, always brave, always smiling.

Above: Proud Aunty Lise. I can spoil him because he doesn't know what spoiling means yet!

Right: 'Nanna, I'm a boy! Why are you reading me *Little Miss Star*?' Mum at home with Jakey, in the last weeks of her life, 2012.

Above: *Scott and Bailey*. Surrane you know how much I love you! Thank God it's only acting, 2012.

Left: Spent the morning sleeping in a cardboard box as a tramp, for *Waterloo Road*. Time to get *Strictly*fied!

Robin and me shooting the famous *Strictly* opening titles, 2012.

First show nerves with Dani Harmer, Colin Salmon, Jerry Hall and Sid Owen.

Loads of fun in the rehearsal rooms.

Above: That lift on tour!

Left: The best door burst ever . . . do you think we're happy?!

Left: Robin and me on a rare night off at the Pride of Britain Awards.

Right: Artem and Robin . . . my sports bra is in the wrong place!

Left: Robin's got food poisoning . . . what a wonderful replacement.

Right: Jennifer Ellison supports me at *Strictly* and the four of us go for a glass of bubbly.

Team Wembley!
We've all got through.

My boys . . . Robin,
why have you got
your shirt on?!

We shook Wembley.
Happy memories and
tears of complete joy.

All my winning
shoes with my
winning girls.

Above: See Mum, I got my name in lights!

Left: A cause extremely close to my heart.

Right: Fully *Strictly*fied with the King and Queen of *Strictly*, Bruce and Tess, 2013.

At the TRIC TV and Radio Awards, right before *Strictly Come Dancing* won the award for Best Reality Programme, 2013.

It put me into a complete and utter daze. Please, can this stop? I was thinking. Can we put a lid on it and stop talking about it? Nick's gone home now. It's over.

I was furious by the time I got into my taxi at Euston. When I reached the BBC at White City, the urge to ring Nick was overwhelming. The sitcom wasn't even on my mind as I dialled his number. 'First, my Sunday was ruined by all these lies about me constantly ringing you,' I told him, when he answered the phone. 'Now, on my way to an important meeting at the BBC, I've just read even more rubbish about us in *Closer* magazine. Look, what we did was bad and wrong, but you've gone back home and it's over. Can you stop talking about it to the press, please?'

'I'm sorry,' he said. 'I've got to make it work with my wife.'

'OK, I appreciate that, but will you please stop telling lies about me!' I said. 'And I've still got your stuff at my house. Can you get it picked up?'

'Er,' he said pathetically.

'Look, we won't speak again,' I said, taking the initiative. 'I'll liaise with your friend to get the stuff picked up.' I put the phone down, my head spinning.

A few minutes later, I met up with several BBC executives and Michelle Smith, the casting director I'd known since I was a kid. Everyone was very friendly, but I was feeling too bewildered and hurt to get my thoughts straight. I went on to make a complete idiot of myself in the meeting. My heart wasn't in it and my mind was elsewhere, so I sat with hunched shoulders and read the script without looking up once. Since I was totally unprepared, I read it haltingly, without conveying any real sense of the character. I left the meeting in a trance, in the sure knowledge that I'd failed to impress on every level.

Back in Manchester, Phil rang. 'Michelle Smith's been on the phone. She's worried about you. Apparently, you weren't yourself yesterday.'

'I didn't get it, did I?' I said miserably.

'Well, they want to give you a second chance,' he said.

At this, I burst into floods of tears. 'After messing it up like I did yesterday, I'm not worthy of a second chance,' I sobbed. 'I'm so embarrassed. I didn't prepare. I feel like my career is over. No one respects me any more. Everyone hates me. My dad's not speaking to me. Oh God, how can I make this better?'

'You can make it better by nailing that script,' he said firmly. 'Be yourself. Do what you normally do. Go and get it.'

I had two days to prepare and this time I learnt the scenes. But when I walked into the meeting and saw the concern and sympathy in Michelle's eyes, I couldn't hold it together. It was a case of, Don't be nice to me, or I'll break! I was so vulnerable.

Bursting into hysterical sobs isn't a great start to a meeting and things went from bad to worse. I think they wanted me for the part, but how could they give it to someone who stumbled their way through the first reading and had tears streaming down their face through the second? I didn't get it. It was a terrible blow to my self-esteem. I was in tatters. I couldn't believe that I was foolish enough to mess up such a great opportunity.

I went to ground after that. For a while, I came off the hamster wheel and stayed at home, moping. I lost all my confidence and self-respect. It was horrific. I couldn't even open up to my friends. When anyone said, 'Are you all right?' I'd say, 'I don't even want to talk about it.' I was crippled by embarrassment. I felt I couldn't say sorry enough. I said it to the point where it became meaningless. I may as well have been saying, 'spaghetti bolognese'.

That time is a blur in my mind. The next thing I remember – but not very well – is Dominic Brunt's wedding to his wife Joanne, which was a beautiful event at a breathtaking venue. We had such a great friendship and still do. Dominic was and is the most amazing mate and I was thrilled to see him so happy. As his fictional ex-wife, it was a little bit surreal to see him getting married in real life. During a working week on *Emmerdale*, I had spent more time with Dominic than Joanne had. What's more, I'd been pretending to be in love with him – and then married to him – for all that time. Even the woman who performed the service made a joke about it when Dominic and Jo were at the altar. 'You've been here before, but in your other life.' We all burst out laughing.

I got absolutely leathered at the reception. I was so pissed that I danced on the bar, drew thick black eyebrows on Paul Loughran's face with my eyeliner pencil and sang along with the band at the top of my voice. Later on, I broke into the hotel kitchen, found several tins of those free biscuits they put in your room and dished them out to all the guests.

The next morning, I woke up slumped on top of the bed, still in my party frock, looking like Alice Cooper because I hadn't taken my make-up off the night before. The phone was ringing and ringing. Finally, I answered it. 'What?' I said groggily.

'It's eleven o'clock, Miss Riley. We thought you'd like to know that everyone in the wedding party is checking out now.'

'OK,' I groaned, and promptly went back to sleep again.

*

Two minutes later, Dom started knocking on the door. 'Lise,' he said, looking a bit worried. 'Are you all right? The only topic of conversation at breakfast was you and the state you were in last night. You wouldn't stop singing.'

'Oh God,' I said.

'As usual, you were the life and soul,' he said, laughing and giving me a big hug. 'But you need to look after yourself, OK?'

Tears sprang to my eyes. Only the very best of friends would be worrying about you the morning after their wedding. 'I love you, Dom,' I said. 'You're the husband I never had. Now, stop worrying and go back to your real wife. I'll be fine.'

I wasn't fine, though. It took me a long time to get over what had happened with Nick Holly. I had serious trust issues for ever after and I was convinced that my career had been tarnished. Still, I'm a Pepper, so I picked myself up and pulled my socks up. There was nothing else I could do. That's how I'm made. I don't do, 'Woe is me!' like the Rileys. I troop on, like the Peppers, and I needed to go back to work. I appeared in *The Afternoon Play* and three episodes of *The Bill* before we started shooting the next series of *Fat Friends*, and when I wasn't working, I spent my time with my friends and family, who helped me to rebuild my confidence and be me again.

I threw myself into the next two series of *Fat Friends*. In series three, Kay wrote a string of intensely gritty scenes for me and Lynda Baron around a storyline involving the death of my character Rebecca's father. Rebecca accuses her mum of never loving her dad and Lynda responds by telling her daughter some home truths. For some of the scenes, we were out filming next to the canal in Leeds at four in the morning, which was absolutely brilliant. I had to pinch myself whenever I turned up on set and saw Lynda and Kay. I never took for granted how lucky and privileged I was to be a part of such a great drama series, right up to the very last day of filming.

Towards the end of our stint on *Fat Friends*, James Corden came up with the idea for a drama based on a wedding he'd been to, where two very different families were brought together by the bride and groom. After that, he was always talking about its possibilities. He and Ruth started thinking about it on set and eventually they co-wrote the phenomenal series *Gavin and Stacey*. I was so proud of them when it aired.

James and Ruth weren't the only ones thinking about a change of direction. I also began to reassess things after a conversation I had with Lynda Baron over pasta in Leeds one night in early 2005. I loved going out with Lynda. I used to sit there in a state of awe, not quite able to believe that she was there in front of my eyes.

On this particular night, Lynda said, 'You, lady, need to get off TV.'

'What do you mean?' I asked, frowning.

'You've done telly now for eleven years straight. You need to get into the theatre.'

I nearly choked on my pappardelle pasta. 'Oh my God, I can't do that!' I said, recoiling in horror. 'I'd have to remember my lines for two and a half hours!'

Lynda's comments seemed to come out of the blue. I didn't know then that she liked to divide her time between the theatre and telly and often did a three-month run in the theatre followed by a three-month gig on TV. Lynda does everything. She's a national treasure. 'I won't be your friend if you don't,' she threatened. 'You're brilliant, but you're forgetting your roots. When this job finishes, lots of offers for TV will come in off the back of it, but you've got to get on the stage.'

Now, if Lynda had asked me to jump fifty yards, I would have jumped, because she's an icon, the crème de la crème of the acting world, both a comedienne and a serious actress. So I wanted to do the right thing. But I was frightened inside. I'd already had theatre offers and turned them down, partly because I was happy doing my TV, but also because the thought of going on stage again petrified me. That night I went to bed thinking, No, I can't! But Lynda said I was letting myself down. That made me think again. She knew which buttons to press.

When *Fat Friends* finished in 2005, I went on doing little bits of TV here and there, but I kept thinking about what Lynda had said. Well, I'm not going to do Shakespeare just yet, I thought, once I'd started getting used to the idea. Let's take it easy. Then I was offered a role in the first tour of *The Play What I Wrote*, a four-handed comedy celebrating the work of Morecambe and Wise that had been playing in the West End. It's a genius play and I could not recommend it more. There's a section in Act Two where the play parodies that famous moment in each Morecambe and Wise show when a celebrity guest makes an appearance. One of the most famous examples of this was when the newsreader Angela Rippon started doing high kicks out of the blue, shocking the nation by playing against type in a classic comic scene. In the play, the role of the celebrity is billed as 'The Guest'.

Deciding that it would be the ideal part to help ease me back into stage acting, because I would only be onstage for the final thirty-five minutes of the play, I took it.

The rehearsal period of *The Play What I Wrote* reminded me of being back at Workshop with David Johnson, because I was literally workshopping the play with the other actors, Anthony Hoggard, Greg Haiste and Andrew Cryer. They were comedically phenomenal actors and we formed a strong bond. It was amazing what we discovered together in the rehearsal room. I was in my element. With comedy, I love finding a way of getting a laugh that isn't in the script. Sometimes this can be achieved by holding a line for a beat longer than you'd expect, or by playing the jester in the way that I did with Mandy Dingle on *Emmerdale*. The key is to believe in yourself and your delivery, and it's the best feeling in the world when you pull it off.

I had kittens before I went on for the opening night at the Swan Theatre in Worcester, but after that the fear went and I loved every minute of it. It's wonderful trying things out on the road and tweaking them until you get the laugh that you think is there. Yet what was weird was that you might do something and get the biggest laugh you'd ever heard at the Newcastle Theatre Royal, but it wouldn't even get a titter at the Southampton Mayflower.

'Last week, you couldn't even hear the next line because of the laughter!' I'd complain, when I came off stage in Southampton.

I soon learnt that you get different audiences in different areas of the country. It's not that they don't like what you're doing, it's that their appreciation just isn't as audible. Audiences seem to get quieter the further south you go, in my experience. Every actor will tell you the same. It can be a bit disheartening when you look at your tour roster and read that you're performing a comedy for a week in Plymouth.

I'm jumping ahead a bit here, but when I toured with another comedy a few years later, the audience in Yeovil barely applauded. People were smiling, though. I could sense they were enjoying the play and found it funny. They just didn't show it.

The worst was one Tuesday night in Plymouth, when I came off stage thinking, That was awful, oh my God! The lines that usually got the biggest laughs – lines from heaven, lines that were breathtakingly funny – didn't even get a chuckle. 'Don't put the crit up on the board tomorrow,' I said. 'It'll only make me cry.'

The next day, the review in the local paper came out praising the play to the rafters and giving it five out of five stars. Why didn't you laugh, then? I thought. I couldn't understand it.

Northern audiences, especially Geordie audiences, are the opposite. They get involved and they're not frightened to show it. I will never forget the two weeks I spent in Sunderland doing *Calendar Girls*. It was mind blowing. The audience wouldn't stop applauding when it came to my character's photo pose scene. All I did was put my leg in the air and they went mental. I felt like Kylie.

Before I get any more sidetracked, I'll return to *The Play What I Wrote*, which was the scene of my worst onstage disaster. We were at Woking and it was the night of the 2005 National Television Awards. Antony Cotton was on the shortlist for the Most Popular Newcomer award for his brilliant work as Sean Tully in *Coronation Street*. It was the award I'd won ten years earlier, shortly after I had joined *Emmerdale*, so I desperately wanted Antony to win it. I couldn't go to the ceremony because I had the play, but I had a television in my dressing room and I put it on so that I could see the results before I went on stage. I was very excited, because the bookies had Antony down to win.

I'm a bit OCD at the best of times and when I'm doing theatre I'm particularly ritualistic. So, whatever I do on the first show, I have to do for the rest of the run. It's like a jinx and it's *so* stupid, to the point where it actually annoys me, but I can't seem to break the habit. Now, one of my hard and fast rituals during the run of *The Play What I Wrote* was that I always went for a wee in the last five minutes of the interval, about half an hour before I made my entrance on stage. I couldn't let anything interfere with that wee. Until the night of the National Television Awards, that is.

I was in my dressing room, keeping everything crossed for my bezzie, when Trevor McDonald said, 'And after the break, we'll find out who this year's most popular newcomer is …'

Oh no, I thought, I can't go for a wee, because I've got to see this! So I held it. Then, to my horror, there was another award after the ad break. I started to panic. I ran down to the stage and asked, 'How long have I got?'

'Nine minutes,' I was told.

OK, I thought. I went back to my dressing room.

Unbelievably, there was yet another award before Antony's. No! I was screaming in my head. You can't do this! I've got to see Antony win before I go on stage.

His was the next award, thank goodness. But as Trevor

McDonald read through the shortlist, I heard the words, 'Miss Riley to stage!'

It was nail biting. Then Antony won. Yes! I legged it down to the stage and went on, without having my usual wee.

Not long after that, there was this bit where Anthony Hoggard and I have a cod fight. He throws me on the floor and I say, 'Hark, hark, thou shalt never be! Thou shalt never cry.'

Just before we got to that bit, I whispered to Anthony, 'I need the toilet.'

'What?' he whispered back.

'Never mind, carry on,' I said.

So he went ahead and pushed me backwards. But, oh God, he pushed me in just the wrong place and the pressure caused me to wee on stage, right there and then. Within seconds, the back of my navy dress was totally wet and there was a puddle on the floor. Andrew looked on in complete disbelief.

The look in his eyes made me corpse so badly that I couldn't breathe, I was laughing that much. I couldn't disguise it. Then the audience started laughing with me. Anthony had to save the situation. He turned to auditorium and said, 'Ladies and gentlemen, this doesn't normally happen. Lisa Riley is supposed to feed me a line now, but she's absolutely incapable of doing so.'

I went to the back of the set and got myself together. But then Andrew set me off again. 'You have actually weed,' he said in astonishment. I had to leave the stage. My whole body was convulsing with laughter. It was the first and last time I've ever lost control onstage and it was hideous, but very, very funny.

I had such a great time touring with *The Play What I Wrote* that I jumped at the chance of going back on stage with *The Vagina Monologues*, an episodic play exploring various aspects of female experience, including sex, love, rape, masturbation, orgasm, menstruation and female genital mutilation. Written by Eve Ensler and based on her interviews with women all around the world, it is often performed by three women, who may or may not be actors.

Sometimes, cast members aren't able to learn the monologues, either because they don't have time, or because they're not actors and they're not used to learning lines. So it's perfectly acceptable to read from cards on stage. In fact, you're supposed to read from the cards.

Of course, the whole idea of not learning your lines goes against the grain for an actress. I felt sick the first time I was told about it. 'You don't pay to see someone read!' I said. 'That's not acting! You can sit in my garden and I'll read to you. I'm not going to charge you for it. '

'Don't completely learn it,' I was told. 'You have the cards there as a prop.'

But I did learn it. I couldn't not. I'd incorporate a glance down at the cards during my performance, but there was no way I was going to sit on stage and read.

There's a long list of big names who have appeared in *The Vagina Monologues* since its New York premiere in 1996. Cate Blanchett, Claire Danes, Jane Fonda, Queen Latifah, Kate Winslet, Meryl Streep, Winona Ryder, Whoopi Goldberg, Susan Sarandon and Melanie Griffith are just a few of them. Still, I thought my agent was joking when he rang and said, 'It's three stints of a fortnight each, in Southampton, Newcastle and Birmingham, and you're going to be working with Sharon Osbourne.'

'Yeah, OK, whatever,' I said.

'No, Lise, I mean it. Sharon Osbourne will be one of the three women in the show, along with you and Jenny Jules.'

Once he had convinced me that it was true, I started to feel nervous. All I knew of Sharon Osbourne was what I'd seen on TV, and she seemed quite an intimidating person. She certainly didn't suffer fools gladly. She could bury you alive. However, Sharon Osbourne in the flesh couldn't have been more gorgeous and mumsy. She was brilliant and I felt very lucky to be working with her. I remember thinking at the time, Don't judge a book by its cover.

Me and Jenny Jules had our own make-up bags. We put the face on, zipped up the black dress and went on stage. Meanwhile, in Sharon's dressing room, she had the hair and make-up person, the PA and the Jo Malone candle going. It was proper LA. Still, she mucked in and was one of the girls. She had the famous orgasm monologue and she'd go for it, spraying her Evian bottle everywhere and dousing herself in water. The audience went crackers. They loved her.

Meanwhile, I had the famous 'clit' speech. Mum was hilarious about it. 'Don't you be telling your poppa what you're doing!' she'd say.

'He's dead proud of me, Mum!' I protested, although admittedly I had also been thinking, How do I tell Poppa that I'm doing a speech about the clitoris?

'Yes, but we're calling it *The VMs*. It's a new play called *The VMs*. Don't even mention the word vagina!'

'But Mum, it's just a word, and that's the point. We're trying to get across in the play that you *can* say vagina.'

'Not to me dad!' she said, shaking her head firmly. 'Never to me dad.'

So that's how I'd find myself listening to Poppa telling people in the family, 'Lisa's doing a play called *The VMs*.'

And all the while, I could see Mum's sister-in-law, Auntie Betty, looking at me and mouthing, 'What?'

13

The naked truth

My thirtieth birthday loomed and I still hadn't found Mr Right. I had a choice. Either I spent the evening sobbing into my mojito or I celebrated like never before. It wasn't a difficult decision. It looks like I'm never going to get married, I thought, so instead I'm going to have the biggest party ever. I wanted it to be every bit as good as all my friends' lavish weddings, with all my family and friends around me.

No matter what it costs, I thought, I want it to be mega. And it was. It was unreal. I got party planners in and organised a party for four hundred and fifty people at the Bolholt Country Park Hotel in Bury. That may sound like a lot of guests, but you have to remember that there are a lot of Peppers on my mum's side! I really went to town. There was a great band. I had a cake made in the shape of a theatre, with a stage and little figures, and I had an ice sculpture made of my torso, with peach Schnapps coming out of the nipples. People were drinking peach Schnapps from my boobs! It was brilliant, really wow. Poppa, Mum and Dad all made amazing speeches and I felt so lucky to have all my loved ones around me.

Among the guests was Andy, my first ever boyfriend. By now he was doing very well and had his own company in Bury. We'd kept in touch and had a few nights out over the years – and in the months leading up to my thirtieth, we started meeting up again more regularly. Mostly he'd come over to the house and we'd get pissed as rats, have a laugh and put the world to rights. We still had a strong connection, although we were just friends. What I liked about Andy was that he always took me for me, even after all this time.

'Be careful,' warned Amanda, when I told her I'd invited him.

'Sod off! Let me have a good time,' I said, like I always do.

It was mayhem at the party. I'd booked several rooms in the hotel for friends like Tiffany, who had come up from London with her husband, and some of my family were also staying, so that no one had to bother with taxis in the middle of the night. Everyone was there. It was fantastic.

At about two in the morning, I was walking back to the residents' bar from the loo when I bumped into Andy. All night he'd been telling me I looked amazing. Now he said, 'You're really special, you know. Look, all these people are here for you.'

'Yeah, so?' I said, looking happily round at all my nearest and dearest.

'Does that not mean anything to you?'

'Of course, otherwise I wouldn't have invited them.'

'Yes, but it's testament to the person you are. You must know that.' The next thing I knew, we were having a snog at the bottom of the stairs. It was a brilliant end to a brilliant night.

The following day, Liam was playing in a huge cricket match and we all went to watch. To be honest, I think everyone was still pissed from the night before. Certainly a lot of the players in Liam's team were a bit the worse for wear, because they'd all been at the party. It was a beautiful summer's day and after the match we decided to go over to the cricket club and keep the party going. It was fabulous. Everyone was talking about the party. Andy was there the whole time, which was fantastic, the icing on the cake.

I saw Andy a little bit after that. We spent a few mad weekends together and had a ball, but that was it. A month or so after my party, we put a lid on it and I've never seen him since. I think that deep down Andy wanted to settle down, but he could never settle down with me, because I was too ambitious, too controlling and too much in the public eye. He hated that side of things. He would tut when people came up to say hi to me in the street.

For my part, I wanted him to be Mr Right because he's such a great person, but I could never see myself watching a movie on a Tuesday night with Andy, or going shopping together at Asda. I didn't want that with him. It wouldn't have suited us, because we were all about having fun and mayhem together. Neither of us was going to get the relationship we wanted from the other. My problem is that I always seem to go for naughty boys. I don't go for John who works in IT. I like them to be a little bit edgy; otherwise I get bored.

I'll never forget Andy. For all I know, he could be married now and it would be a lie to say I'm not curious about where he is and what he's doing. If he's still with the girl I think he's with, then I'm happy because she's good for him. I wish him well and hope he has a wonderful life. If I bumped into him on the street, I think I'd sigh like Holly Golightly, because I'm such a sad romantic. He was such a great part of my life.

There I was, thirty and single. I seemed to have it all, except Mr Right, and I accepted that this was the way it was going to be from now on. I'd had enough of looking for love, so I stopped thinking about it and instead threw myself into my work, touring relentlessly for the next few years. It was fantastic. Instead of finding a boyfriend, I fell deeper in love with acting every day.

The next part I was offered was the most phenomenal comedy part any woman could want to play. Even better, Dave Simpson, the writer, had written it with me in mind. 'You have to play Bev,' he said when we met up. 'I can see you playing her, I can *hear* you playing her.'

This was the boost I needed. How could I resist? To create a part in a brand new play is an incredible challenge and involves a lot of experimentation and workshopping, which I love. Dave had been a writer on *Emmerdale* and he had always written brilliantly for Mandy Dingle. After he left the show, he wowed audiences all over the country with his smash hit play, *Girls' Night Out*, before his attention turned to pole dancing. At the time, everyone was obsessed with pole dancing as the new form of exercise, so Dave jumped on the bandwagon and wrote a brilliant pole dancing play called *The Naked Truth*, with an all-female cast.

The script was fantastic, full of gritty Northern humour in the vein of *Stepping Out*. It made me laugh out loud when I read it, but it had a real edginess to it as well, and it explores lots of big themes, like the power of friendship and the importance of living life to the full. Funny and farcical, yet also poignant and moving, it's set around a pole dancing class and tells the stories of a group of women with different lives and backgrounds. When one of the characters discovers she has breast cancer, the others put aside their differences and join forces to do a fundraising pole dance. Since you don't know if they're going to be able to pull it off or not, there's a little bit of *The Full Monty* and *Calendar Girls* in there too. My character Bev is a proper Northern slapper, a big girl with a heart of gold and a cheeky sense of humour. It's a role that requires lots of physical comedy, which is just the kind of challenge I relish.

When we launched, we decided to link the play with the Breakthrough Breast Cancer charity, which made me very proud and Mum really happy. Mum loved the theatre and was thrilled that I'd decided to focus on stage acting. She was still doing amazingly well. She kept getting the all-clear at The Christie Centre and everyone was hoping that she'd be able to beat her illness, although we were all aware that things could change at any time.

The Naked Truth was a huge success everywhere we toured, all round the country. The reviews were fantastic and everyone was talking about it. It went through five cast changes and I stayed in the production for three of them, because I was having such a great time. It was hard work, though. I was away for big clumps of time, from January to May, say, and then from September to Christmas, with only Sundays off, when I'd race back to Bury for a few precious hours with my friends and family. I had toured before, but I'd never toured as intensely.

While all this was going on, the general public assumed I'd left the acting profession, because I wasn't on TV. I'd go into Asda and the girl on the till would say, 'Are you not working any more? What are you doing now?'

'I'm in a play.'

'Really? I thought you'd stopped, because I haven't seen you in anything.'

I was still being recognised a lot and there were always fans at the stage door asking me to sign autographs, but it wasn't anywhere near as crazy as it had been. I had taken a step back from the limelight. I've always felt guilty when my friends get asked to take snapshots of me with fans when we're out in a wine bar. I know they're proud of me, but it's no one's idea of a good night out.

Now I was doing theatre, there was far less of all that. Someone might come up and say, 'Is it you from …?'

I was happier than I'd been in a long time. Mum instantly noticed a difference in me. I loved the work and felt I was expanding my horizons. The people you meet in theatre are quite different from the people in telly. I've often found that they're more interested in you than what you bring to the table. You don't feel like someone's talking to you because you're a stepping stone in their career, and when you have a drink after work, you don't talk about famous people or TV programmes, you talk about everyday things and what's going on in the world. It feels much more real than the telly world. I ended up meeting loads of new friends who really excited me.

People always ask, 'Don't you get bored doing the same thing every night?' But it's impossible to get bored with theatre acting, because every performance is completely different, day by day, venue to venue. It means that you're constantly adapting and adjusting what you're doing. If the audience don't react to a line in the way I expect, or want them to, I'll rethink the timing. If I don't get a certain laugh when I think I should, it just makes me work harder. Your performance is always developing.

You start to get an idea of what an audience will be like about twenty minutes before curtain up, when the relay comes on in the dressing room and you can hear all the hubbub outside. The purpose of the relay is to enable actors to hear what's happening on stage in their dressing rooms, but it also means we can hear the audience arriving. You can sense an atmosphere simply by listening to people milling around before a performance and it definitely gives you an idea of whether you've got a good crowd or not.

A more accurate way of judging your audience is seeing how they react to a certain winning line or physical gag. In *The Naked Truth*, I used to do a fake fall quite early on, where I went to the top of the pole, slid down and made it look like I'd fallen on my back and hurt myself. I was taught how to fall and make the appropriate noise with my heel, so it was very realistic. That generally used to get an absolute whopper response from the crowd, but if it didn't, it often meant that we were in for a more difficult show.

There are all sorts of variables when you're on the road. The cast changes could sometimes make things a bit difficult, although that was a good thing really, because it made me think on my feet and learn to accommodate the new actors. But I would rely on getting a certain delivery of a feed line and it would drive me crackers when a new actress came in and fed it in a different way. The timing's messed up now! I'd think. It was frustrating, because you get a rhythm with comedy and if the rhythm is broken, you might not get the response you want. I always wanted that big laugh. If it didn't work on the night, I'd be a bit quiet in the bar afterwards.

'All right, I'm going up to bed now,' I'd say.

The girls would take the mickey out of me. 'Oh God, she's in a mood because she didn't get that laugh tonight.'

It really mattered to me. I was in such a great, funny production that I wanted it to work every night. I was touring the country, bringing it to audiences everywhere and I wanted to do it to the best of my ability.

I'm known for being fun and giddy, but I take my work very seriously. I've always had a thing about arriving on time to the theatre, to the point that other actors tease me for it. 'You're here an hour before the half!' (The half is what actors call the thirty-five-minute countdown to curtain up.) It's partly because I like to feel I'm settled before the half starts. I can get my cup of tea, have a fag and put my face on, allowing time for me to get into character during the half. Some actors come in at six twenty-five, leaving themselves thirty minutes until the half. That's too late for me. Some people even come in on the half, slap their face on and walk on stage. David Johnson would never have allowed it.

He put the fear of God in me when it came to getting to work on time. I could never forget how he refused to teach me, Antony and Emma when we were late to Workshop after being delayed by a car crash on the M62.

David Johnson has come to see everything I've ever done on stage. To this day, I find it nerve wracking to know he's in the audience, as do all his other ex-pupils, by all accounts. He came to see *The Naked Truth* after the first cast change. The producer had asked me to stay on, but for a while I was the only confirmed member of the second cast.

Alison King had played my character's stooge in the original cast and she was phenomenal. 'Do you know any brilliant comedic actresses that you feel you could have the same rapport with?' Dave, the writer, asked me.

I didn't hesitate. 'Gemma Wardle,' I said.

So they approached Gemma and she came on board, which was fantastic. It also meant that David Johnson was able to see both his girls the night he came to see the play. Oh dear, though, if you'd seen Gemma and me before that night's performance! We were like fathers-to-be, pacing up and down the waiting room. We were so jittery that we couldn't even get our make-up done. 'David's coming!' we kept saying nervously.

The show opened with the two of us on stage together. 'Good luck, babes,' I said, under my breath.

'Good luck!' she whispered back.

The fear he instilled in us both! You talk to any of the Workshop kids and they'll probably do an impression of his booming voice. 'YES?' he'd say. 'Speak up! You're sorry? Well, so am I!' After all these years, we were both petrified of him coming backstage afterwards with notes for us both, which of course he did. But, by God, I took every single one of them, because every single criticism was spot on.

Obviously there were nights when things didn't go according to plan. When, say, one of the other actors corpsed and the rest of us would scramble to cover up for her. I often seemed to get the blame when that happened, for some reason. The cast were always accusing me of having a cheeky twinkle in my eye on stage, although I was completely unaware of it. 'Don't look at me like that again!' they'd say.

'Like what? I didn't do anything!'

'You did!' Apparently, I've got a look in my eyes that makes people laugh.

One night I farted onstage. You know when you think it's going to be a small one? Well, I got it wrong. It was a big loud trump! Even the audience heard it. The other actresses all came out of character and stared at me. What could I do? I couldn't explain that I hadn't expected it to be a loud one. Inevitably, I corpsed.

I become very breathy when I'm trying not to laugh. I speak through my breaths, which just about works, but sounds a bit weird. Someone told me that there's a nerve on your hand you can bite to keep yourself together. I've tried it and it doesn't work.

Laughing on stage is like laughing in church. You're not supposed to do it, so you can't help yourself, and the nerves make it worse. I'll never forget being at a friend's mother's funeral when Samantha got her kitten heel stuck in a grid as we solemnly made our way out of the church. I instantly lost it; I couldn't stop laughing, because we were holding up the whole procession at a desperately sad and serious moment. In the end, Sam had to take the shoe off and walk hobbledy, with one shoe on and one shoe off, so that people could carry on down the aisle with the casket.

I did four stints of *The Naked Truth* over the next couple of years. Mum came to watch me all the time. She'd often jump in the car and drive halfway across the country to see me perform and spend a few days with me. One night she was in the audience with one of my best mates, T. All through the first half I could hear Mum saying, 'Get ready for this bit,' and 'Wait for this!' She was giving away every punch line.

Mum was always there along with loads of my family and friends when I performed anywhere near home. It was a special thrill to appear at Manchester's Palace Theatre and it always will be. I will never forget my awe at its grandeur and beauty when I went to see Les Dawson there in panto when I was a kid, or my utter joy at the age of sixteen as I watched Gary Wilmot and the rest of the cast camp it up in Barry Manilow's musical *Copacabana* – although Mum slept through the whole thing. Whenever I find myself in Dressing Room Number One at the Palace, I feel like I've arrived. No wonder – I've read interviews with Shirley Bassey that have taken place in that dressing room!

Bury doesn't have a theatre on anywhere near the scale of the Palace, but I still have a great affection for the 170-seater Bury Met Theatre in Market Street. It's kooky, with an offbeat, fringe programme of plays. I love it and I've been involved in quite a few Bury Met fundraisers over the years.

At the end of the spring 2008 tour, after a successful season of *The Naked Truth*, I had an idea. I said to the producers, 'I'd love to do two charity nights at the Bury Met Theatre. None of us will earn a penny, but the proceeds will go to Bury Hospice. How about it? We'll raise a fortune. I'll get some mega auction prizes as well, so we can hold an auction and raise even more money.'

I'm a patron of Bury Hospice because of my gran, who went there for a while before she passed away in Fairfield Hospital. The people who work at the hospice are so kind and compassionate that it breaks my heart. They do their utmost to make patients and their relatives comfortable by offering everything from practical care and pastoral help to massages and reflexology, which can give you a real boost when you're going through chemotherapy. Since *The Naked Truth* confronts the topic of breast cancer and its consequences, which had affected Mum and my family so directly, it seemed like the ideal vehicle for a fundraiser. So we went ahead and did it and it completely sold out.

There's a moment from our first charity performance of *The Naked Truth* at the Bury Met Theatre that will always stand out in my mind. It took place during Act Two, when my character becomes forlorn and you only understand the reason for it at the end of the play. She sits in the corner for a good five pages of dialogue, which gave me time to scan the crowd for my mum, who knew every line in the play by this point. When I found her, she was looking at the audience with the biggest smile on her face. It was an amazing moment for me, because she was literally beaming with pride. Theatre was such a huge part of her life.

That Christmas, I did panto at the Southsea Kings Theatre in

Portsmouth, which is a wonderful venue that's very close to my heart. In all, I've done three Christmases at the Southsea Kings and I'm now a patron there. Mum loved it as much as I did and often came down to see me there. She had a favourite seat in Row B of the stalls. There's now a plaque there that says, 'Always in our hearts. Theatre was a huge part of Cath Riley's life.' It's a beautiful, old, landmark theatre, so Mum will be part of history now, which is lovely. The arts meant everything to her.

One of the brilliant things that came out of doing *The Naked Truth* was that the writer Dave, his wife Diane, me and my mate Teresa (aka T) created our own production company, because we realised that between us we covered every aspect of the arts. Diane was a TV producer, T was a musical director and I was an actor who had begun to develop directorial abilities on the various tours of *The Naked Truth*.

I love performing, but my heart also lies with the production company, which I hope will feature hugely in the next chapter of my life. I know I can juggle the two. Producing is all about ideas and giving back, which is what makes it so stimulating. My dream is to take theatre to people who wouldn't normally think about going to see a play, because they think it's just about people wearing corsets and talking in old English. I want to create theatre that we can bring to a new audience, and in the process change their minds about what it is.

I'm talking about people who are staunch football supporters, both women and men, and women who go out with the girls every Thursday. They love *Big Brother*, which absolutely is theatre, if you break it down. It's planned and directed! The producers give the characters involved a topic to speak about. It's like a form of very commercial improv. My other aim is to promote new writing and playwrights. And I mean brand new writing – not just a modern take on a classic.

I went on to direct one of Dave's plays, a musical called *Pop Star The Musical*. It was about the corruption intrinsic to some reality shows and the script was brilliant, but it didn't work out. Still, it didn't put me off directing theatre and I definitely see it as part of my future. Although I think I'll always act, I can't help watching productions with a director's eye these days. I'll go and see a play and think, If only they'd done this or that! I may not be right, but I have strong ideas. I love concepts and doing things differently, although not in an Edinburgh Fringe way, I hasten to add.

In a gap between tours of *The Naked Truth*, I did another run of *The Vagina Monologues* in Leicester, Nottingham and Plymouth alongside Sue Holderness and Shobna Gulati. A year or so later, in 2009, I set off on a three-month stint of one-nighters with Sarah Jayne Dunn and my wonderful friend Sally Lindsay. This was my best and final run of the play, even though you don't have a life when you're touring from town to town.

Every single day was the same – structurally, at least. Meet in the lobby at ten past ten in the morning. Check out of the hotel. Get on the tour bus. Drive to the next venue. Check in to the hotel. Get back on the tour bus ten minutes later. Go to the venue to sound check. Eat your food. Do the show. Go to sleep. (Or in mine and Sally's case, have a bottle of rosé and go to sleep.)

We travelled in a long Mercedes van that reminded me of the

Scooby Doo bus. Behind the wheel was Charlie, our Rastafarian driver. Me and Sally sat right at the back like naughty schoolkids. Sarah Jayne and our understudy, Naomi, sat in the front. Oh, the fun we had! Me and Sally caused mayhem wherever we went. We found we had loads in common, including David Johnson, who had taught Sally at Stockport University. We also shared several friends and – at times – a very silly sense of humour.

Touring became my life. Getting back up to Bury for my day off became vitally important. When you're on tour, you need your day off. You need your own space and your own bed. It may sound trivial, but you want more than anything to wash your knickers. A lot of actresses take their laundry into the theatre and wash it there, but I can't do that. It doesn't seem right. Instead I carry around billions of pairs of knickers so that I never run out of clean pairs.

I overpack when I go on tour, because I need my things around me. Otherwise, it can feel like a very lonely life. You wake up in another Radisson hotel and they all look exactly the same. You have to roll over and look at the label above the telephone to find out where you are, because you've no idea. 'Oh, I'm in Bristol, am I?'

So, on Sundays, I wanted to go home more than anything. But there was a problem. I still couldn't drive, which made getting back from somewhere like Yeovil for the day nigh on impossible. In fact, in 2009, I only managed to spend a total of twenty days back in Bury. How mad is that?

Believe me, I have done my best to learn to drive. I've even passed the theory test. It's the practical side that's the problem, purely because I never seem to have time for lessons. To date,

I've had thirty-one hours of instruction, but there's been no continuity. It's been six hours one year and seven hours the next. I haven't had a lot of luck with my instructors, either. One guy told me off so badly that I nearly got out of the car and left him to it, just because I didn't realise that you're not allowed to use the horn to honk someone. It was all perfectly innocent. I was driving up Bury Old Road when I saw Granddad walking down to pay the newspaper bill. Well, I was over the moon to see him and I hit the horn several times to attract his attention.

'That's illegal!' the instructor yelled hysterically.

'Why?' I said. 'Granddad, look!' I yelled. 'I'm driving.' Granddad started waving back.

'Harrumph,' said my instructor, after he'd told me off. 'You'll be one of those drivers who fiddles with their radio on the motorway – and then anything could happen.' What sort of thing is that to say to a novice driver? Meanwhile, I wasn't any nearer to passing my driving test.

Before I knew it, I was back on the road again for another tour. I loved the work, but it was around this time that I started to feel small pricks of loneliness when I was alone in my hotel room at night and first thing in the morning. By now, most of my friends in Bury had been married for ages and already had or were having kids. When we went on a night out, all anyone seemed to talk about was sleep patterns, weaning, potty training and schools. The one exception was Flossie, who had been my mayhem friend forever, the mate I could ring at a moment's notice and say, 'Do you fancy coming to London this weekend?' Flossie would always share one more bottle with me when everyone else had got a taxi home. Like me, she is free and easy.

Then Flossie got together with Dan, another good friend, on my thirty-first birthday, when Samantha organised a barge trip from Macclesfield to Manchester and back for all our friends. We had a whole day on the booze barge and it was seriously good fun. It rained torrentially, which made it even more fun, because we were totally filthy and mud-splattered by the end of the day.

I was so happy when Flossie and Dan got together. OK, Flossie was the last of my closest single friends, but we could still have fun together. But then it wasn't long before Flossie was ringing me excitedly to say she was pregnant. That hit me hard, because I knew it meant that in some way I'd lost her. She certainly wouldn't be dropping everything to come and party with me any more. It also meant that I was the only one among my closest friends who hadn't settled down – and was nowhere near to settling down. When's my fairy tale going to happen? I wondered for the billionth time.

I had the occasional one-night stand on tour, usually with people in the industry. Sometimes I'd snog a random. But I hadn't had a boyfriend for years. My boyfriend was my suitcase as I schlepped here, there and everywhere. I was constantly alone. When I went to a fundraiser back home, I'd be the eleventh person on a table for ten with the five couples who were my nearest and dearest. It often seemed like I was the one having the best laugh, but I had to question my role in life. Am I here just to be the jovial, funny one? I wondered. The stereotype of the fat, happy person drives me crackers. I've fought against it all my life.

When you're in a hotel on your own, you have a lot of time to think. Is this it? I started to wonder. Just me, on my own, having to fill my day with this and that until it's time to go to the thea-tre? Am I going to be living out of a suitcase forever? Am I going to be alone for the rest of my life?

14

Don't leave me, Mum

When you're doing this tour and that tour, a year can fly past without you even noticing. Then you look back to find that several years have passed. I was still fun-loving, jolly Lise, but time was ticking on. I'm getting older, I realised, and I'm still not with anyone.

It started to get me down. It's not going to happen, I thought. How can I possibly meet someone on the road?

I was tired of dragging myself round the country. It felt like I was plodding, which I'd never done before in my life. Every day was the same: get up, have breakfast and hang around until it was time to go to the theatre. My heart wasn't in it and I started to let myself go. I'd get out of the shower and shove my hair in a wet knot at the back. I'd leave the hotel without putting any mascara on. I didn't bother with my clothes any more, which was unheard of for me. I usually tried to do a daily exercise class or put in an hour at the gym when I was on the road, but that all stopped. I piled on the weight.

I was longing for a boyfriend again. Looking round at other members of the cast who had boyfriends or husbands and kids, I'd wonder why it hadn't happened for me. Is it true? I wondered. Do men only want a size ten woman on their arms? The only time I've ever wanted to be slim was to discover how men would treat me. I'd still like to try it for just one day, just to see.

I wouldn't admit to myself or anyone else that I was unhappy. 'I'm fine,' I'd say, but I wasn't.

Mum tried to get me interested in my appearance again, but nothing worked. I think she was alarmed by how I let myself go, because Mum was a real class act. She wore lipstick everywhere she went. 'Get your bloody lipstick on!' she'd tell my Auntie Joyce. 'You don't leave the house without lipstick!' That was Mum all over, very finished.

Mum and Dad were worried about me. Eventually I admitted to Mum that I wasn't happy, but I was ready with an excuse: 'You can't have it all.'

I told myself that you can't have the mega career, the boyfriend and the child on the way. It doesn't work. Something has to give, and I was never willing to give the job up.

I'd done little bits of TV over the years, but I preferred doing theatre. So, even though it was lonely on the road, I kept on touring. In 2010, I went on tour with a genius play called *Waiting for Gateaux*, written by Ed Waugh and Trevor Wood, two Geordie writers who are passionate about theatre. *Waiting for Gateaux* is a satirical play about weight loss, but not in a *Fat Friends* way. Set in a slimming club in a church hall, with one cycle, one yoga mat, one exercise ball and one muscle stretcher on the stage, it's about four seriously dysfunctional people who come to the club more out of loneliness than a desire to lose weight. They're there to make friends and have a gossip, much like people at real slimming clubs, I suspect. There's definitely a dark side to the play, but it's also very funny and a real crowd pleaser.

It's a wonderfully clever piece. Its title makes you think of *Waiting for Godot*, and it was my character, whose husband is having an affair, who is doing the waiting – for gateaux. The phenomenal Sally Banks, genius Royal Shakespeare Company actress, played the team leader, who doesn't stop eating throughout the play. We toured for five months and everywhere we went, audiences and critics loved the play.

I was non-stop on the road in my early thirties. When I wasn't touring, I'd be doing a pantomime somewhere, living away from home. I loved the different audiences, but it was hard to fill the empty days in Yeovil or wherever. Some afternoons when you're on tour, the cast will go out shopping together, but there would be days when I'd think, I literally cannot go to Boots again, just for the sake of getting out of the hotel.

But when Mum came to visit, it was lovely to have the days free. It was great. We'd go round the shops, have a nice lunch or watch a movie and chat in bed together at the hotel.

After seeing us together, another actor said, 'I've never seen a closer mother–daughter relationship. It's almost weird how strong the connection is between you two.' Me and Mum leant on each other for everything. She needed me and I needed her. We wanted to spend as much time together as we could and Dad never minded. He was wonderful about it. 'I miss your mum telling me the stories about your little adventures,' he said the other day.

In February 2010, my beloved Poppa began to fade away. It was a rocky year for me and my family. It was difficult to see the patriarch of the family getting older and weaker. Everyone found it hard, especially Mum.

'The leaves need sweeping in your garden, Lisa,' Poppa said, eight days before he died of stomach cancer.

He had always liked to do things for me around the house. When I was away, he'd fix any bulbs that needed changing or do a bit of wallpapering. He'd see things before I did. 'One of the chandelier bulbs is out in the dining room. I'll sort it out while you're away,' he'd say. Now he barely had the strength to hold a broom, but he insisted on sweeping up my leaves. Me and Mum watched him sadly out of the French doors at the back of the house. Mum couldn't bear to see him crumbling.

Two days later, Poppa went into hospital. He went downhill fast and for the last four days of his life he floated in and out of a coma. I knew it was important to keep talking to him and we organised a roster of visitors to keep his spirits up. But the inside of his mouth had become sore because of the constant vomiting and as a result his speech was dreadful. Poor Poppa. I knew he would hate being cut off from his family, so I started a system of signals with him. Two squeezes meant he was happy. One squeeze meant he wasn't. If he was in pain I told him to squeeze my finger. Next I came up with an idea for a letter board, so that he could spell out words by touching the letters. We got this rapport going that meant we could communicate and suddenly everyone was asking me to translate. Even the nurses were asking what he was trying to say. I was the only one who understood.

The night before Poppa died, he wouldn't let me leave his hospital room. As other visitors came in and out, he kept reaching for me. 'Where's my Lisa?' I felt guilty at the thought of leaving him, even for a moment. I felt I couldn't even go home and have a bath, although I'd been in the same clothes for two days.

Then Uncle John and Betty arrived. 'Please translate!' they pleaded, so I felt I had to stay.

At one point Poppa said, 'Can we please hurry up, because I want to sort things out for the wedding.' Ever the family leader, he was thinking six months ahead to Liam and his girlfriend Nats' wedding, which was planned for the September.

'Don't worry, Poppa, we've got lots of time,' I assured him, trying not to cry.

The sister on the ward said, 'You should pop home for a little bit.'

In the end, I decided that I had to go, even if only for an hour or two. I rang Liam and Nats and asked them to take over from me. 'Uncle John is going to be here with Auntie Betty,' I explained. 'Mum needs to come with me and sleep for a bit.'

Liverpool had a big football match that night, so I set up the telly in order that they could watch it at the bedside. I explained Poppa's signals and how the letter board worked. 'I don't want Poppa to know I'm not here, so if anyone asks, say that Lisa's gone to the loo.'

It still makes me sad to think that I didn't get to hear Poppa speak for the last time. It's Sod's Law, isn't it? I'd done everything

I could – the signals, the signs and letter board – but when I got back to the hospital, he had stopped communicating. Luckily Nats was astute enough to write down everything he had said while I was away.

In his final hours, Poppa had a vision of his beloved sister Nelly sitting in the chair in the corner of the room. Apparently he said, 'Nelly's there and she's safe.' It's as if Nelly had come to take his hand and lead him to heaven. I love the thought of him leaving this world with his favourite sister as his guide.

I stayed with Poppa for the rest of the night. In the morning, it was just me and him in the room. I talked non-stop to him and gave him a running commentary of the sudoku I was doing. I was chatty and bubbly, but I felt broken that that I'd missed his last words. It mattered so much at the time and it still affects me. I should have been there.

Around lunchtime, a young trainee doctor came to see us. 'I'm not supposed to say this but your poppa's my favourite patient ever,' she said. 'I've never met a gentleman like him, or seen anyone keep their dignity like he has, right up to the last hours.'

The rest of the family arrived at about half past three and Poppa passed away at just gone six. At his funeral, I had reams and reams of Peppers coming up and thanking me for staying by his side in his final days, but all I could think about was the fact that in the two hours that I slipped away, I missed his final words.

Poppa's death hit Mum badly. She crumbled and during the summer of 2010 she had tests that showed changes in the status of her health. We couldn't help suspecting that her cancer was back. Until then, she had been doing brilliantly. Her check-ups had gone from being every two months, to every three months, then every five months and finally every nine months. She'd had the all-clear after five years, but now the oncologists organised a raft of tests for her at The Christie. She was due to have them shortly after Liam's wedding.

For the time being, we tried to forget about what the future held for Mum and focus on the wedding. My little brother was getting married! It totally brought out my controlling side. I said to him, 'Do you want party planners? Because I'm fine doing it.' In other words, Just leave it to me, please! I oversaw everything, until Mum said, 'You've got to step back! It's not your wedding.' We laughed about it, but we both knew that deep down I wished it was me who would be going down the aisle on that September day.

The wedding was amazing. We held it at the Bolholt Hotel, where I'd had my thirtieth, and it was the best wedding ever. Everyone drank and danced and laughed all day and night. You would never have known that there was anything wrong with Mum, who sat on the top table holding court, like she always did. I think she knew what was coming, but the rest of us hadn't caught on yet.

After the wedding, Mum's tests showed that her cancer was back. I was distraught. We all were. Nothing's going to take her away from me, I thought, but deep down, I had a horrible sense that history was repeating itself. Mum's mum had died young, of cancer. Now it was happening again.

On the flip side, Mum was very strong. She didn't say things lightly, so you believed her when she said, 'This cancer is not going to beat me.'

She had another lot of chemo up at Christie's and she lost her hair again. It didn't affect her anywhere near as badly as it had ten years before, though. She was still brimming with energy and fun. 'It's a walk in the park this time!' she kept saying. She was incredibly positive about it.

'It's not good, Lisa,' the oncologist told me while Mum was getting changed one day.

'OK,' I said.

I told Dad what the oncologist had said. 'That can't be true,' he said. 'She's feeling better all the time.' He was in denial and he stayed in denial for the next year and a half.

The chemo flatlined Mum's tumours, but it didn't shrink them. Later, the doctors discovered dispersions in her ovaries and pelvis. When they didn't suggest a hysterectomy, I knew that they were no longer planning to save Mum's life, only to keep her alive as comfortably as possible. I did panto in York that year, so that I could be close to home. My life revolved around Mum now. I wanted to be there for her as much as I possibly could.

Mum seemed well in herself and I suppose that lulled me into a false sense of security, so in early 2011, I went ahead and accepted the role of Ruth in *Calendar Girls*, a play based on the decision by members of the real-life Knapely Women's Institute to pose virtually naked for a calendar and raise funds for a cancer charity. The rest of the cast included Ruth Madoc, Gwen Taylor, Lynda Bellingham and Jennifer Ellison, so I was really looking forward to getting into rehearsals.

However, the process of *Calendar Girls* was not at all what I envisaged. As far as I was concerned, there was too much talking and not enough acting. We spent days and days sitting around a table with the director, nine-thirty to six-thirty, talking about the play and our characters. 'Can we please get on the floor?' I begged. 'I want to find this character and I can't find her just by talking about her.'

One evening, I rang Mum in floods of tears. I was crying my eyes out on the phone. Earlier in the day, we had spent more than four hours discussing the meaning of friendship and exploring how each member of the cast related to all the others. It made me feel hemmed in. We got on the floor in the second week, but by then I'd thought about it too much.

In my experience, you find a part by doing it. There's only so much talking you can do. If you can act and you believe in yourself, just go and do it but I'd started to have real doubts about my ability as an actress. I thought back to my Workshop days and tried to keep it simple.

Perhaps my approach has been shaped by several years of acting in a soap, where you might get a script change moments before you film a scene. You haven't time to think, Where's my back story? Where have I been? Being in a soap is a bit like playing by numbers, but you're still acting. You can adapt at the last minute because know your craft inside out.

Off we went on tour. Most of the other cast members had husbands or boyfriends. Lynda and Ruth even had their partners travelling with them, and Jennifer Ellison, who became my nearest and dearest on the job, had her husband Rob, who is amazing. Looking at the people around me highlighted how lonely I was, yet I wasn't sure what kind of relationship would be right for me. I knew I wanted someone independent, but I also felt I needed a lot of support. Was that too contradictory?

What's more, I couldn't see myself becoming a mother unless I was able to have the kind of relationship with my child that my mum had with me, which would mean giving up acting. But if I gave up acting, wouldn't I resent my child? It was all so confusing.

After years of loving theatre, I started yearning for some steady telly work again. I remember saying to my agent, 'I'd love a year in *Casualty* now.' But the phone wasn't ringing half as much as I wanted. I did a little bit. I did an episode of *Doctors* and joined *Waterloo Road* for four series, dipping in and out of the show between runs of *Calendar Girls* to play Tina Allen, one of the mums. Scout, my character's daughter, was a regular and they'd bring me in for four episodes of every series to cause mayhem.

'I think I've had enough of touring,' I told Mum. She soothed and comforted me every time I rang her in tears.

I didn't have a boyfriend and now the job wasn't doing it for me, either. It was sending me under and I became quite subdued. As I arrived at the theatre, I'd say to Jen, 'I can't be arsed today,' and when you're saying that, it's time for a change. That's not me. Can't-be-arsed doesn't flow in my blood. I felt confined. What next? I thought. Which box do I want to tick?

I confided in a director friend, Hannah Chiswick, who I had met years before when I was doing panto at the Stoke Regent Theatre. Hannah was now working at the Hull Truck Theatre Company in Hull, a highly respected company known for its quality productions. Being a commercial actress, I didn't think Hull Truck would be interested in me, but it turned out they were. Hannah asked if I would consider playing Sadie in *Little*

Voice, which happens to be a favourite play of mine. I'm also a big fan of Annette Badland, who played Sadie in the film. 'But I doubt your agent will take Hull Truck money,' she said. 'It's £490 a week with actor's union minimum and you have to pay for your own board.'

'You watch me!' I said. 'This is exactly what I want. It's not all about money. I've done the big jobs in order that I can do jobs like this.'

We did *Little Voice* for five weeks at the Hull Truck Theatre and then we took it on the road for five weeks. The whole experience restored my belief in acting. I loved it so much. The writing was incredible and I never tired of listening to the other actors while they were on stage. Helen Shields, who played LV's mother, Mari, was unreal.

Over the time I worked with Hull Truck, I became good friends with an actor whose father passed away during the run. I remember thinking, How on earth can you go on working when your father has passed?

He even came to work the night his father died. It seemed unbelievable. 'I couldn't do that,' I said to one of the other actors.

'Maybe not. It's down to the individual,' he said.

I know I couldn't. Yet I really admired him for carrying on.

I was pleased I'd been in *Little Voice*, because there was a lot of respect for the production and we got great reviews in papers like the *Daily Telegraph*, where I don't usually get a mention. Afterwards, with a sinking heart, I went back to *Calendar Girls*. Don't get me wrong – I never took work for granted. I knew that I was fortunate to keep getting jobs, considering how many actors are unemployed. When the chips were down, I never sat at home festering and wondering when the phone would ring, because it always rang. Even when I tried to take three months off, a job would come in and I'd jump to take it. There's definitely a part of me that hungers for work and being around creative people. It's obviously something I need. Still, at this point I had to resign myself to being a touring theatre actress. If this is what I've been put on this earth to do, I thought, then I've got to go with it. That's why when the phone rang offering another run of *Calendar Girls*, I took the job.

Around this time, a magazine that I won't name approached me offering to pay for me to have a gastric band operation. In exchange, they wanted photos of me before, during and after the procedure. Yes, before, *during* and after. How sick is that? I turned them down flat. It was offensive. OK, I had put on a lot of weight in my thirties, but so what? This is me, this is who I am, I thought, after I sent them packing. I'm different and people need to get over it, because it's OK to be different. In a way it did me good to be reminded of that.

Far and away the highlight of 2011 was the birth of Liam and Nats' son, Mum's first grandchild, my beautiful nephew Jakey, in September. Now, I'm not good with babies from birth to nine months because they don't do anything, but I doted on Jakey from the moment I first held him in my arms. I'm so glad that Mum got to see him. Her eyes used to light up whenever she was with him and he brought the biggest, happiest smile to her face.

I'd rush home whenever I had a day off and Mum was sometimes still well enough to come to me. One afternoon we were lying in bed in my hotel room watching *The Help* together when she said, 'I'm going to close my eyes for a minute. I'm tired.' That instantly told me that her illness was getting worse, because it was unheard of for Mum to nod off halfway through a film. I took her hand and clasped it in mine. 'I can still hear it. I know the story,' she kept saying, but she missed a good fifty minutes of the film.

Mum took a huge turn for the worse on her birthday, 10 January 2012. We all saw a massive change in her. She began suffering from constant vomiting, which caused dramatic weight loss. It was agonising to see. I was careful to avoid most of the 'how to deal with cancer' sites on the internet, but I found the Macmillan and Cancer UK sites very helpful, because they tell you the truth. Every patient is individual and every case is different, but from what I was reading it looked as if Mum could go quite quickly. Still, she kept fighting. 'I look in my babies' eyes and I'm not going into no coffin,' she used to say.

I'd done panto again at Christmas and then I went back to *Calendar Girls* at the end of January, which was hard, especially knowing Mum was so ill. I didn't want to panic Mum though by pulling out of the play. She never realised how poorly she was, right up to the end, and I wanted to keep it that way. But after a few weeks, I found I couldn't cope with the play, not least because its main topic is cancer. It was incredibly difficult sharing the stage with a character who dies of cancer every night, so I came out three months earlier than planned. I wanted to be with Mum every second of the day. Within a week of getting home, I moved her into my house so that I could care for her day and night.

Mum loved my house. She always said there was a real sense

of fun about it. I've even got a green room. The walls are green, the bedding is green, everything is green. It's completely kooky, so that's where Mum stayed, because she loves all of that. The nurses who visited every day loved it too. 'This house is bonkers!' they'd say.

Mum's personal nurse, Jo, used to time her visit so that she got to spend her lunch break with us and have some fun. She said it would set her up for the rest of the day. Mum was utterly different from all the other patients she saw. Even when Mum was at her most ill, she was taking the mickey and saying things like, 'You hurt me, you bugger, and I'll jab you back!'

It was the same at The Christie Centre when we went for checkups. 'Here comes Trouble and Big Trouble,' the staff would say when they saw us. They were amazing. They'd hug us when we arrived.

Mum always made them laugh. They deal with nothing but cancer, twenty-four hours a day, and all of a sudden they had this exuberant woman coming in and causing mayhem. She never moaned or whinged. 'Just give me a paracetamol, that'll do,' she'd say. 'Call me Cath! I don't like being called Catherine.' I was so proud of her.

Back at home, I took on nursing Mum because I knew it was what she wanted. I'm very proud that I was able to do that for her, to help her retain her dignity. It was a huge responsibility, but we had such fun. It was like playing doctors and nurses. I'd wake up, put her in the shower and we would role play from the start to the finish of the day. I'd walk into her room and say, 'Hello, my name's Ebony and I'm going to clean your wound today.'

I learnt so much about cancer during that time. If I went on

Celebrity Mastermind to answer questions on oncology, I reckon I would win. I could be a Macmillan nurse. Mum had sites in her neck and stomach where various tubes went in and I became expert in cleaning them. I did a tutorial at The Christie Centre so that I could change the pipe that drained off the fluid that kept building up inside her. That pipe caused all kinds of complications because it kept breaking and the site would get infected, but we got through it, laughing and joking all the way.

There's a rat called Fat Rat in the film *Ratatouille* and I had the soft toy version. That toy brought us so much happiness, because I put bandages on it wherever Mum had a wound. I made pipes out of cotton wool buds and stuck them into Fat Rat's neck and stomach. 'Mum, meet Mum. This is you,' I said, the first time I showed it to her. She thought it was absolutely hilarious. Every time Mum had a jab or a new site put in, so did Fat Rat.

'What are you doing?' the nurses would ask in astonishment.

There was one brilliant time when a supersonic doctor came to see Mum at my house. 'Doctor, thank you for coming to see me,' she said. 'But I'm not the patient. It's Fat Rat, over there.' She pointed to the armchair in her bedroom, where Fat Rat was sitting.

The look on his face! You could see he was thinking, What? You're pointing to a soft toy that's got plasters and fake tubes stuck on it?' We were crying with laughter as he examined her.

Inevitably I had major moments of frustration, when I'd thump things in the kitchen, thinking, Why Mum? She'd done nothing but good all her life and surrounded herself with beautiful, loving people. It destroyed me that I couldn't fix the situation. I had to accept what was happening, which was so, so hard.

In March, my agent called and said, 'Lisa, they want to see you for *Strictly*.'

'Really?' I was amazed.

Mum didn't seem a bit surprised, though. 'I've always said you'd be brilliant on *Strictly*! People need to see you dance.'

I had been approached several times about going into the jungle, but I'd always said, 'No, I don't eat bugs. I'm an actor. It's not what I'm about.' They were throwing thousands and thousands of pounds at me, but I wouldn't do jungle. *Strictly* was different though, or was it? I felt that some of the contestants – like John Sergeant and Ann Widdecombe – were simply there for people to mock. They were chosen to add a bit of old-time circus entertainment and there was an element of the bearded lady about them. Being a bigger girl, I knew full well that was probably the role I was being considered for.

I went to London for a meeting with the executive producers. I told them I could do the splits. I'm very supple for my size. When they asked if I had rhythm, I said yes. 'I can feel the beat. I'm not awkward and I've always loved going clubbing.' I had to admit that I had never ballroom danced in my life, though.

I was with them for an hour. 'I don't think I've got it,' I told my agent later.

I didn't hear anything for ages and forgot all about it. Then my agent had a call about a month and a half later to say that I was on the *Strictly* shortlist. I was surprised to hear I was still in the running. I hadn't stopped to think about it.

My life then was completely consumed with looking after Mum. I didn't even think about work. We had our daily routine that revolved around pills, bandages and tubes. Everything was Mum, Mum, Mum, the whole time.

There was a lovely girl who came in to give Mum her daily bath, but eventually I took over from her, because Mum preferred me to do it. She had lost a huge amount of weight by then. 'Look at me, doing a Posh Spice,' she'd joke. 'Don't bash my Posh Spice knees!'

I had to be really careful placing her in the bath. There was nothing there but bone. She looked like someone who had just walked out of Belsen. 'No lipo needed on these thighs now, Lise!' she'd say. She still took the mick all the time.

We never lost our sense of humour. It was Mum's wish that we referred to her cancer as 'cheesecake'. I used to tease her and Dad about all the 'cheesecake' in our family. Gran Pat, my nana and my poppa had all died of it. 'Thanks for the gene pool you've given me!' I'd say. That's what we're like in my family; that's our humour.

One night towards the end, I had some friends over and Mum shouted down for a yoghurt. She constantly needed sips of drink or spoonfuls of yoghurt, because the morphine she was taking dried out her mouth. 'Oh, shut up you whinge bag,' I shouted back. 'Anyone would think you were dying.'

My mates couldn't breathe for laughing. 'If that doesn't sum up the relationship you and your mum have, nothing does. It explains everything.'

In the last week of June, my agent rang and said I was on a shorter shortlist for *Strictly*. 'Mum, what does it mean?' I said. 'What's a shorter shortlist? You know, I think I could be in with a chance of doing it.'

'It's a given,' Mum said, laughing. 'You're going to get it.'

I had a feeling she was right, but did I really want it? Admittedly, my life was at a crossroads and my career needed a shake up. But would it work for me, or go against me? I wondered. Would it change my life forever?

A part of me was terrified at the thought. 'My partner won't be able to lift me,' I said to Mum. 'I'm too heavy. They'll have me on cables in the air.'

'Just do it your way, darling. Just be you and everything will be fine,' she said. It was the best advice.

Two weeks before Mum passed, my agent rang and said, 'They want to see you in London. They need to see you dance.'

I didn't hesitate. 'I won't leave my mum,' I told him. 'If I lose it, I lose it.'

Mum loved *Strictly* and we always watched it together. Poppa always watched it too. He was a huge fan of Brucie. 'Who's the gorgeous hunky dancer?' Mum asked. 'The one I love. He's one of the pros.'

'Robin Windsor,' I said.

'I hope you get him. Can you imagine being with him all the time? That smile! He was wonderful with Anita Dobson.'

Mum's illness didn't change her. She never lost her marbles. Even when she was having whopper injections at the end to help her fall asleep, she was still concerned with other people. My Auntie Joyce came round and she said, 'Joyce, how are you doing? Are you feeling OK?' She was amazing.

Towards the end of July, Mum was taken into hospital for three days. I stayed by her bedside day and night. There was no way I was going to leave her for a minute and I could tell Mum didn't want me going anywhere. I could see it in her eyes. 'No matter what happens, don't go!' I will never know what I was running on that week. One of the doctors said I was going a bit delirious because I was so tired. Thankfully, when Liam and Dad were there I could go into the family room and lie down for an hour or two.

Together with the Macmillan nurses, the doctors decided that we could bring Mum home. Dad and Liam were in denial about how poorly she was, but I knew that she could pass within a matter of hours once we left the hospital because you can't take the intravenous drip with you. The plan was for the Macmillan nurses to come in every fourth hour to give her medicine and change her dressings. We also had a night nanny system. I didn't need help with the practical side of things, but I wanted someone around in case Mum stopped breathing.

'We don't need her! I've got you,' Mum would say when the door went in the evening.

'No, Mum, she's for *me*. I'm going to need a brew sometimes if I'm upstairs with you.'

'Is it OK if you go and sit in my office and watch telly?' I'd ask the night nanny.

Mum left hospital on the Thursday and she was still going strong on the Saturday, joking away. She needed a lot of pain control and the nurses were fabulous. 'What's that jam they're mixing up for me?' Mum asked on the Saturday morning.

'They're going to give you an injection to help you fall asleep, so it doesn't hurt. I don't want anything to hurt you,' I said.

I did my best to comfort her in those last hours. That night, I told her, 'Poppa's up there with the biggest whisky and ginger in his hand to welcome you. And you've missed him, Mum. You turned when Poppa died. Your dad was your world, as are your children. We're all here.'

Around her bed, she had the people she loved most in the world: Liam, her baby; me, the apple of her eye; and Dad, who loved her every bit as much on the day she passed as he had on the day they married, if not more so. We stayed by Mum's bed throughout the Saturday and Sunday, laughing and joking with her, hugging and kissing her. She was her exuberant self right up until the end, which is extraordinary, considering what was happening to her body. It was absolutely proof of who Mum was.

Mum passed away in my arms at 7.27 p.m. on the Sunday night, 29 July. It was heartbreaking. I had lost my best friend in the world, my rock, the light of my life. I didn't know how I would be able to live without her.

Two days later, Phil my agent rang. 'Are you sitting down?' he said. 'They want to offer you *Strictly*.'

15

You. Can. Dance

'They want you in London today,' Phil said.

'You know I can't go. Mum passed two days ago. I don't even know who I am.'

'I explained that to them, but will you do me a favour? Will you ring one of the producers for me?'

I spoke to the producer. She was very understanding. 'We're so chuffed that you're on board. Welcome to the world of *Strictly*,' she said.

'Thank you,' I said vacantly. I couldn't take any of it in. I was going to be on *Strictly Come Dancing*. What did it mean?

My first instinct was to go and find Mum and tell her, but she wasn't at home any more, she was in the funeral parlour. I had left her lipstick with Lisa, our guardian angel there. 'Whatever you do, keep putting her lipstick on,' I told her. 'She'd go mental if people came to see her and she didn't have her lipstick on!' Mum always took a lot of care over her appearance and I knew she wouldn't want to let that slip, even after she'd passed.

I sort of forgot about *Strictly* while I focused on Mum's funeral. It was decided that I would write Mum's eulogy, which wasn't easy. Two weeks earlier, Mum had said to me and Auntie Joyce, 'If I die, which I don't plan on doing for a very long time, there won't be a spare seat at Guardian Angels Church! And whilst I'm at it,' she went on, 'there are not enough trees in England to produce the paper for my eulogy, so be warned, the pair of you!' She was spot on, of course. The church was packed to the rafters and, although I was supposed to keep the eulogy to five minutes, it ended up lasting for twenty-two. I was too broken to read it on the day, so my friend T read it for me.

A fortnight after Mum passed, I went to London for the first stage of *Strictly*. I was in a complete daze as I entered the huge dance studio at Battersea, in South London. The celebs were all given Bruce Forsyth masks to wear as they went in, to add to the mystery around the 2012 line-up. No one knew who the other contestants were, although there were rumours going round in the press and they got a few of them right. We went upstairs to find all the pro dancers waiting for us in a room. I looked around to see who else was there. 'Denise Van Outen, fantastic! Look, it's Michael Vaughan! Wow, that's Nicky Byrne from Westlife!' I was a little bit excited when I spotted Nicky Byrne, who turned out to be an absolute dreamboat. I thought, I've seen you in concert, but I'm never going to tell you, because it's not cool! It was amazing to see Colin Salmon too, and Johnny Ball, bless him, a face from years gone by.

We met all the pros and then started dancing one on one,

switching pro partners. It was a bit like speed dating, except we were dancing, watched by a group of executives and Karen Bruce, the choreographer. Over the next three days, Karen switched us all around and gave us different routines. She and the producers had an idea of who they wanted to partner everyone with, but they were still piecing together the jigsaw.

After about half an hour, we had a break. I started chatting to Robin Windsor on the fire escape, where I went to have a fag. We hit it off immediately. He's camp, I'm camp and I love all the camp banter. 'It's all about wearing a vest, is it?' I teased him. He found it really funny. You're fabulous, I thought. The sun was shining and I felt happy for the first time in ages. The other person I instantly got on with was Dani Harmer. She's a bit younger than me and something about her brought out my mothering instinct. I know I've got a friend for life in Dani, which is lovely.

On the second day, I was out on the fire escape with one of the associate producers, when he said, 'You're the talk of the professionals. They're saying you're not what they thought you'd be. You can dance.'

'Can I?' It was high praise and I felt deeply humble.

'Yes, and you're keeping up,' he said.

Of course I can keep up, I thought. Why would I not be able to? Then the penny dropped. People put you in envelopes, so if you're bigger, they think you'll be unfit and wanting to sit down every twenty minutes. That wasn't the case with me. I had energy to spare. Also, when Karen Bruce gave us a new section to learn, I found I could pick it up quickly.

On the final day we did a dance circle that included a lift with each dancer. Oh no, I thought with a sinking heart. Please don't let this go wrong. My great fear was that they would have to do things differently with me, because I was heavier, and I didn't want that to happen. I wanted to go out there and do it exactly the same way as everybody else on the programme. I felt I had a right to do that. I had a lot to prove. I didn't want to be this year's comedic figure.

'No one's going to be able to lift me,' I said to Dani. 'It's going to be embarrassing.' I was scared. I imagined everyone apart from me flying up into the air.

They put me with Robin first and he lifted me sky high. 'Oh my God, you got me off the floor!' I said breathless with excitement. 'Thank you, thank you!' I felt like Jane to his Tarzan.

We did the circle again and this time Brendan Cole lifted me off the ground, no trouble. I loved Brendan for that. He was very charismatic too. When James lifted me up, I loved him for it as well, but when I got to little Vincent, I said, 'Babe, you're smaller than me. Let's not even go there!'

'I don't want to give you a hernia,' I told Anton. 'Let's just do a twizzle.' And I wouldn't try it with Pasha, because I fancy Pasha a little bit and I didn't want to look an idiot.

They were all lovely, but it was Robin's personality that I was most drawn to. We couldn't stop giggling together. On the second morning we had a fitting for shoes and I said, 'I'm not wearing the ones with ankle straps. I'll do myself a disservice in those!' It really made him laugh.

'I love your accent,' he said.

'What's your accent?' I asked. 'Are you really from Ipswich, because you sound Australian.' When he said he'd picked up the intonation in his voice while living in Australia, I said, 'Nah, you're just putting it on, aren't you?' We constantly had a cheeky banter going.

There were cameras everywhere and we were being watched all the time. The execs sitting on high chairs at the back of the studio were suddenly seeing *Will & Grace* before their eyes. Since they hadn't envisaged me and Robin together, the jigsaw they were planning had to be rethought.

'Who would you like to be partnered with?' I asked Robin.

'I'd really like Kimberley,' he said.

'That would be great,' I said. Kimberley wanted him too, as did Victoria Pendleton and Fern Britton. He was hugely popular.

The next stage of the process was to shoot a teaser for the show: 'Coming soon to BBC One ...'

This was the first day I got *Strictly*fied, with fake hair and massive lashes. We tried on different dancing dresses and everything sparkled. It was all giddy. I wore a pink dress for the shoot and I had half pink hair and a load of extensions. It was completely thrilling. There was no argument that I was having the best time of my life, although it was obviously the worst time of my life as well, because I'd just lost Mum. But after everything I'd been through in the previous few months, I could feel myself opening up and having fun again.

Then came the pairing show, when we would be told who our partners were. Afterwards, the show was scheduled to come off air for three weeks while each couple trained intensively for their first dance. The pairing show rehearsal was the first time we saw the *Strictly* set. Every single person said, 'It's a lot smaller than it looks on TV!' I've worked in TV all my life, but I heard myself saying it along with everyone else.

The other thing we all said was, 'Isn't the judges' table a bit close to the dance floor?' I spent ages trying to find the number 10 paddle underneath the table. I really wanted to have my photograph taken with the 10 paddle.

As we rehearsed, I was hit by one of the most powerful bouts of nerves that I've ever experienced. I can't begin to explain how strong it was. The routine we were rehearsing was quite simple, but I was a wreck. I think it's because I'd suddenly realised I was part of *Strictly*. It was such a massive thing.

The line-up had been officially announced now and every paper I picked up seemed to have something negative to say about me. They were all predicting that I'd be voted out first. The expectation was that I'd be the joke figure of the series, the one who couldn't get her feet around the steps. The internet forums were saying the same thing about 'her from *Emmerdale*'. Part of me thought, Fine, I will probably be going after a couple of shows, but I'll have fun in the meantime.

Another part of me thought, You just wait! I'll show you.

I had a panto in Southsea booked to start in December and I rang the producers to reassure them that I'd be starting on time. 'The *Strictly* final is on 23 December and so contractually I need that day off, but I'll be out well before that, so it will be the only day I can't perform.'

'No problem, we'll put an understudy on for that day,' they said.

The day of the pairing show arrived. You were allowed two guests in the audience at each show and I invited Sam and Kate, my best, true heart friends. 'If Mum can do anything tonight, she'll give me Robin,' I told them. 'But Robin wants Kimberley,' I added.

Robin has since told me that he was hoping he didn't get me or Jerry Hall. Meanwhile, I was hoping that I wouldn't get Anton because he was the one who usually partnered the comedy characters. It's a standing joke that he never gets past week eight.

Me, Jerry Hall, Denise Van Outen and Kimberley Walsh made up the final group of contestants to be paired. On the staircase, were Anton, Pasha, James and Robin. First up was Kimberley.

Bruce said, 'Kimberley, you'll be making sweet music with …'

I waited breathlessly. Would it be Robin?

'… Pasha Kovalev!'

Wow, I was still in with a chance! I sneaked a look at Robin. He was still smiling, so maybe he wasn't too disappointed that he hadn't got Kimberley.

Next it was Jerry's turn. Bruce said, 'Jerry, you'll be strutting your stuff with … Anton Du Beke!'

Breathing a sigh of relief, I caught Kate and Sam's eyes in the audience. 'Wow,' I mouthed at them. It was my first step away from being a Widdecombe.

Now it was my turn. I stepped up to join Bruce with a pounding heart. Please, please, please let it be Robin! I thought.

'Now then, the dancer you'll be enjoying life with, Riley, is …'

Please say Robin Windsor! I thought. I had nothing but admiration for James Jordan, the other professional still standing on the staircase, but me and Robin had a special connection – and he was my mum's favourite too.

Finally Bruce said, '… Robin Windsor!'

'Yes!' I yelled, thrilled beyond belief. Gorgeous, funny and kind, Robin was my dream partner. I was on cloud cuckoo. He ran over to me, lifted me up and span me around, kissing me on the cheek and looking every bit as happy as I did.

But once we'd gone up the stairs, Craig Revel Horwood said bitingly, 'Robin Windsor, good luck.'

'What did Craig mean by that?' I asked Robin.

He shrugged. 'Just what he said, I think.' He was thinking the same thing, I later learnt. He went home to his partner Davidé and said, 'What on earth am I going to do with Lisa Riley?'

We shot the *Strictly* opening titles the following day. It was a real laugh, because we played on the idea of me being with the body of Adonis and his six pack. Me and Robin got on brilliantly and found we had loads in common. We had that music conversation, the one that I always start with, 'I love Motown and musical theatre ...'

'Fantastic, I love all that,' Robin said,

'I don't really like grunge or what I call Glastonbury music. I'm the queen of pop.'

'Me, too,' he said with a laugh.

Everything changed for Robin when we did a shot where we had to walk towards the camera looking straight into the lens. Robin did a move called the Cuban walk and I followed his lead, mimicking him exactly.

'Jesus Christ!' he said.

'Have I done something wrong?'

'No, quite the opposite.' Later, he rang Davidé and said, 'This is going to be fine. She can move.'

It was time for us to start our intensive training, so we booked a rehearsal room. By now we had been told that we'd be dancing a cha-cha to Aretha Franklin's 'Think', which was really exciting. However, I also had another commitment to fit in to our agenda, which involved travelling to Greenock in Scotland for two weeks, where I was due to film my character's dying scenes in *Waterloo Road*. Surreally, a mere four weeks after my own mother had died in my arms, I had to play a mother dying of tuberculosis with her daughter by her side.

Obviously, I found it very hard. I did a lot of crying in my trailer because it brought back Mum's passing every time I went over my lines. The stage direction was, 'She takes her last breath.' All I could think about was Mum. I knew exactly what happened when someone took their last breath. Very recently I'd seen it for real, so it was very, very raw.

'I know what I'm doing here,' I said to the director. 'I've just been through this, a month ago.'

Kate, who played my daughter, was brilliant. She's so mature for her age. 'You'll learn as an actress to use stuff from your life,' I told her. 'You'll bring it to the table when needed, for certain roles. This, more than anything, is the time when I'm going to thank my mum, because I know how it happens.'

The scene seemed a bit overwritten, because they had to include certain facts for the storyline. I wanted to get it right. There's nothing worse when someone's dying on screen than the actor speaking the words and then falling back on the pillow. 'We've got to cut this down,' I said. 'The final scene should just be about her death, so let's dissect what you need me to say and put it in the scene before.'

The director went with everything I suggested and we put all the stuff about Tina and Scout's mother–daughter relationship into another scene. There was a lot to explain. My character feels she has been a bad mother and is full of regrets. She is in Scotland to say sorry and ask for forgiveness. 'But when I get better, we'll get that flat I promised you,' she says. In the deathbed scene, she frantically asks, 'Where are you?' When she sees Scout, she says, 'You shouldn't be here. You should be at your exam. I want you to be a teacher.'

My last line was, 'I want you to make me the proudest mother …' Then it cuts to the monitor screen, which flatlines. The crash people come in and give her a shot and then the camera stays on Scout, who is missing a crucial exam to be by her mother's side.

The day I filmed that final scene was one of the most bizarre and painful days of my life. In the morning I was practising my cha-cha with Robin and in the afternoon I was dying. It was especially weird because I was using my recent experience with my mum for work. What on earth is going on with my life? I thought. It was crazy and confusing to have to replicate Mum's death. I asked Mum for her help getting through it, because by then I'd started talking to her in the ether.

I've never had a reaction to my work like I did when the episode was aired, many months later. All my family and friends felt the agony of reality that I'd put into it. I hadn't told anybody that the character was dying because it had to be kept secret contractually. People kept saying how moving it had been. I was chuffed with that.

When my friend T rang, she was crying that much down the phone that I could barely hear what she was saying. 'I've never seen you die before. It was so real,' she sobbed.

259

'Bless you! But I've not died. You're talking to me now,' I said gently.

Life felt as if it had gone back to normal while I was filming *Waterloo Road*. You can't phone people when you're filming, so it didn't feel strange that I wasn't on the phone to Mum ten times a day. The penny hadn't dropped that she wasn't there.

I had warned my friends to leave me alone for a little bit, because I desperately wanted to get on with *Waterloo Road* and *Strictly* without breaking down. 'Don't ring me,' I'd told them. 'I don't want to be asked if I'm OK. I'm fine.' They respected that. I had to get on. I knew it was what Mum would have wanted. She wouldn't have wanted me crying in my pillow.

My rehearsals with Robin were going well, I thought. It could have gone either way and I was scared. So I was like putty in his hands. 'Show me what you want me to do and I'll do it to the best of my ability,' I told him.

He couldn't believe how much energy I had. I told him that Dominic Brunt had always been amazed by my energy levels on the set of *Emmerdale*. 'With Lisa, what you see at six in the morning is exactly the same as what you see at six in the evening,' Dominic says. 'She never, ever runs out of battery.'

Robin kept saying, 'Do you want to sit down?'

'No, I'm fine. Shall we carry on?' No one can understand how I'm the size I am, because I'm always on the go.

Robin came up with a wonderful routine that we both believed in. We agreed that it would be funny to spank my bum in front of Craig Revel Horwood's face. It would be one in the eye for Craig, because he'd so nastily said, 'Robin Windsor, good luck.' We also continued to play with the idea of Robin as a sex god.

Actually, as far as I was concerned, Robin *was* a sex god. He was in vests the whole time, which was wonderful, and I was the envy of the country, because I got to stroke him 24/7. Everyone wants a piece of Robin, but I literally had him for nine hours a day and then afterwards at the hotel socially. I was in my element.

I'd hear myself asking him, 'Can I please just have one feel of your thighs?'

He took advantage of my slavish adoration. 'If you don't get this right, you can't have a touch today,' he'd say, his eyes twinkling. It was like he was bribing a little doggie with a treat. One day, I was struggling with a section of the cha-cha called the drag, where I stroked him from shoulder to ankle. After we'd tried it for four hours, he said, 'If you don't get this bit right, I'm cutting it out.'

'I'll get it right, no problem,' I said, and I did. God loves a trier.

My first videotape was hilarious, because I was just being myself, and me and Robin were mucking around. We were getting on insanely well, having a riot. At one point I said to him, 'Don't worry, I'll lick the sweat off your back!' A bit later we were practising the drag down his body and I turned to the camera and said, 'My job's really hard!'

Every now and then, I'd look up and say, 'Look what I'm doing, Mum. Look at me!' I genuinely believed that she was guiding me through everything. When I mastered a section I'd been struggling with, I'd say, 'Look, Mum, I've done it.'

It was especially hard to cope with her absence because this would have been the proudest time of her life. Talk about taking a kid to a candy shop – if she'd been alive she would have insisted on watching every minute of my rehearsals with

Robin. I kept thinking about how she wouldn't be seeing me live on *Strictly* dancing the cha-cha. My mates got lots of tearful phone calls from me, despite promising myself and them not to call. 'Why is she not here?' I'd say tearfully. It seemed so unfair.

About ten days before the first show, we went into the BBC to look through costumes. There were racks and racks of what I call 'thimble dresses' and not much else. I need a lot more fabric than that, I thought in a panic. I don't show my thighs!

By then, our routine was decided, if not polished. 'But we need an ending,' Robin said. There were two lots of eight counts to get to an end tableau, as it were. We could have used props or staging, but he didn't want to. 'I just want raw dance,' he said thoughtfully. 'I can't think what to do.'

I thought back to how Mum had told me to do things my way. 'How about I lift you?' I suggested.

'Don't be ridiculous,' he said. 'Look, leave it with me tonight. I'll think it through. Certainly you can't lift me.'

'I had to lift my body weight every night when I was pole dancing in *The Naked Truth*,' I said. 'I am very, very strong.'

'Are you really?'

'Try me. Jump on my back.'

He did. 'That was quite easy,' he said. 'But you're not lifting me. This is the world of structured ballroom where the woman has to be ladylike.'

'Where is the written rule that the woman can't lift the man?' I asked.

'Look, it just doesn't happen!'

He went back to Davidé that night and said, 'She must be

mad.' But then a bulb went on in his head and he thought, Why not? Why can't we?

He came into rehearsals the next morning and said, 'I love your zest for life. You have an energy that's unbelievable. I went home and doubted everything. I thought, Is she crazy? She's going to lift me? But maybe it could work, you know.'

I jumped up excitedly. 'Let's be different!' I said. 'Let's make this about us. I haven't conformed for my whole life. My mum *never* conformed. Why do I have to conform just because I'm doing *Strictly Come Dancing*? I don't. *We* don't.'

'I love you!' he said. 'What are you thinking?'

'How about I run to you at speed at the end of the routine?' I suggested. 'We'll make it look like you're petrified. Then we hold the beat, one shrug, up, pop, and I'll catch you.'

'You can't do it! It will kill you. You'll fall over.'

'Let's try it,' I said. 'We don't know until we've tried it.'

'You're unreal,' he said. 'I've never met anyone like you in my life. But let's simplify it. Let me jump on your shoulders from behind.'

'No, that's boring! If I'm going to catch you, I want to catch you on my neck at the front.'

Robin looked aghast. 'That would be very difficult. Let's try on the hips.'

I was adamant. 'I want your bum on my boobs,' I insisted. 'If it's not on my boobs, it's not the end frame we want.'

He laughed. 'You blow me away.'

First we tried it on my hips. 'Come on, let's go a bit higher,' I said.

'No, I'll lock round the waist,' he said. He didn't think that I could hold him any higher than that, but I knew I could.

Three days before the live show, we shot the routine for what was known as a director's cut. It was only to give the producers a sense of how we were doing, so we did it in training gear and I wasn't wearing any make-up. I hadn't seen my frock yet. I didn't have a clue what they had in store for me. Would I get a thimble dress and look a bugger, or would they cover me up completely?

The following day, we were in the rehearsal room when Robin's phone went. He came away from the call smiling like a Cheshire cat. 'You've obviously had some good news,' I said. 'What is it?'

'Nothing.'

'Tell me!' I insisted.

'OK, but don't say anything. They've just watched our director's cut tape and the entire office stood up and clapped.'

'Wow,' I said.

Little did I know that word had been getting back to the office from the camera crew that was trailing us. 'He shows her something and she picks it up straight away,' they were saying.

'We've been given a slot on the Saturday show,' Robin said. That put the pressure on. The Saturday show was the one with by far the highest viewing figures.

He didn't show it, but he was nervous about our first show, because he didn't know how I would react to dancing live on TV. Would I be thinking, Oh God, thirteen and a half million people are sat at home watching me! Would I forget the entire routine?

'I'll still be going home after the first week,' I said, resigned to my fate.

He smiled. 'I think we'll be safe the first week. It's when we get to the ballroom that we'll be tested,' he said. We had already tried some ballroom steps together, without much success, so we knew it was going to be an uphill struggle. I started feeling more and more nervous.

On the day we went in to do the first camera rehearsal, I instantly noticed that Robin was wearing a yellow vest. 'Why are you wearing that?' I asked.

By now, I'd spent a lot of time with Robin, but so far everything had been fun, fun, fun. We talked a lot about fashion, because I love clothes and he's very funky and trendy. I had instantly picked up on the fact that his vests were his trademark, but I also knew his tastes quite well. One thing I knew for sure was that yellow would never, ever be on his colour palette.

He looked sorrowfully down at his vest. 'I've been so busy that I haven't been able to do any washing,' he explained. 'I was scrabbling around this morning to find something to wear and I found this. I got it on holiday with Davidé. I've never worn it before.'

'Yellow's not your colour, is it?'

He smiled. 'I don't think I own anything else that's yellow.'

'OK, thanks,' I said, instantly welling up. I went over to the corner of the room and poured myself a cup of tea.

He followed me. 'What's the matter?'

'Nothing,' I said, smiling through my tears. It's just a little sign that everything is going to be OK. It's brilliant. Mum's made you wear that today.'

Robin knew my mum had passed away, but he didn't know a lot about her at this point, and he certainly didn't know her colour was yellow. It tripped him out, because he never usually wears yellow. I truly believe that it was Mum saying, 'Everything is going to be fine.'

Thinking about Mum really helped me on the night of the show. I'm not sure if I could have got through it if I hadn't felt she was there at my shoulder, guiding me. My nerves were unreal. I was drowning in nerves.

Thank God for distractions like stocking shimmy, I thought. Stocking shimmy is an amazing iridescent spray that makes your legs look like they've got stockings on.

'Is it OK to put stocking shimmy on your legs?' someone asked as I was getting ready.

'Yeah, whatever,' I replied breezily, not knowing what on earth it was, but willing to give anything a try.

'I've got stocking shimmy on,' I told Amanda on the phone. 'Check my legs out when you see me dance!' As I say, it was a brilliant distraction, as was the phenomenal blue crystal encrusted, knee-length dress they had selected for me to wear, and the huge fake eyelashes. I sparkled all over and it felt fantastic. But would I be able to dance? That was all I could think about as we were called to the stage and took our positions on the famous staircase.

Unless you've been a contestant on *Strictly Come Dancing*, you could never know how it feels to hear the theme music start up. The music tells you that you are minutes away from D-Day. It's horrific, the most nerve-wracking sound you could imagine. But I had Robin by my side and my mum looking down at me and they both gave me the strength and courage to go out there and do my best, just as I had determined to do from the start.

And lo and behold, we nailed it. When Robin was sure that

everything was working and we had the audience on side, he did the final lift exactly how I had originally pleaded with him to do it, which is why the most famous picture in *Strictly* history shows us with his bum on my boobs.

The whole thing went by in a blur. One minute, thirty-seven seconds of the most pumping adrenaline high ever. As I held Robin in my arms, the entire studio gave us a standing ovation. The judges were gushing with their praise. 'Three words, darling. You. Can. Dance!' Craig Revel Horwood said.

From that moment, my life changed forever.

16

I've been Strictlyfied

I will never forget Sunday, 7 October 2012, the day after my first *Strictly* appearance. It was one billion per cent amazing on every level. I felt like everybody was talking about me. I was on the cover of every newspaper. It sounds crazy, but I felt like Kate Middleton as I walked to Euston station in the morning. Truly, I did.

I'd watched the Royal Wedding on television and, like everyone else, I was entranced by the moment when all of those hundreds of thousands of people outside the palace were chanting 'Kiss, kiss, kiss!' at William and Kate on the balcony. I remember thinking how incredible it was that this girl who'd had a very normal life was now the most loved and adored creature in the country. Now something similar had happened to me. I'd had my very own fairy-tale moment. It was total insanity.

I was walking on air as I made my way through the London streets with two of my best mates, Lizzie and Amanda, who had been my guests at the show. I'd barely had a chance to speak to them or Phil, my agent, the previous evening. They had spent three hours sitting on a couch in the BBC bar, watching in amazement as people dragged me here and there.

'I'm sorry!' I mouthed at them.

'Don't worry,' they mouthed back.

People kept surrounding me and saying, 'Wow! Do you understand what you've done?'

'No,' I kept saying.

At one point I caught Robin's eye and whispered, 'What's going on?'

Then my phone went. It was my dad and he was crying. 'I'm so proud of you,' he said. 'Your mum would have been so proud of you.'

It took everything in my power not to break down. 'Thank you, Dad. I love you so much,' I said. 'Tell Liam I love him. Kiss Nats and Jakey for me. I'll see you tomorrow.'

Then Antony rang. He was so emotional that he had trouble getting his words out. 'I cannot tell you how much I love you,' he said. 'Do you know what you've done? Your life will never be the same again.'

'That's what everyone here keeps saying. What do you mean? How do you know?' I asked. I didn't know what everyone was going on about.

'I'm telling you, babe, I know,' Antony said. 'You're going to win this.'

Apparently, the bookies thought it was a possibility, too. Overnight the odds on me winning *Strictly* went from 88/1 to 6/1. One minute and thirty-seven seconds of dancing had changed everything.

I was in a daze on the train back to Manchester the following day. Robin kept texting me. 'Have you seen this picture? Have you read this article?' Everywhere I looked there were photos of us doing our catch at the end of the cha-cha. On the front page of the *Mail on Sunday*, there was a photo of me doing a pose with my knee up. Oh my God, I thought, I look like Cha Cha DiGregorio from *Grease*! Yes, from Kate Middleton to Cha Cha DiGregorio in one morning – that's how mad that Sunday was.

I felt proud as anything. I've shown you! I thought, as I remembered all the nasty tweets and negative newspaper and online forum comments. You judged this book by its cover, because I'm a bigger girl and you've only ever seen me looking like a minger in the roles I've played. Then, all of a sudden, I've surprised you by appearing in a sexy, beaded dress, with my hair all done and make-up to die for, dancing a cha-cha to the best of my ability.

It was my dancing that made the difference. It was a dancing show, after all. I could have been funny in the videotape and looked sexy on the night, but if I'd gone out there with two left feet, or been dragged around the floor like a Hoover, people would not have reacted in the way they did. Twitter was on fire with comments about how surprised everyone was. All kinds of compliments were being bandied about, including a couple of bonkers marriage proposals. It was hilarious.

During the week that followed, me and Robin trained up in Manchester. One afternoon, I went off to do a photo shoot and on my way back I popped into Tesco in Bury, half forgetting that I was still done up to the nines, with the full socket eyes, the crinkled hair and wearing a lovely outfit.

I bumped into Antony in the vegetable aisle. 'Oh my God,' he said, looking astonished.

'What?'

'You look amazing!' he exclaimed.

'It's smoke and mirrors, babe,' I said, almost apologetically. 'I've come straight from a photo shoot and I'm getting some supper for tonight.'

'Lise, I'm telling you. I have never seen you look so good.'

When we met up in Manchester later in the week, he kept saying to Robin, 'Thank you! It's just what she needed. I was sick of seeing her with her hair in a wet bun.'

He turned to me. 'You should always get your hair blow dried. You're Lisa Riley!'

It was then that I realised how much I had let myself go while I was schlepping around the country on tour. Your gay friends want you to be their princess, but for years I had been anything but a princess. Since I'd given up on finding Mr Right, I didn't think it mattered all that much whether I took care over my appearance outside of my job, but of course it matters. It's incredibly important. Now that I was dressing up and wearing make-up for the show, I started getting excited about clothes again. It helped that beautiful designer outfits kept arriving for me at the BBC. I felt very lucky and I vowed never to let myself go again.

It killed me that I couldn't ring Mum and tell her about everything that was happening to me. My grief and sadness hit me so badly during that week, it was horrific. A hundred times a day I wanted to tell Mum about all the different ways my life was transforming and getting better, but she wasn't there. She couldn't see how I'd become a princess overnight. She wasn't around to gasp over the beautiful clothes that kept arriving for me, or laugh at my stocking shimmy. That hurt so much. I was so sad that she couldn't share it all with me, because she would have had a ball. She would have adored Robin and all the other people I met during the series. She would have loved my costumes and dances. I missed her so much it felt like my heart was bleeding. And yet I was having the time of my life.

Robin was the most amazing support. He could always tell when I needed to take a break and have a cry over Mum. Sometimes it would suddenly hit me like a baseball bat and I'd crumble before I had the chance to excuse myself and run off to the loo. Robin knew exactly when to offer me comfort and when to back off. He was completely brilliant and seemed to understand what I was going through.

We were practising hard to master his Viennese waltz routine, which we would be dancing to 'Never Tear Us Apart' by Paloma Faith, an absolutely beautiful song. We toyed with various ideas when we were asked to come up with a theme for our set and then I said, 'Over the years, I've done panto after panto where I've either been the Fairy Godmother or the Wicked Queen. I'm never the princess and I'd like to be a princess, just for once. So, can I be Cinderella?'

Robin started laughing. 'That makes you my Prince Charming,' I added.

Well, I thought, if you don't ask, you don't get.

To my joy and delight, the producers went with it and let me be a princess, so I was set to fulfill my dream of playing Cinderella.

At last! I thought. I'd always imagined that my own personal fairy tale would involve Mr Right, but this felt every bit as wonderful. I felt incredibly lucky and privileged.

But first I had to learn how to Viennese waltz, which was far from easy. I couldn't get the steps. Robin tried everything with me and I started to get really cross with myself. I felt I was letting him down. We'd had this massive response to the cha-cha and now I was going to mess up the waltz and get egg all over my face.

Finally, I asked Robin if he could do me a favour. 'Would you mind dancing the routine with your feet being my feet, exactly how you want them to be, so that I can record it with my iPhone and practise at home?'

'What? Nobody has ever done it like that before,' he said.

'OK, well I'm just asking. Would you mind?'

'Of course not.'

That night in my lounge I mimicked my video of his feet until I knew the steps inside out. Robin was amazed the next day. 'What happened?' he asked. 'Did you eat a pile of Popeye spinach or something?'

'This is what happens with me,' I explained. 'Can't means won't in my book. I get so cross with myself that I have to find a way.'

'You have absolutely nailed it!' he said excitedly. After that I knew that I had a solution if ever I was struggling with the steps.

I didn't have the time or the inclination to learn all the correct dance terminology. Instead, I gave some of the steps my own names. We'd get to the studio and Denise would ask, 'Have you done a fallaway in your routine?'

'Robin, what's a fallaway?' I'd ask.

'It's what you call a wafty woo,' he'd say, much to everyone's amusement.

Robin still calls one of the main ballroom steps an elastic band, because that's what I christened it. To this day I don't know the correct name for it, but I always found it a struggle. After a while, we had our own little dictionary of dance terminology. Robin would say, 'Right, do two elastic bands, a washing machine and a wafty woo.' He was totally on my wavelength. I'd write down each sequence in my lingo, go away and learn it like a script.

Once I'd nailed the steps, it was time to work on my frame and posture. The big problem I had with the ballroom dances was that my boobs are so massive that it's very difficult for me to achieve a ballroom arch, which is essential in the promenade position. At one point, Robin had me with a pole behind my neck to correct my posture, but it didn't work. Nothing worked. Ballroom dancing didn't come naturally to me.

Despite this, my agent Phil had a phone call from the *Strictly* producers asking if I would agree to be part of the *Strictly Come Dancing* live tour in early 2013. 'You're the first celebrity they've asked,' Phil told me when he rang with the news. I couldn't believe it. I was over the moon. The producers believed in my dancing! What's more, it meant that my *Strictly* journey wouldn't end when I left the show.

Right now, though, I had to concentrate on my waltz. We didn't know the running order when we arrived at the studio on the Friday for our first rehearsal, so I immediately went to find Daisy, one of the gorgeous producers. 'Please, where are we in the order?' I asked.

'You're last.'

Oh no, I thought, feeling prickly with the pressure. It was going to be much harder to look good after everyone else had shown what they could do, especially as I knew the audience and judges would have far higher expectations of me this week.

It's an indescribable feeling waiting for everyone else to do their dance before you go on. It's the worst. I've never known fear like it. Time goes so slowly. You do your best to try to disguise how you're feeling and if anyone asks you how you are, you smile and say, 'Fine!' But you're thinking, You have no idea what is going on in my head and stomach right now.

All kinds of thoughts keep whirring through your brain. The greatest worry of all is that you will let your partner down, after all the work you've both put in. If I mess up, how will I get myself back into the routine? Will one step out of place wreck the piece? The answer is that yes, it probably will. You can't fudge the steps.

Thankfully, all our practice paid off. Even though I was the non-conforming princess, the chubby one, and Robin was my gay Prince Charming, we managed to bring a huge amount of romance to the waltz. My fairy-tale mind kicked in and I really went for it. It was like we were kids playing dress-up and I let my imagination run away with me. I was floating on a cloud of childhood dreams. Right at the end of the dance, a huge clock up on the stage struck midnight and away I dashed, Cinderella style, stopping to hold a wistful pose on the stairway. Then, as soon as the music stopped, I bounded back down the stairs, threw myself into Robin's arms and gave him a big smacker on the cheek. I felt so happy. We'd done it!

The judges' comments were brilliant. Unsurprisingly, Len said I had to work on my hold and Bruno agreed, adding that I needed to fight my tendency to try to lead Robin. But he also said, 'What I love about you is that we're always getting full-on entertainment.' That was amazing.

Then Craig said, 'I thought you danced that with great dexterity. I thought it was light … and graceful. But it's true that the man should lead, darling!' The judges gave us a score of 25 and the public voted for us in their millions. We were safely through to week three.

Our next dance was the jive, which was obviously going to be really upbeat. It was movie week and we thought hard about which movie we wanted to do, which genre and era.

'Who is your dream movie star?' Robin asked me.

'Actually, I want to be a pop star.'

He laughed. 'Only you would say that. You are so camp.'

'Can I be Madonna? Can we do 'Hanky Panky' from *Dick Tracy*, please?'

We put the idea forward to the producers and they said yes. 'Right I'd like Madonna's cones,' I said, getting carried away.

'That's not from 'Hanky Panky', you idiot.'

'I want the blond ponytail.'

'No! We have to stick to the movie.'

It turned out to be one of my favourite dances and I loved my look. My curls alone took two hours and fifty minutes to get right, which was crazy. Even madder was my costume. When we went for the try-on, on the Friday morning, I noticed a gorgeous beaded mini dress as I was looking through all the rails of costumes. 'That's nice,' I said to Vicky, who designs all the outfits. 'Is it Ola's?' I assumed it must be Ola's, because she always wears thimble dresses.

'No, darling, it's yours,' Vicky said.

Oh my God, I thought, gulping. They don't want to cover me up! I'm going to be wearing what the normal girls wear. It boosted my confidence to think that they wanted me to be sexy and thought I had the right to be sexy. It was an incredible moment.

It's funny to think how worried I had been before the show started about what they would dress me in. What had changed? I suppose I started going with the flow of the programme and thinking, Well, why can't I get my legs out? It's everything I believe in: you do what you want to do in life. That's how I've always been. Still, I never thought it would happen. It was brilliant.

Things went smoothly in the practice room and we arrived at the studios ready to sail through the Saturday rehearsals. What could possibly go wrong? Well, while we were practising the leapfrog at the end of the dance, I lost my concentration for a second and forgot to bob my head down as Robin leapt over me, which meant that his meat and two veg whacked me in my nose and forehead. Ow!

Robin was in agony. He had to go and lie down in his dressing room with a little cushion over himself, bless him. He also banged his knee and thigh because he landed awkwardly, also my fault, so I felt absolutely terrible. He was in such pain that we weren't sure if he would be fit for the show. Understandably, he was quite cross with me for not putting my head down at the crucial moment. If I'm honest with myself, it was because we had been told that they would set off seven flares at the end of the leap and I lifted my head for a fraction of a second to see what they would look like. It was stupid of me. Luckily, he recovered in time to go on. I was so relieved.

I felt really sexy in my dress. Sexy beyond belief. So, when Jo was doing my make-up and suggested putting a black beauty spot beneath my nose, I said, 'Right, we've got the legs out, the boobs look phenomenal, this is the shortest dress I've ever worn in my life, so let's go for it. When in Rome ... let's go the whole hog.' So I had the beauty spot as well.

The jive went well and we scored 29 with the judges, which was amazing. We had another standing ovation from the audience and Craig said, 'That was brilliant!' I think Robin forgave me after that.

Afterwards, I told Tess Daly, 'I never thought my thighs would be on British television! I feel like a sex kitten.' I couldn't get over what was happening. I felt like the ugly duckling who had turned into a swan, the beautiful butterfly emerging from her dull cocoon.

Later in the day we began rehearsing for our first big group number, which we were set to dance the following week, Halloween week, to Michael Jackson's 'Thriller'. It was desperately exciting, because they brought an American choreographer in specially. He arranged us all in a V shape and put me and Kimberley right at the front.

As soon as I got the chance, I grabbed Robin and said, 'I don't want to be at the front. Why have they put me at the front?'

'Shut up and get on with it!' he said.

'But why?' I insisted, starting to get a bit panicky. 'It's just me and Kimberley.'

'Why do you think, you idiot?'

That was a real penny-drop moment for me. It dawned on me that it must be a reflection of how popular me and Robin were, and how much they believed in my dancing. I left the rehearsal thinking, Wow, the producers have faith in me. It made me more determined than ever to work my arse off. I wanted to get better and better.

There was a move in the routine called a tango break, which I hadn't come across before. When I heard someone call out, 'Tango break,' I thought that perhaps I had my own name for it, but it turned out that we hadn't covered it yet.

'What am I going to do?' I asked Robin, totally panicked.

'Don't worry. Just follow me.' That was the moment I began to let him lead, instead of trying to lead him, because I didn't have a choice.

Liam and Dad came to London to watch me jive and they stayed for the whole weekend. We had a lovely time together. I was very conscious of keeping Dad busy, because I knew from my own experience that the baseball bat moments – when my grief blindsided me – came when I stopped and thought too much. I didn't want that happening to Dad. I knew it was best for him to keep going and it helped me to know that he was OK.

I was so relieved when Liam and Nats decided to move in with Dad. He wasn't himself after Mum died and he would have been rattling around in the house without them. Still, not a day goes by when I don't hear a cold shudder in his voice when I speak to him. We joke about it, but it's painful at the same time. I'll say, 'Hi, Dad, it's me. I'm checking up on you,' or, 'Hello, it's your free therapy session.' I can always make him laugh. It's a family tradition to turn everything into a joke to try and lighten even the darkest moments.

I didn't show my worries or grief to the public, because I didn't want anybody to know what I was going through. It wasn't the side of me that I wanted people to see. The hardest part of it was that I kept wanting to say to Mum, 'Look what I'm doing! Look at me.' I believed that she was on my shoulders, guiding our success, but I longed to see her in the practice room. Please, Mum, walk in here now, I'd think. Had she been alive, she would have been sat there watching every single minute. It would have been the proudest time of her life.

Robin was always looking out for me, bless him. There were nights when we would finish at around seven-thirty and instead of rushing home, he'd say, 'Shall I come for dinner at your hotel?' He seemed to sense the times I didn't want to be alone for the entire night. He was a phenomenal friend, such a sweetheart.

Imagine the guilt I felt when I caused Robin an absolutely horrific injury during the rehearsals for Halloween week. It was the worst thing that had happened to him on *Strictly* and it was all my fault – again. We were dancing the Charleston to a song called 'Witch Doctor' by David Seville and the Chipmunks. Robin had choreographed a brilliant routine in which he played a geeky student and I was teaching him witchcraft. At the end of the dance, the big flourish Robin had dreamt up involved me flipping him up from the floor into a cartwheel and then sliding down his body. First, he lay on the floor on his back with his arms out and then I hopped into position and rolled forward, taking him with me.

It was an ambitious move. As Robin said, 'If you go for it, you go for it. If you half go for it, you will go wrong.'

And, boy, did I go wrong when I half went for it on the Thursday of that week. I lost concentration for one moment, mistimed my fall and tripped over my own foot, accidentally stabbing the heel of my three-and-a-half inch stiletto dance training shoe straight into Robin's arm joint on the inside of his elbow. That's a very tender part of the body and my entire weight was pressing on my heel. It was horrendous. I thought I'd done him lifelong damage and was beside myself with worry.

I could see he was cross. That's it now, I've buggered everything up, I thought. I was devastated.

Robin had a massive pro number to practise at the BBC that night. The Girls Aloud choreographer had arranged a funky routine and it was a big deal for the pro dancers, so it was awful for Robin that he spent the rehearsals struggling to lift his pro partner Christina because he was in so much pain. By the end of the week, he was still suffering. Nothing seemed to help, not even strong painkillers. We went out and did our routine live on the Saturday night and the judges were very positive about us, but Robin wasn't himself the entire night because of the pain he was in. His whole demeanour had changed. He was very withdrawn and I thought he wasn't speaking to me because he was angry.

Antony and his partner Peter were in the audience that night and I was crying by the time I met them in the BBC bar, I felt so bad. I couldn't bear the thought that I had caused Robin pain or upset him. I knew it was an accident, but it was my fault and it shouldn't have happened. What haunted me most was the look of utter shock on the camera crew's faces when they realised what I'd done. From where I was standing, I could see their reactions as it happened – it was like watching the whole thing in slow motion.

Robin went for a scan on the Sunday morning and it turned out that he had torn four tendons. I felt totally responsible and full of remorse. Would he even want to dance with me again? I wondered. I think he knew how worried I was about him, so being the gorgeous person he is, he and Davidé asked me to Joe Allen in Covent Garden that evening, where we put the world to rights over dinner. It was lovely. We talked about what had happened and he explained that his way of dealing with pain is to withdraw inside himself – and he had been in agony for days. I could tell that he had also been cross with me, but having dinner that night somehow made everything all right again.

When me and Robin were originally paired up, I wore a beautiful royal blue dress in the picture that was taken for the press pack. Seven weeks later, after training for nine hours a day, the wardrobe department asked me to wear the same frock for another picture, because it had looked so good the first time. It didn't fit me. There was a massive bunch of loose material on both sides. What's going on? I thought. It's hanging off me. Even though the room we practised in was walled with mirrors. I hadn't noticed how much weight had dropped off me. I'd lost three and a half inches off my waist and shrunk several dress sizes. After that, the costume people had to keep taking in my dresses.

It was now that the media became completely obsessed with my weight. All the interviews I'd done so far had focused on my size, of course. I can't count how many journalists tried to make me confess that I was unhappy with my weight. They'd needle me with questions, on and on, until they finally had to backtrack and admit that I am fine and very positive about the way I look. There was one journalist who had found me to be upbeat about my body image back when I was playing Mandy Dingle in *Emmerdale* but, meeting me again more than a decade later, she was sure that I wouldn't have been able to stay positive for all these years. 'But I have to hold my hand up and say that you are happy in your own skin,' she admitted. 'I've never met anyone like you.'

I totally clocked that the BBC press office kept organising my press interviews over the lunch hour. 'We'll do the shots of you dancing, half an hour before lunch break and then we'll do the chat while you're eating,' the journalists all said. 'Is that OK? Do you mind chatting while you're eating?' They clearly wanted to see me eat. Was I having a bowl of lettuce? Evidently I wasn't. I was still having creamy mushroom sauce on my pappardelle pasta and a Twix bar for afters, believe me. I think I was losing weight because all the exercise I was doing kicked my metabolism into a faster gear.

What the press couldn't do was go for the health angle. They always go on about obesity putting pressure on your heart, but it was clear that I was super fit. Apparently our Charleston was the fastest Charleston in the ten-year history of the show. Afterwards, I was standing talking to Bruce with Robin wheezing beside me like Muttley the Dog, and he's been a professional dancer since he was three, whereas I wasn't even breathing hard. No one could say I was unfit or unhealthy.

I was happy to lose the weight because it was different. Clothes started looking different on me. My face looked different. But that's all it was: different. The magazines began to run pieces showing before and after pictures and talking about 'Lisa's no-diet slim down'. I find the obsession with my size hilarious, but there's a part of me that feels like I'm letting women down by losing weight, because my weight is not important to me. I want to say, 'I'm just a person! I'm me and my size doesn't matter.'

What does matter to me is that I've been able to inspire people to feel good about themselves, especially the bigger girls like me. One day I tweeted that you can be sexy and be who you want to be, even though you don't look like Helena Christensen. Robin cried when we got a tweet back from someone saying, 'Thank you so much. My husband has fallen in love with me again.' I felt so proud that I was in a position to have such a positive effect.

17

Will I Make Wembley?

In week five, I started to have crazy thoughts about appearing in the live show at Wembley in week seven. I didn't tell anyone what I was thinking, not even Robin. It was my secret dream. I knew it was bonkers. After all, I hadn't expected to make it past week two. And yet Wembley was on my mind constantly.

One minute I thought, Maybe I can make it. Then I'd think, Don't be stupid! Little Lisa from Manchester, dancing in front of thousands of people at Wembley Stadium? As if! I couldn't help hoping, though. I couldn't help dreaming.

The first time Robin mentioned the possibility of going to Wembley was when I told him I could do the splits. 'Really?' he said. 'Go on then.'

There and then, I dropped into the splits for him. It was a trick I'd learnt while doing the pole dancing play, *The Naked Truth*.

Robin's eyes lit up. 'We'll save that for Wembley if we get there,' he said.

Wow, I thought. He thinks we might actually be in with a chance!

Determined to stay in the competition, I worked so hard it was ridiculous. There was absolutely nothing going on in my life outside the programme. I lived, ate and breathed inside the *Strictly* bubble. I didn't have a second to spare. I remember texting friends and saying, 'Please forgive me,' because I knew they were probably thinking, God, she doesn't even text back! Who does she think she is? I wanted to explain, but if I texted one, I'd have to text them all and a round robin text felt too generic. It was mad – I didn't even have time to worry about it.

The phones were always off in the practice room, but me and Robin got an app that made our phones flash if a family member was calling. I always answered when it was Dad or Liam. Sometimes Dad would ring in tears and then that would set me off. Dad was struggling beyond belief around this time. Everywhere he went, people wanted to talk to him about Lisa on *Strictly*, but Mum's passing was so raw for him that he found it hard. Often he rang just to hear my voice, because I sound a lot like Mum.

Every time I spoke to Dad, I'd be thinking, Oh God, I should be practising! Then I'd get upset, about Mum, about Dad, about everything. Robin never tried to push me on when I crumbled. 'Come on,' he'd say, 'let's break for half an hour.' He was amazingly patient and sympathetic with me, knowing that I was torn between my need to give Dad time on the phone and my need to practise.

Apart from speaking to Dad and Liam, I always found a few moments for FaceTime with my nephew Jakey every week. That was a big priority for me. I also managed to squeeze in a couple of phone calls to my mates, for late-night reassurance. There was a pattern to my calls, apparently, although I didn't realise it until we got together after the series had finished. I would phone Sam in a panic on a Tuesday night and say, 'I can't do this! I can't remember the steps.'

Here we go, it's the Tuesday night phone call again, she would think.

Samantha was my Tuesday call and then I'd ring T every Thursday. 'I'm going to be thrown off the show this week, I know it!' I'd say. 'Oh my God, I know for sure I won't make it past this week.'

Despite my worries and sadness, I hung in there, battling my grief. Robin was my main source of strength and encouragement. He was an amazing friend to me. The other contestants were lovely, too. Dani Harmer could make me laugh, no matter what, and Denise Van Outen was a huge support to me, in a strong, silent way. Denise always seemed to know when I was having a terrible day. It was like she was telepathic. She'd send a text saying, 'I'm thinking of you right now, Lise.' Or she'd come over and wordlessly give me a cuddle while we were in hair and make-up, as if to say, I'm here should you need me. On the staircase before we went live, she'd give me a wink and tap her shoulder, as if to say, 'Mum's there.' I appreciated it so much and I love her for it. She's a great person.

Next up was the tango, which meant that me and Robin had to knuckle down, because the tango is a serious, complex dance with intricate footwork. I was conscious that we'd only done one ballroom dance so far, and ballroom was difficult for me. All our other numbers had been upbeat, fast and funky, but we couldn't do the fun, fun, fun thing now. There was no messing around in rehearsals this week. We had to nail it. The atmosphere in the practice room was totally different, because the need to get it right and express the severity of the dance took some of the fun out of things for us, although we still had a laugh in our lunch break.

I felt I had to prove myself worthy of staying in the competition and I was worried I would look very exposed when I did the tango. I had a real fear of going home that week – and I was desperate to avoid going home. We worked our arses off in the practice room. As the days went past, I grew to love the tango for its passion. It was the one dance in which I fully played a character. I didn't smile once during the whole routine, which was a first for me.

Being Will and Grace meant that we were never going to be able to get down and dirty with our tango, so we did it our way, which is what we did with all our dances. Our video that week was all about how we couldn't be serious or overtly passionate, because we'd burst out laughing. There was a bit in the routine where we had to lock eyes and we couldn't keep straight faces. 'You're like three-year-olds,' Denise told us at the weekend. We had a reputation for being the pranksters on the show.

The press had gone insane and there were constant demands on us to do shoots and interviews. People wanted to read about us; photographers were always popping in to get a shot of us in the practice room. One day, I did *Lorraine* at 8 a.m., followed by a photo shoot until 11.30. I made it to the practice room by 12, but then I had to leave early to record *It Takes Two* with Zoë, so we only managed to fit in four and a half hours of training. *It Takes Two* finished at 7.30 and then I had another photo shoot until 11.30. Meanwhile Robin did the front cover of *Gay Times* that week, which was massive for him, and there was a lot of PR stuff to slot in between training and press. The sudden focus on us meant that we were being pulled here, there and everywhere. It was exhausting.

I mustn't get too tired, I thought. It's not the press stuff that's important, it's the dance. I have to get it right for Saturday night.

You have to realise what matters. It's all well and good doing press and it was probably helping us with the live show votes, but on the flip side, it's ultimately what happens on the Saturday night that decides your fate. You have to nail your routine, and this was a ballroom dance, which was always going to be harder for me.

We pulled off our tango, but only because Robin was so good at choreographing our routines to accommodate my size. He was wonderful. I struggle with the gapping side of ballroom dancing because my boobs get in the way and I can't get that line with my partner. On certain phrases of the routine you should be close and there should be no gapping when you do turns – and we had gapping. People didn't understand it was because my boobs got in the way and pre-watershed I couldn't say, 'It's because I've got big boobs!'

There was also the problem of my frame. I did countless exercises to improve my arch in the promenade position. Back at the hotel I'd lie on my back on the bed and go into the crab position to try to get more bend in my back. Several times I watched

EastEnders upside down. For another exercise, aimed at keeping my frame up, I'd soak two gigantic bath towels in the bath to make them really heavy and then I'd stand up straight with my arms stretched out and the towels draped across them. I often stood there until the pain was unbearable. It improved my frame, but I was a long way off getting the 'giraffe neck' posture that I needed.

Our tango went well on the night. The judges were positive about it and Darcey Bussell gave me a 7, which made my week. What's more, we were one step closer to Wembley! But Darcey also said that my footwork could have been cleaner and sharper, which made me determined to focus on my feet when it came to the foxtrot the following week. The foxtrot – or 'trot on' as I called it – is all about the footwork.

Barely pausing to take a breath, we plunged back into rehearsals. I never stopped working. Even at night, I'd be going over the steps in my hotel room. I wanted to impress Len more than anything, because he was always complaining about my technique. He'd say, 'You're light on your feet … you're wonderful to watch … you make everyone at home feel happy … but your technique …' and he'd grimace and start listing the places where I went wrong.

In training for the foxtrot, we focused on the heel turn, which is Len's favourite move. Once you've mastered a heel turn, you've won Len over, apparently. 'Come on then, Robin, let's put two heel turns in,' I said.

Robin loved that idea. 'Yes! If he doesn't notice the first one, then he'll definitely notice the second.'

The comedy was, I broke three pairs of shoes in training that week, because a heel turn involves putting your entire body weight on your heels as you turn on the spot, leaning back. In my case, that's a lot of weight!

We were working harder than ever in the practice room. We kept going at it, relentlessly, because we were both conscious that doing a good foxtrot meant getting through to Wembley week. Could we do it? I was determined to give it my absolute best shot. In order to improve my frame, Robin put me in a neck brace collar, which was another way of keeping my head up like a giraffe. We laughed so much about my toilet-roll neck.

The foxtrot took us back to what we loved, which was pure camp fun. We danced it to the Natalie Cole song 'This Will Be An Everlasting Love' which I was flattered to hear has since become a favourite for the bride and groom's first dance at weddings. It was a fantasy moment for me to come down the staircase like a Broadway star. Robin was in tails and a top hat and I wore a top hat and black dress with white cuffs. I felt super confident that week. After all our hard work, I knew we were going to dance a great foxtrot, and we did. Every backbreaking moment of practice paid off. It was far and away my favourite dance of the series.

'Feet on fire!' Bruno yelled at the end. 'Talk about showbiz pizazz! I thought you were going to do a Liza Minnelli number. It was pure Broadway.'

Craig was also very complimentary. 'As always, impeccable timing. Ferocious footwork, darling,' he said. Was I hearing right?

'Wow, Lisa, you have worked hard on cleaning up that foot-work,' Darcey added. She thought it was my best ballroom dance by far.

And Len? What would Len say? I held my breath. 'For me, I don't know about the X factor, you've got the F factor: good foxtrot, good footwork and fun!'

Well, that was the cherry on the trifle. I started bouncing up and down with elation. I couldn't help myself. When the scores came in, each of the judges gave us an 8, so our total was 32, our highest score yet. I instantly knew what that meant, even without the public vote to confirm it. We were going to Wembley! I was indescribably happy. My dream had come true.

It was an amazing week for me, because a couple of days later Phil had a call saying that Craig Revel Horwood wanted me to star in a show he had written and was planning to direct. 'You what?' I said to Phil. 'Craig? Are you sure?' I knew Craig had changed his mind about me since he had made his scathing remark after I was paired with Robin, but this was an unexpected development.

Craig needed someone who could dance and act, because he'd had an idea for a play called *Strictly Confidential*, which would give audiences an insider's view of *Strictly*, as well as ballroom and Latin dancing. Why me? Well, I could act, he believed in my dancing and he loved my attitude, so he felt that he'd found the right person to star in the show. His plan was to build the show around my experiences of *Strictly*, as well as the ups and downs of my life to that point. Pro dancers Artem Chigvintsev, Ian Waite and Natalie Lowe were also set to be in the cast and the plot would include autobiographical elements from their lives too. I was amazed. It was a huge honour to be asked to appear in a production with some of the world's best ballroom and Latin dancers.

I was very flattered that Craig wanted me to be a part of *Strictly Confidential*. It's the ultimate compliment when someone says they think your story is strong enough to build a two-hour show around it. It also gave me great satisfaction to think that I'd proved Craig wrong about my ability to dance. I happily said yes to his play. It was yet another thing to look forward to, after the *Strictly* arena tour. I loved the fact that I was going to go on dancing well into 2013.

But first, the live show at Wembley. Yes, Wembley, Wembley, Wembley! I gasped when I saw the auditorium. It was ginormously enormous! I'd always wanted to be a pop star and now I felt like Beyoncé, J-Lo and Madonna all in one.

The remaining contestants in the series apart from me were Denise, Dani, Kimberley Walsh, Nicky Byrne, Michael Vaughan, Louis 'Lou-Lou' Smith, Victoria Pendleton and Richard Arnold. There was a real closeness between us once we all knew we were going to Wembley. We were in this thing together and we were all doing well. Since we had two massive group numbers to rehearse, one for the Saturday live show and the huge *Grease* medley for the Sunday, we started spending a lot of time with each other.

I was excited about dancing the samba to 'Car Wash' by Rose Royce, because it was a totally upbeat number, which was what me and Robin did best. 'Will I be doing the splits?' I asked him.

'Of course. When in Wembley, do it big,' he said, laughing.

Doing it big was in his mind when he suggested bringing in two hunky guys to lift me into the air at the start of the routine. He knew all about my fears around being lifted. 'You will be lifted, my darling, you will be lifted!' he said excitedly.

I've seen the footage showing the moment Robin's dancers first lifted me up and carried me forward in rehearsals. My little face is a picture of joy. I was being lifted, at last. Fine, it took two boys, but it put me on a par with the other contestants. It was another dream come true.

We also had another drama that week, when Robin went down with horrific food poisoning after eating a dodgy tuna melt one lunchtime. Poor Robin, he was so ill! Artem had to replace him in the practice room for a day and a half. I missed Robin, but it was nice training with Artem, especially as I knew we would be dancing together in Craig's show *Strictly Confidential*. We did loads of work on my arms, which I enjoyed.

I was glad when Robin came back, though. It meant I could collapse in a dead faint in his arms when we were told that we were opening the show at Wembley. What? OK, I didn't collapse in a dead faint, but it gave fear a whole new meaning for me. It should have instilled me with confidence, because the producers trusted us to open the show, but instead it filled me with terror. Christina, Robin's pro partner, said that in all her *Strictly* experience she had never seen someone look as scared as I did before we went onstage.

I experienced so many different emotions that amazing night of 17 November, at Wembley. Two hours before I went on, I met up with Dad, Liam and Nats in the friends and family room backstage. 'I've never been more proud of you in my entire life,' Dad said, giving me a big hug. We both had tears in our eyes, thinking of Mum.

Standing in the queue into the venue, Dad had heard people

saying, 'I can't wait to see Lisa and Robin!' His pride kept build-ing and building inside him until he was in turmoil. All evening he had this vision in his mind's eye, of me aged six, singing along to T'Pau's 'China In Your Hand', pretending to be a pop star. Now here I was at Wembley.

'Dreams do come true, they really do,' he said. Oh God, it took every drop of strength I had not to break down there and then.

I was so, so nervous. I was used to performing live, but I had never in my life stepped out in front of so many people. The pressure hit home as I stood on the huge Wembley stage wait-ing for our samba routine to start. I'm a big girl, but I felt tiny in front of that massive audience, wearing nothing but a bright orange and pink mini dress. All I could hear was people scream-ing our names. Thousands and thousands of people chanting, 'Lisa! Robin! Lisa! Robin!' It was mind blowing.

The music started. Here goes, I thought. The crowd roared and cheered as I was lifted up by the hunky guys Robin had drafted in. It was exhilarating on every level. The audience kept cheering and calling out all through the dance and they went mad when I went into the jump splits at the end. The atmosphere was completely wild. If I could bottle anything and sell it to the world, it would be the feeling I had as I listened to six and a half thousand people clapping and stamping and yelling at the end of our routine. It was the best feeling I've ever had in my life. The entire audience were on their feet. The whole of Wembley shook.

The noise was deafening. Bruce could not do his opening link because the entire audience was shouting for me and Robin. You could see the floor manager going mad. It was unbelievable. Me and Robin started crying because of the immensity of the emotion. To say I was overcome is an understatement. Till the day I die, I don't think I will ever feel that pure, pure emotion again. Obviously we all learn new emotions as we get older and experience new ups and downs, but I'm certain that nothing will ever compare to that. You just don't have moments like it in your life – well, not if you're me, anyway.

Why on earth are we so popular? I kept thinking. It was wonderful and confusing and brilliant, especially knowing that Dad, Liam and Nats were sat in the front row, watching me. I'm in tears every time I think of it. Sometimes I find it hard to believe that it actually happened. I was so lucky to be there.

Eventually the noise died down enough for Bruce to introduce the judges. 'My darling, you were funky, frisky and frothy!' Bruno said, getting up to wave his arms about enthusiastically. 'Your personality shone through the whole performance.'

People were still shouting and screaming our names. It was hard to take anything in and I was having trouble containing my excitement and amazement. I was incredibly grateful to have Robin's strong, steadying arm around me.

Craig spoke next. 'It was big, darling, it was bold and it was beautiful.'

'I'm glad you saved those splits for Wembley,' Darcey said.

'The performance level is great. You make everyone feel fabulous,' Len said.

Wow. I was totally dazed by it all. Robin gave me a squeeze and led me off to Tess's area, where the judges' scores came in:

32, again, our joint highest score! It couldn't have been any better.

In the function room afterwards, my big, strong brother was welling up despite himself. Nats gave me a huge hug. Dad said, 'There's no sponge big enough in this world to soak up how I'm feeling now.'

I was in tears again when Craig turned to my family and said, 'This girl is so special.' None of us could find anything to say to that.

Meanwhile, Denise was sitting opposite us with her family. Her mum came up to me and she was so beautiful in what she said about me losing my mum. At one point, me and Denise sat there smiling as we listened to our parents talking about what they'd just witnessed their children doing onstage. It was really special, all thanks to *Strictly*. I went back to my hotel on a total high, feeling proud and happy.

'Did you see me up on that Wembley stage?' I asked Mum, as I talked to her in the ether, just before I went to sleep. 'Can you believe it, Mum? Cos I can't!'

18

My life's changed for ever

The high of performing at Wembley lasted for days. Being a part of *Strictly* was brilliant in every way and Wembley was a massive layer on the trifle. People started coming up and saying, 'You can win this, Lise,' but I didn't take them seriously.

I think it irritated Robin a little bit that I didn't feel competitive. He comes from an incredibly competitive world and not only did he start to believe we could win, but he wanted to win, whereas I just wanted to be accepted. I wanted people to see that I could move and I wanted to break down all the barriers that the press had put there with their comments about me being too big.

The following day I was on the front cover of three national newspapers, this time doing the splits. Where once they had tipped me to lose and lose badly because I was big, now they were saying, 'This girl! Is there no end to what she can do?' I couldn't help flushing with pleasure.

I still do the splits every now and then. Usually when me and my mates are having a drink in a bar. 'I can do the splits,' I'll say to a group of lads.

'Yeah, whatever,' they say.

'Bet you a fiver I can.'

'All right.'

Then I drop into the splits. It's pure comedy value for me and my mates.

There was no time to bask in our samba success however, because it was back into the practice room on the Monday for more relentless training. This week we were dancing the rumba, the dance of love. It didn't warrant our usual big, funky, camp treatment, so we took that edge off our dancing and made it more serious. We chose a song from *Sunset Boulevard*, 'As If We Never Said Goodbye' by Barbra Streisand, and I focused on using my acting skills to give it a *Sunset Boulevard* feel. It felt special to be dancing to Barbra, who has been my idol since I was young. My mum played Barbra throughout my childhood, so her voice and music have beautiful memories for me.

I wasn't feeling the best that week. I don't know whether I was run down, but I somehow picked up conjunctivitis and was sent to a posh doctor's on Harley Street. The comedy that came out of that visit was priceless. The doctor put luminous dye in my eye to help him examine it, with the unfortunate result that I cried neon orange for the rest of the day. I was often crying at that time – either through sadness or when Robin made me giggle so much I couldn't hold back the tears of laughter. It was an extreme time. We were practising this passionate, sexy dance and Robin couldn't even look me in the eye, because I was crying orange.

I felt confident about my rumba, because I was totally on top of the steps. So I didn't feel as nervous as I usually did when we went into the studio to rehearse, and when I went for my costume fitting, I liked the orange dress I was set to wear. But then I had a change of heart. When I looked at myself in the mirror after being fully done up, the dress suddenly felt too tight and clingy. There was no flow to it. Who am I trying to kid? I thought. I look like an orange sausage!

Robin picked up on my worries immediately. 'There's something the matter. What is it?' he asked.

'I'm fine!' I said quickly.

'No, you're not. What's the matter?'

'Well, do you like my dress? Do I look OK? You've got to tell me the truth,' I asked.

We were that in sync with each other by then that he went straight to the wardrobe department without even consulting me. 'I'm sorry, but we need to change Lisa's dress. She's not happy,' he told them. Within forty minutes, the wardrobe department had cut the dress up and added more fabric, to make it more floaty. I felt so much better – and so grateful to Robin.

I adored dancing the rumba live and felt I'd done well. Afterwards, the other pro dancers said that technically it was my best dance, but the judges didn't pick up on that. They didn't like it and they went for the gullet. They probably wanted to bring me down a peg or two after Wembley and, by God, did they?

It seemed that they wanted the whole camp thing from our routine again and yet that doesn't suit the rumba. 'It wasn't exciting, so I can't get excited about it, unfortunately,' Len said. My heart sank. It was a massive disappointment.

Bruno said that he'd been expecting something a bit more fiery. Darcey and Craig were also downbeat. 'This isn't your dance, sadly,' Darcey said.

My face said it all as they were giving their comments. I was devastated, because I felt I had used my acting to portray real emotion as I danced to the music of my idol, Barbra Streisand. My performance couldn't have been more me if I'd tried. I also felt that it had been one of my best dances technically. The final stance was hard: I had one leg in the air as Robin span me around on the ball of my foot. I'd been desperate for Len to say something about that move, but he didn't.

I felt deflated when we went into Tess's area. We're in danger, I thought. But, thankfully, the people at home picked up their phones and we were saved by the public vote. I was always grateful to people for voting for me. It meant so much.

After rumba week, I started worrying that we'd be going home soon. Of course, I didn't expect everything to be plain sailing, but I wasn't expecting the judges to take the wind out of my sails quite so dramatically, either.

I was determined to pick myself up and march on, Pepper style. Unfortunately, quickstep week turned out to be the week from hell, because me and Robin both got chest infections. We were both on antibiotics and missed a whole day in the practice room. The quickstep isn't called the quickstep for nothing. The speed of it uses all of your lung capacity, and yet when we were at our worst that week, we were having trouble just breathing.

Aware that the judges' reaction to my rumba had knocked me

off my perch, Robin did something special for me in quickstep week. He went to the wardrobe department and said, 'This week, we dance in yellow.' He hadn't forgotten that it was Mum's favourite colour. It was a beautiful thing to do. It shows what kind of man he is.

We had a major panic before the live show. Because we'd missed so much practice time, I still didn't know the routine on the Saturday morning and they had to give us our own studio to train in, so that I could get on top of the steps. My chest was starting to improve slightly by then, but Robin was getting worse. The medicine wasn't working. He was coughing and wheezing. He couldn't breathe. He felt so ill at one point that he started crying. I was really worried about him. I was relying on him to get me through and it was scary to think he was only about twenty per cent fit. The fear of messing everything up was overwhelming.

Robin was feeling the pressure too. In Tess's area before we went on, he kept telling himself, 'It's just a minute and a half, that's all.' He was willing himself to get through it.

Unfortunately, it was a minute and a half of top-speed quickstep, so it was insane. On the upside, we were dancing to the Morecambe and Wise signature song 'Bring Me Sunshine', and we'd put a little Morecambe and Wise tribute into the routine by kicking up our heels every so often. It was brilliant to be allowed to dance to that song. It meant so much to me, even though Robin had no idea who they were!

'That's what you bring to this show every week, a bit of sunshine,' Len said afterwards. 'It was fast, it was fun. I bet you Eric and Ernie are looking down cheering you on. Well done!'

That was the best compliment I had on *Strictly*. I was totally gobsmacked by it.

I felt weak and ill and made loads of mistakes during the routine, so I didn't warrant a score of 31. I even slipped at the end and dive-bombed behind the sofa where I was meant to be taking my final position. Added to this, it was Robin's jinx week, because he had never got into the quarter finals before, so we were elated when Tess shouted our names out on the results show. 'We've done it!' we yelled, hugging each other, and then we broke into another round of coughing.

Robin began to recover towards the end of the weekend and we were back in the practice room working harder than ever on the Monday. We had a particular challenge ahead of us, because this week we had to fuse a Latin and a ballroom dance. It was the first time this had been done on *Strictly* in the UK. We decided to combine a tango and a cha-cha, which wasn't going to be easy. 'Have you guessed what we're going to do at the end of the cha-cha?' Robin asked, his eyes twinkling. 'I'm a big boy and I'm going to catch you!' So we recreated the catch at the end of the cha-cha that made us so famous, only this time it was the right way round.

It was at this point in the series that I started to feel exhausted, less because of the show itself than everything that goes with it. Every week there seemed to be more press and more filming to squeeze into our schedule. As much as I was loving it, the time kept whizzing along and we never seemed to have got anything done. Almost every day I'd look at the clock and think, Oh my God, it's half two! Please rewind and make it half ten again. We've not got enough time to learn the routine.

In previous weeks, I generally knew my routine by the Tuesday. Now, the time frames were changing and it was scary. To make things worse, we couldn't make a certain section of what we called our 'cha-chango' routine work, because of my body shape. It was the part of the routine where the tango fuses into the cha-cha and I couldn't get in front of Robin's body for a crucial move. 'Sorry, babe, we're going to have to lose that move,' he said.

Oh no, it's Friday! I thought. I was worried I wouldn't get to grips with the new move in time. I had a strong sense that this would be my last week on *Strictly*.

More than ever before, I felt I needed my mates from Bury. 'Girls,' I said when I rang them. 'I desperately need you all in the audience this week. Sam, Kate, Amanda, Lizzie, Sara.'

'You're adamant, aren't you?' they said.

'Yes, because I'm going home. It will be a miracle if we get through this week.'

They all came. I was so grateful. I've got the best friends in the world, I thought, as I winked at them all from the staircase before I went on.

I made some quite big mistakes in the routine. As I'd feared, I had a total blank when we got to the section we had changed at the last minute. 'I'm sorry,' I said to Robin afterwards. I was devastated. My original cha-cha had changed my life forever. Now I had buggered it up.

After you've gone through Tess's area, you go down the stairs and burst through a door, where a camera is waiting to capture your reaction to the judges' comments. They call these shots 'the door burst' and there's a famous picture of me from fusion week looking totally dejected and downhearted. I definitely didn't burst through that door. I felt like I'd gone a step back and I don't do that. It's not what I'm about.

When it came to the results show, I was one billion per cent convinced that I was going home. I looked at Kate and Sam in the audience and waited for the news that I would have to dance against another contestant to win a place on the following week's show, in what's known as the dance-off. But my name wasn't called. Instead, Denise and Nicky Byrne and their partners had to battle it out.

I couldn't believe it. I started screaming Robin's name over and over again. Then I jumped that far into the air that my microphone came unhooked from my dress and ended up dangling between my legs. I am forever indebted to the British public because that week, people voted for us in their millions.

We were over the moon to reach the semi-finals. Words can't express how brilliant it was. I felt it was an incredible achievement for both of us: for me, because no one had expected me to survive beyond the first few weeks of the competition, and for Robin, because he had steered me through choppy waters and several storms and helped me shine as a dancer with his wonderful choreography and steadfast patience.

We had to learn two dances for the semis: the salsa and the American Smooth. What can I say? It was a huge amount of work! In fact I was practising so hard that it felt like I was becoming delirious. In the middle of the week, I arrived at the practice room and saw what looked like my nephew Jakey's pushchair through the door. My brain was so overloaded that at first I couldn't work out what was going on. What is Jakey's pushchair doing there? I wondered. I shook my head. Don't be stupid, Lise! I thought. You're seeing things.

But I wasn't seeing things, because the *Strictly* producers had brought Liam and Jakey down to London for a surprise visit! I totally lost it when I realised they were really there. Seeing my brother and darling baby nephew was just what I needed after this major rollercoaster I'd been through. I'd had FaceTime with Jakey, but I hadn't held him in my arms for all the time I was in *Strictly*. It was wonderful to be able to hug him and shower him with kisses. Even though I was tired and preoccupied with the two dances I had to learn, it somehow recharged my batteries.

In the end, I picked up the two dances pretty quickly. But although I'd nailed the floor spin in our salsa rehearsals, I completely mistimed it in the live show. I lost my view of Robin for a moment and I ended up in a bundle of mess on the floor, which was a bit embarrassing. Still, we pulled off the handstand, which was fantastic, and we ended up with a score of 31.

Now for the American Smooth. They had told us we could choose any musical theatre and we'd picked 'All That Jazz' from *Chicago*, an absolute all-time favourite of mine.

'Are you ready for this?' one of the producers said to me. 'We've had this idea. We're going to put your name in lights on the stage.'

My heart started thumping. 'What? I'm just a girl from Bury,' I said. How could life get any better? It was every little girl's dream to see her name in lights and, at thirty-six, it felt exactly as it would have done if I'd been four years old. It was fantastic. The letters were massive and my name dominated the set.

I loved our American Smooth. I was very proud of it. But I

didn't have any illusions about staying in the competition. When it was over, I hugged Robin and said, 'I'm sorry, but thank you.' I knew. He knew. We were going to find ourselves in the dance-off and I'd be going home, because whoever I was up against, there was no one I could beat.

Although I scored 31 in the salsa and 32 in the American Smooth, it wasn't enough to avoid having to dance against Denise and her partner James. 'How are you feeling?' Claudia asked me, before we danced the American Smooth for the second time.

'I'm going to go out there with Robin and enjoy every single minute of it, just like I've enjoyed the whole series,' I said. And I did. I went for it and loved every second of it.

After Denise and James did their dance, it was down to the judges. They called it on pure merit, which is right and proper. I was going home and it was the right time to go, because the four best dancers were left in the competition.

Denise, James, me and Robin had a group hug. 'There's no one I would prefer to go out to than you,' I told Denise and James.

Tess called me and Robin over to speak to her. 'The judges called you "our people's champion" and you've been one of the most popular contestants we've ever had on *Strictly*,' she said. 'How has it been for you?'

The crowd was going mad, cheering for me and Robin, and I was overcome with emotion and gratitude. 'It's been the best time of my entire life and I can't thank you all enough,' I said, tears pouring from my eyes. 'I've had the time of my life.'

At that moment, my mind was full of Robin and everything he had done for me over the course of the series. More than anything, I wanted people to know what an incredible, amazing person he is and how I owed everything to him. 'There's one person I need to thank above everyone,' I said, trying my best not to break into sobs. 'And that is Robin Windsor. Because what no one knows is that having me as a partner is a really, really tough ask. Week in, week out, he's done everything, and he's helped me through one of the toughest times of my life. I owe every inch of *Strictly* to Robin. He's just amazing.' I turned and hugged him.

'We know you've had a very special relationship and it's been very special for us to watch. Thank you for all the joy you've given all of us,' Tess said. The audience was still going mad. The atmosphere was totally charged. Tess turned to Robin. 'What would you like to say to Lisa?' she asked him.

'I just want to say that from day one, this whole experience has been absolutely amazing,' he said. 'Lisa's come out and shown that you don't have to be a certain size to be able to dance and she has inspired everyone.'

Oh my God, Robin, thank you so much! I thought, as I hugged him again. For the hundredth time, I felt incredibly lucky to have found in Robin the big brother I'd always wanted. He had summed up exactly what I was feeling, because the best thing by far about appearing in *Strictly* was having the chance to challenge the idea of judging a book by its cover. I know that a lot of people looked at me at the beginning of the show and thought, Oh, here we go. Here comes the comedy one. But I'm proud to say that I proved them wrong. I went out and proved to everybody that no matter what size you are, you can dance. I showed that it's fine to be different. That meant the world to me.

Epilogue
Dreams do come true

24 July 2013

Sitting in my dressing room at the Birmingham Symphony Hall, *Strictly*fied to the nines, I can't help smiling to myself in the mirror. This moment always reminds me of the frantic, anxious minutes I spent in the BBC dressing room before I first went out and danced live on *Strictly Come Dancing* in October 2012. I'm almost as amazed now as I was then to find myself wearing a crystal-encrusted dress, with eyelashes like claws and iridescent stocking shimmy on my bare legs, just minutes away from doing the cha-cha in front of a vast audience. Only this time I'm not worried about looking stupid or being laughed off the stage. We've had standing ovations every night on the *Strictly Confidential* tour so far, so I'm not fretting about making a laughing stock of myself.

I feel a bit dizzy when I look back on my first *Strictly* performance. It's only now that I realise how much of a risk I was taking that night. If things had gone wrong with my cha-cha on live television in front of thirteen million people, I definitely wouldn't be here now, sparkling with glitter and sequins, about to step out on stage in the best show I've ever done. In fact, I think I was probably so fragile back then that if I'd ended up with egg on my face after that first *Strictly* dance, my whole world would have come crashing down. It was just a few short weeks since my mum had passed and I was walking a tightrope between survival and emotional collapse. Thanks to Robin Windsor, I survived that night. Thanks to *Strictly*, my life was transformed. And with the support of my beautiful friends and family, I was able to make it through the ups and downs of the past year to end up here, in my dressing room at the Birmingham Symphony Hall, feeling happy and excited. (And yes, a little bit nervous too, because I'm always nervous before I go on stage.)

Appearing on *Strictly* changed everything for me. A year ago, I would never have dreamt that people would actually pay money to come and see me dance, act and sing in a show that tells the story of *Strictly* through my eyes. Never in my wildest dreams could I have imagined that I'd be on stage alongside some of the best Latin and ballroom dancers in the world, including Ian Waite, Natalie Lowe and Artem Chigvintsev, or that I'd get to sing two exhilarating solos, recite a passage from *Romeo and Juliet*, dance with a bevy of muscular bare-chested men or devote a whole section of a sold-out show to my beautiful, wonderful mum. Can this really be happening to me, little Lisa from Bury? No one could have predicted it, least of all me. Sometimes I have to pinch myself to make sure I'm awake.

My life has been a whirlwind ever since I started *Strictly*. Every week I raced to learn a dance, or two dances, and then in the final week I spent every spare minute learning my lines for the part of the Evil Queen in *Snow White* at the King's Theatre in Southsea, Portsmouth.

'Please run this scene with me,' I kept begging Robin.

'We don't have time!' he'd exclaim, but I think he secretly enjoyed reading out all the different pantomime characters' lines.

The day I finished shooting *Strictly* on 23 December, I got straight in a car to Portsmouth and arrived at the theatre just in time to watch the evening performance of *Snow White*. My lovely friend Adele Silva was standing in for me as the Evil Queen and she was utterly brilliant in the part. During the performance, I stood in the wings and frantically took notes of all the entrances and exits. Afterwards I did a short run-through with the rest of the cast, trying to memorise where I was supposed to stand in each scene. My mind was whirring with stage directions and lines from the script by the time I got into bed.

The following day, I got through the first Christmas Eve show by the skin of my teeth, guided by the rest of the cast, who were wonderful to me. 'I'll just stand here, is that all right?' I kept whispering. Fortunately, the audience didn't seem to notice.

I had played the role of the Evil Queen the year before, so I thought I knew what to expect from the audience. But everything was different after *Strictly*. Nobody wanted to boo or hiss me, because they found it hard to see smiley Lisa from *Strictly* as a baddie. I should definitely have been playing the fairy godmother instead!

Since I only had one day off over Christmas, my family came to me. It had become a family tradition to stay in a gorgeous hotel in whichever town or city where I was appearing in panto each year. It always felt like a treat. We'd have an amazing Christmas dinner and open our presents in Mum and Dad's room. But Christmas 2012 felt dark and surreal in comparison with the Christmases that had come before. It was horrible without Mum, horrible. If it hadn't been for little Jakey running and bouncing all over the place, it would have been absolutely unbearable. As it was, we all had our moments of heart-rending despair that day. I wanted to hold it together for Liam and Dad's sake, but I wasn't able to, perhaps because I'd had to bottle things up quite a bit while I was on *Strictly*.

I totally lost it at the breakfast table on Christmas morning. 'Where's Mum? She should be here. I miss her so much,' I sobbed. There was a huge gaping hole at the heart of my family on the most important family day of the year. It was devastating.

We somehow managed to get through the rest of Christmas Day. I was comforted by all the messages of support my friends and family wrote in the Christmas cards they'd sent. 'How proud Cath would be of what you've achieved,' they said. 'Imagine what your gran and mum are thinking as they look down on you now!' It helped to think of Mum and Gran shining down on me like stars, but it was still a rotten time. Mother's Day the following March was even worse and I imagine that the first year anniversary of Mum's passing in a few days' time will probably be the worst of all. I still miss her so very much.

After my only day off in six months, I went back to work on Boxing Day and played the Evil Queen in two shows a day until 6 January when the panto run finished. At 6.30 p.m., straight after the final show, I got a car to London and started rehearsals the following day for the *Strictly* live tour. Eleven days later, we opened at the Birmingham NIA. That first night was incredible. The live show at Wembley had prepared me for the live tour to a certain extent, but I was still blown away to hear the sheer volume of the crowd noise. I couldn't believe it when I saw people in the audience waving banners with mine and Robin's names and photos on them. Wow, I thought. Someone has actually gone out of their way to make a banner to show us their support! I felt so honoured. The audiences were amazing every night. You could tell they were having a fantastic time, which made everybody feel happy. The atmosphere at the venues was always electric.

We went on to perform twenty-six dates at massive arenas around the country. I really, really loved it, but I couldn't tell you what I was running on during those weeks. There was never enough time to eat properly and I remember scoffing a mountain of Pot Noodles, chocolate bars and M&S sandwiches. And yet the weight continued to drop off me because I was doing so much exercise. I had to have my costumes taken in twice over the course of the rehearsals and tour. Where's it all going? I kept thinking. Every day I felt lighter on my feet.

Everyone on the tour was brilliant. We all gave each other nicknames. Among the celebrities, Fern Britton was 'Mum',

Michael Vaughan was 'Dad' and Phil Tufnell was 'Naughty Uncle Phil'. Denise was 'Eldest' and we called her 'Eld'. I was 'Mid', for middle child, and Dani was called 'Tiddles', because she was the youngest. Then you had Louis, who started off being 'Brother' and then became 'Neighbour'. I got on really well with Louis. I was very cheeky with him and I loved to shock him by saying the unsayable. He was always gaping at me in outrage. 'You can't say that, you're a girl!' Of course, that made me want to shock him even more.

Eighty-eight friends and family came to see me at the Manchester Arena on 1 February. That was definitely my favourite night of the tour and it was also the one night that me and Robin won the audience vote. The tour followed the format of the TV show in that each couple was judged on their dance by a panel of judges – we had Len, Bruno and Craig on our panel. After the judges had spoken, we had a chat onstage with Kate Thornton, just as we did with Tess Daly on the TV show. Then the audience had the chance to vote by text for their favourite couple's dance.

Before we got to Manchester, Louis and his partner Ola Jordan had won every night, except for in Glasgow, where Denise and James were voted the winners. In Manchester, unbeknownst to me, while they were having their onstage chat with Kate Thornton after their dance, the other contestants asked the audience to vote for me and Robin. Well, you can't buy that. What a great bunch of mates! I was over the moon when we were declared the winners on the night. I was in my hometown, with my nearest and dearest in the audience, having the most brilliant time ever.

314

These things don't happen to me, I thought in wonder. What's going on?

Everything in my life was changing. 'The day will come when you'll have to get off the hamster wheel,' my mates started saying. Knowing how much I loved my mum, knowing how much I missed her every day, they were worried I'd suddenly collapse with the weight of it all.

'Well, I'm not getting off it at the moment,' I'd say.

In fact, being busy helped me to cope with my grief over Mum. I went on having desperate moments of pure sadness – usually late at night, alone in my hotel room – but I was also having the time of my life. *Strictly* had given me and my career such a boost. Suddenly there were loads of different job offers and opportunities coming in.

I've seen a massive difference in my body since I started *Strictly Come Dancing*, even more so while I've been touring with *Strictly Confidential*. I always have a little smile to myself when I look at photos of me at the start of the series. I was around a dress size 28 when I began *Strictly* and now I'm about size 18–20, so I've dropped almost ten dress sizes. It's insane. I've had to buy a whole new wardrobe, because my old clothes were hanging off me. Strangely, though, I keep coming home from the shops with clothes in bigger sizes than I need – I think it's because I quite like wearing clothes that are too big as a reminder of how much weight I've lost.

I feel really good about my body. I'm so toned! I'm almost all muscle now. I love looking in the mirror and seeing my 'samba calves'. Even the professional dancers have noticed them. The only downsides to losing so much weight are that my boobs have shrunk and I've got loads of excess skin on my stomach. I get the feeling that it's skin that's not going to spring back, so maybe surgery is the only way to get rid of it. I don't know. I've been so busy that I haven't had time to ask anyone!

I have to be honest with myself and say that I do love this exceedingly active life. I'd like to remain at this weight, but I'm not sure how I'll be able to stay so fit once the tour finishes. I know that I'll still have my chocolate bars, as I can't ever imagine giving them up. I don't monitor what I eat and I'd be cross with myself if I did, because that's not me. Hopefully, I'll go on dancing, since I can't see myself going to the gym for an hour and a half every day. There's not enough fun to be had at the gym! I think the key is to stay busy and interested. When I piled on weight while I was touring in plays prior to *Strictly*, it was partly because my days were so monotonous. Having a nice lunch was a way to pass the time; I'd sit down to a slap-up meal even if I hadn't moved from my room all morning and didn't need feeding up. I don't want to fall back into that routine again, so I need to make sure I'm happy and fulfilled in what I'm doing. Luckily, there's a lot in the pipeline right now, including a primetime Saturday night show, a sitcom, a West End show and a return to *Strictly*. Plus, I'm going on holiday to New York with the gorgeous Robin Windsor and his partner Davidé three days after the *Strictly Confidential* tour ends! It's all exciting beyond belief, so I can't see myself getting depressed and going back to my old ways any time soon.

As for Mr Right – even though I'm mortified when I look back at my disastrous love life over the years, I'm still hoping he'll come along. I've made so many mistakes romantically that it's ridiculous, but you've got to keep hoping, haven't you? Loads of men showed interest when I finished *Strictly*, which was brilliant and very flattering. I started dating a guy, a friend of a friend in London, but we realised that I can't settle down at the moment. I'm so busy that I don't come up for air. I'd see him at the weekend if I had a night off, but the occasional dinner isn't enough to keep a relationship going. I think I'll need a guy who's happy for me to go off and do my own thing, so maybe it will have to be someone who's in the business and understands this crazy life. I feel a trillion per cent ready to meet him and I keep saying to Mum, 'Come on, pass him my way!' but I know it can only happen when the time is right.

I never forget that I'm already incredibly lucky. It's beyond thrilling to get up on stage every night wearing sequins and glitter and dance the cha-cha with five gorgeous men. It's a dream come true and it makes me feel like Cinderella, even though I haven't found my Prince Charming yet! The truth is, I've felt like a princess ever since the day after my first *Strictly* dance. I get to wear beautiful make-up and sparkly frocks, meet different, amazing people, do the work I want to do and be who I want to be. I've got the best friends in the world and a wonderful, loving family. I feel very, very grateful.

I'm unbelievably happy with my life as it is right now, so how can I ask for more? I love what I do and it's what I want to do. Now that being on *Strictly* has given me the opportunity to do more of what I love doing, my life is exactly where I want it. Meeting Mr Right will be the cherry on the trifle, not the be-all and end-all. So, as long as I have the chance to live my dreams and love my work, I will go on doing what I do. I'm living the fairy tale I longed for all those years ago at Oldham Theatre Workshop and I count my blessings every single day.

Index